Robert Blackley Drummond

Erasmus: His Life and Character

Volume II.

Robert Blackley Drummond

Erasmus: His Life and Character
Volume II.

ISBN/EAN: 9783742846495

Manufactured in Europe, USA, Canada, Australia, Japa

Cover: Foto ©Andreas Hilbeck / pixelio.de

Manufactured and distributed by brebook publishing software (www.brebook.com)

Robert Blackley Drummond

Erasmus: His Life and Character

ERASMUS

HIS LIFE AND CHARACTER

AS SHOWN IN HIS

CORRESPONDENCE AND WORKS

BY

ROBERT BLACKLEY DRUMMOND, B.A.

With Portrait

IN TWO VOLUMES

VOL. II.

LONDON
SMITH, ELDER, & CO., 15 WATERLOO PLACE
1873

CONTENTS

OF

THE SECOND VOLUME.

CHAPTER XIII.

Erasmus's Views of Reform—The Needs of the Time—Luther—Rome's Doctrine of Justification—Her Sacramental System—Purgatory—Faith and Grace—The Indulgences—Luther's Theses—Position of Erasmus—His Letter to Luther—To Wolsey—To Albert—To the Pope—The Bull—Its Effects—Egmund the Carmelite—The Fat Monk—Erasmus at Cologne—Letter to Campeggio—The Burning of the Decretals—Letters illustrating the Views of Erasmus 1

CHAPTER XIV.

Erasmus thinks of leaving Louvain—Meeting with Aleander—Starts for Basle—Taken ill at Worms—Arrival at Basle—Visit to Constance—Accession of Adrian VI.—Erasmus's advice to him—Ulrich von Hutten—Erasmus declines an Interview—Letter to Laurinus—Hutten's Expostulation—Erasmus's Sponge—Hutten's Death—Judgment on the Controversy 90

CHAPTER XV.

"The Familiar Colloquies"—Origin of the Work—The Maid that would not Marry—The Penitent Maiden—The Soldier and the Friar—The Shipwreck—German Inns—The Inquisition of Faith—The Old Men's Colloquy—The Poor Rich Men—The Abbot and the Lady—Ichthyophagia—Charon—The Seraphic Obsequies—Success of the Work—The St. Hilary—Accession of Clement VII.—Erasmus and the Reformers—Farel—The Doctrine of Free-Will—Correspondence of Erasmus and Luther—The "De Libero Arbitrio"—Reception of the work—Letter to Fisher—To Melancthon—Luther's Reply—The "Hyperaspistes" 151

CHAPTER XVI.

Erasmus attacked on both Sides—Bedda—Louis de Berquin—Persecuted by the Sorbonne—Warned by Erasmus—Thrown into Prison—His Sentence—And Execution—Correspondence between Erasmus and Bedda—Reply to Sutor—Erasmus addresses the Sorbonne—Answers Bedda—Appeals to Francis I.—The "Familiar Colloquies" condemned—Erasmus's Declarations—Bedda makes the *amende honorable*—The Prince of Carpi—His attack on Erasmus—Reply—The Prince's Death—The Spanish Monks—Erasmus accused of Heresy—His Defence—Letter to Fonseca—Erasmus's Farewell to his Persecutors 219

CHAPTER XVII.

Erasmus at Home—His Income—His Sufferings—Letter to Warham—Jokes at the Reformers—Death of Linacre—Longolius—Froben—Tract on Confession—Devotional Works—The "Lingua"—The Institution of Christian Marriage—The "Christian Widow"—Pliny—Irenæus—St. Chrysostom—St. Athanasius—St. Ambrose—The "De Pronunciatione"—The "Ciceronian"—Bembo and Sadoleti—Julius Cæsar Scaliger's Orations—Quarrel with Eppendorf—Conduct of Erasmus—New Edition of Seneca—St. Augustine . . . 267

CHAPTER XVIII.

Progress of the Reformation at Basle—The new Dogma—Conrad Pelican—Œcolampadius—The Mass abolished—Erasmus removes to

Friburg—Invitation from Fugger—Letter to Pirckheimer—Troubles of Housekeeping—Erasmus's Health gives way—His Edition of St. Chrysostom—The Diet of Augsburg—His Apophthegms—Preface to Aristotle—To Livy—Edition of St. Basil—He buys a House—Death of Pirckheimer—And of Warham—Various Works —Paul III.—The "Ecclesiastes"—Erasmus returns to Basle—His last Illness and Death—Estimate of his Character and Influence . 309

ERASMUS:

HIS LIFE AND CHARACTER.

CHAPTER XIII.

ERASMUS'S VIEWS OF REFORM—THE NEEDS OF THE TIME—LUTHER—ROME'S DOCTRINE OF JUSTIFICATION—HER SACRAMENTAL SYSTEM—PURGATORY—FAITH AND GRACE—THE INDULGENCES—LUTHER'S THESES—POSITION OF ERASMUS—HIS LETTER TO LUTHER—TO WOLSEY—TO ALBERT—TO THE POPE—THE BULL—ITS EFFECTS—EGMUND THE CARMELITE—THE FAT MONK—ERASMUS AT COLOGNE—LETTER TO CAMPEGGIO—THE BURNING OF THE DECRETALS—LETTERS ILLUSTRATING THE VIEWS OF ERASMUS.

FOR many years Erasmus had now been toiling, with the most unwearied self-devotion, for the reformation of the Church. At length the time was at hand when his object was to be accomplished, but in a way which he had neither expected nor desired. He had fondly hoped that a peaceful reform was possible. He had hoped that by the advancement of learning and the diffusion of the Scriptures the superstitions of the monks might be abolished, their manners purified, and the corruptions of the Church, both in doctrine and discipline, be purged away, while her integrity, and the unity of Christendom under one visible Head, the Bishop of Rome, should remain unimpaired. Vainly, as it proved. He was hardly to blame, however, if he could not see, what indeed was seen by very few, that the corruption was too deeply seated to be healed by gentle remedies—if he, an old man, was unwilling to despair that the aim of his life might yet be reached in his own way. But—

> Non tali auxilio, nec defensoribus istis
> Tempus eget.

The time, in truth, demanded one of a far different stamp—one cast in a more heroic mould—who should not merely command the intellect, but master the heart of the great German people, and hurling defiance at the old Popedom, lead them on to smash into fragments that splendid fabric of power and glory which fifteen centuries had reared and perfected. It is not from the learned and the wise, as was said in the beginning, and as many an example since compels us to confess, that the help of humanity comes. It is not usually they who live in kings' houses and bask in the smiles of the great, who can grasp and wield with effect those fundamental ideas by which the world is moved. Out of the heart of the people the great movements of humanity come. And the leader for whom the world was now waiting must be of the people and from them.

About the time that Erasmus was pushing his way among the great men at Rome, or labouring at those classical studies, which effected so much for the revival of letters, a young Augustinian monk was passing painful days and sleepless nights, scarce noting the difference between night and day, in the monastery of Erfurth, engaged in grim struggle with his own soul, and earnestly seeking deliverance from the weight of sin, which seemed to be crushing him down to hell. An intense and passionate nature, the solitude and weariness of the monastic life, and the continual introspection of a mind convinced of its own helplessness and intent on finding salvation, a glimpse which had been opened for him, through the sudden death of a companion, into the eternal world, the spiritual barrenness of the fasts and prayers and other religious exercises, which he practised with a zeal which almost destroyed him, had all contributed to give Luther an exaggerated sense of the reality and consequences of sin, until at length he came to believe with all his heart, what others were content to profess with the lips, that he was by nature a child of wrath and doomed to everlasting perdition. This, indeed, was no more than his Church taught him to believe. Only it seemed to Luther that the state of man, apart from Divine grace, was more absolutely helpless than the Church had hitherto taught, while the machinery provided for the application of the great remedy for sin appeared to him to be needlessly or wickedly complicated with mere human devices. And here it will be necessary to state briefly the more important points of difference between the Roman and the Lutheran doctrine of justification, because, without having these in mind, it would be impossible to understand the position of Erasmus, or his relation to Rome upon the one hand, and to Luther upon the other.

The remedy for all sin, both original and actual, was to be found, according to the Catholic Church, in the merits and suffering of Christ; and so far therefore there was no ground for revolt on the part of the Reformers, who not merely carried this doctrine with them from the Mother Church, but applied it more rigidly and consequentially. For the Catholic teachers certainly did not push the vicarious theory to the extreme to which it was carried by Luther; they laid more stress on the humility of Christ in condescending to our nature than on the mere endurance of pain, and although they attributed a penal character to his death, and held that the sacrifice upon the cross was demanded by supreme justice, they were equally careful to impress the view that in the triumph of Christ the power of evil was vanquished, that being, no doubt, the significance of the quaint notion, according to which the Devil, having by mistake taken a life to which he had no title, and that too a life of infinite value, thereby forfeited his right over the guilty, and thus justly lost his hold upon the sinful world.[1] It was, however, when she came to apply this remedy to human needs, that the Church

---

[1] "Peccata quoque nostra, id est, pœnam peccatorum nostrorum dicitur in corpore suo super lignum portasse : quia per ipsius pœnam, quam in cruce tulit, omnis pœna temporalis, quæ pro peccato conversis debetur, in baptismo penitus relaxatur, ut nulla a baptizato exigatur, et in pœnitentia minoratur. Non enim sufficeret illa pœna, qua pœnitentes ligat Ecclesia, nisi pœna Christi co-operaretur, qui pro nobis solvit."—*Pet. Lomb. Sen.* III. xix. 4. "Decreverat Deus in mysterio, ut ait Amh., propter primum peccatum non intromitti hominem in paradisum, id est, ad Dei contemplationem non admitti, nisi in uno homine tanta existerit humilitas, quæ omnibus suis proficere posset ; sicut in primo homine tanta fuit superbia, quæ omnibus suis nocuit. Non est autem inventus inter homines aliquis quo id posset impleri, nisi leo de tribu Judæ, qui aperuit librum et solvit signacula ejus implendo in se omnem justitiam, id est, consummatissimam humilitatem, qua major esse non potest. Nam omnes alii homines debitores erant, et vix unicuique sua virtus sufficiebat et humilitas ; nullus ergo eorum hostiam poterat offerre sufficientem reconciliationi nostræ. Sed Christus homo sufficiens et perfecta fuit hostia, qui multo amplius est humiliatus, amaritudinem mortis gustando, quam ille Adam superbiit per esum ligni vetiti noxia delectatione perferendo. Si ergo illius superbia omnium extitit ruina, ipsum de paradiso mittens foris, aliisque

found the occasion of introducing practices which opened the way for all manner of superstition, and which, so far as they tended to make salvation marketable, could not but lead to fearful abuses. It was all very well to tell men that they could be saved by the merits of Christ, but what if those merits were quite beyond the reach of human search or human endeavour? The doctrine of Rome was that the merits of Christ could be applied only through the sacraments, and that the sacraments could be administered only by the priest. There lay the whole of that immense power which Rome wielded for centuries over the human mind. The birth-sin by which every human being born into this world was doomed to perdition, was cancelled by means of the sacrament of baptism, and this was refused to none, but, on the contrary, eagerly pressed as being simply essential to salvation and to the enjoyment of the other privileges which the Church had to

occludens januam; multo magis Christi humilitas, qua mortem gustavit, ingressum regni cœlestis omnibus suis, impleto Dei decreto, aperire valuit, atque decreti delere chirographum."—*Ib.* III. xviii. 5.

Lombardus further cites Augustine, lib. 2, *de baptismo parvulorum*, to show that Christ offered the Devil a bait by presenting him with his blood on the cross, and as the Devil was foolish enough to take it, although there was no cause of death in him, our sins were thereby blotted out.—*Ib.* III. xix. 1. But this theory was evidently not considered inconsistent with the doctrine that the death of Christ was a sacrifice to God, for in the next section we are expressly guarded against the consequence which might seem naturally to follow, that the sacrifice was made to the Devil; and here accordingly is a statement of the doctrine of justification which, so far as it goes, does not differ at all from that of Luther or Calvin: "Christus ergo est sacerdos, idemque et hostia, pretium nostræ reconciliationis; qui se in ara crucis, non Diabolo, sed Trinitati obtulit pro omnibus, quantum ad pretii sufficientiam; sed pro electis tantum quantum ad efficaciam, quia prædestinatis tantum salutem effecit."— *Ib.* III. xx. 3.

bestow. But after baptism there still remained the daily, hourly sins, venial or mortal, which every human being continues to commit up to the very moment of death. For these other sacraments were provided, and of these the most awful was the Holy Eucharist, in which the penitent sinner was taught to believe that he received between his lips, under the form of a piece of bread, the very body, soul, and divinity of his Lord. But this sacrament could not be lightly administered; it could not be administered at all except after confession and penitence. Now penitence in the view of the Church was of two kinds—internal and external. Internal penitence was a virtue; but external penitence or penance—there is but the one word in ecclesiastical language—was a sacrament; and it was in this sacrament, if anywhere, that the Church's power was concentrated. The theory of all the sacraments was that the sinner must through them be conformed to the likeness of Christ; and the theory of penance in particular was that as Christ had suffered the sinner must suffer too; not indeed that it was necessary for him to endure sufferings commensurate with his sin, but such as with the co-operation of Christ's satisfaction might suffice.[2] Hence the fasts, the prayers, the pilgrimages, the almsgiving insisted upon by the Church, all of which were meritorious works and effectual to prepare the way for the application of the perfect atonement. Thus every priest, however humble, nay, however wicked, held in his hands the keys of the kingdom of heaven. There stood the awful words, addressed, as he might fancy, to himself—"Whosoever sins ye remit, they are remitted unto them; and whosoever sins ye retain, they

[2] *Pet. Lomb. Sen.* IV. xiv.—xvii.

are retained"—by which his Lord had delegated his power to his Church. Through the confessional the Church imposed such penances as she would, remitted such sins as she would; and is it any wonder if, in a corrupt and ignorant age, she sometimes sold the privileges with which she was entrusted, for such sums of money as she could get? Nor did the Church loose her hold upon her children even after their departure from the world; for, in one part of the infernal regions, there burned for the souls of the good a purgatorial fire, through which they must pass before they could be so perfectly pure as to be fit to enter the realm of eternal bliss.[3] Why, indeed, if the merits of Christ be all sufficient, any purgatory should be necessary, is a question which may well raise scruples in the Protestant mind. The answer may be found in the distinction drawn by Aquinas, according to which every mortal sin incurred not merely the eternal punishment which might be cancelled through the sacraments in their ordinary operation, but also temporal punishment which must either be endured or avoided by some special remedy; or else, it may be, in the notion that however complete the satisfaction for sin, some traces of it still remained in the soul and needed to be purged away.[4]

[3] The general impression among Protestants probably is, that purgatory is for the wicked. Such clearly was the idea of Dean Milman, who seems to have taken it for a modified hell (*Latin Christianity*, vol. ix. p. 91, ed. 1867). But the Catechism of Trent is clear upon the point: "Præterea est purgatorius ignis, quo *piorum* animæ ad definitum tempus cruciatæ expiantur," &c.—Pars I. Art. v. 5.

[4] *Summa Theol.* Pars III. Q. lxxxvi. 4. The Council of Trent adopts the distinction of Aquinas, declaring that after justification there still remains the liability to temporal punishment, which must be discharged either in this world or in purgatory.—*Canones et Decreta:* Sessio VI. Can. 30.

At all events the Church believed that she had scriptural warrant for this doctrine in the words of St. Paul, —" the fire shall try every man's work " (1 Cor. iii. 13)— and claiming for herself the power of opening the gates of purgatory no less than those of heaven and hell, she extended still further her influence over the living by appealing to their feelings on behalf of the departed. Then again, to pass to another point, or rather, perhaps, to look at this same subject of justification under another aspect, the question naturally arose, seeing that salvation was of grace, whether man could do anything to merit grace, and whether, having obtained grace, he could do anything towards meriting reward. To this the church answered that he could do very little, but still something. Man, in his fallen state, was, indeed, in a very helpless condition; but although he must wait for the coming of grace to make him capable of attaining salvation, he might, notwithstanding, prepare himself for grace by good works; and this the schoolmen called "congruous merit." Again, after grace, while still dependent upon the Divine assistance, he might, by his own effort, co-operate with God's grace, —while, on the other hand, having free-will, he might also resist it—and in this state he could perform good works which were actually deserving of reward, and as it were put heaven in his debt. This the schoolmen called "condign merit."[5] Another distinction, the nature

---

[5] "Utrum homo in gratia constitutus possit mereri vitam æternam ex condigno?" is one of the questions discussed and answered in the affirmative in the *Summa Theologica*, Pars II. Q. cix. Art. ix. Conf. Luther, *Commentary on Gal.* ii. 16: "Wherefore the wicked and pernicious opinion of the Papists is utterly to be condemned, which attributes the merit of grace and remission of sins to the work wrought. For they say that a good work before grace is able to obtain

of which will be apparent from what has preceded, was that between operating and co-operating grace. Thus it might be urged in favour of the Catholic doctrine, that if it opened the way for great abuses, it had at least the merit of throwing some responsibility upon man, and inciting him to exert such powers as he possessed to do his duty in the world and reach heaven at last. And if it be said that it was this very notion that man could of his own will perform any meritorious work, which gave birth to the very worst corruptions of the Church, it might still be replied, by an impartial onlooker, that unless the Church had introduced arbitrary penances and invented artificial sins, and if she had confined herself to the inculcation of natural duty, no practical evils could have followed from this speculative doctrine, whether it be true or whether it be false.

But now what did Luther, under his monk's cowl, wearing himself to a skeleton with fasting and prayer in his lonely cell at Erfurth, think of all this? Luther, earnestly seeking the light, and reading devotedly his St. Augustine and his Bible, and helped, it must be added, by the counsel of John Staupitz, the vicar-general of his order, came to the conclusion that there was a nearer way to a participation in the merits of Christ than that commonly pursued, that faith, and a faith which no effort of man could attain, but which only the grace of God could impart, was the sole means to this

merit of congruence (which they call *meritum decongruo*), because it is meet that God should reward such a work. But when grace is obtained, the work following deserveth everlasting life of due debt and worthiness, which they call *meritum de condigno*." I quote from the London edition of 1616.

end. His own experience taught him that it must be so. For, by-and-bye, whether through the natural reaction of the over-strained mind, or by the influence of books, or by the operation of some power beyond, which we may still venture to call the grace of God, the burden under which he had groaned was lifted off, the light poured into his soul, and peace and joy succeeded to the fierce tumult which had torn his very being. The idea which now possessed Luther was that which possessed St. Paul, when he said, "Thy grace is sufficient for me." All things come from grace, and without grace it is impossible to do any good work. If grace be given, good works will follow; if it be not given, man remains necessarily under sin: by no effort of his own can he keep God's precepts, or even prepare himself for grace. This master idea, it will be seen, must, when carried out to its legitimate consequences, strike at the very root of the Catholic system, scatter to the winds all Popish ceremonies, condemn the entire hierarchy of bishops and priests, and leave every man free to be dealt with according to God's mercy or displeasure. It destroyed in a moment those school subtleties about congruous and condign merit, operating and co-operating grace, and came home in its grand simplicity to the heart of a people weary of vain ceremony and longing for some faith which should at once appeal to and satisfy their conscience and their heart.

That this idea of man's simple and entire dependence upon grace was true upon all sides of it, probably no one would now undertake to affirm. It is, at all events, a question on which the biographer might well be excused from pronouncing judgment. This much, however, may be said, that, besides having some very plain texts of Scripture in its favour, it is so far rooted in the nature of things as to make it exceedingly difficult to evade the reasoning which can be urged on its behalf. Its merits as a practical instrument against the usurpations of the spiritual power, and its adaptation to the necessities of the times, are indubitable: and these certainly had their share in recommending it to the German princes and people. But how far, it may be asked, was this idea to be carried? Was it to be carried to the point of affirming that a man's conduct was so absolutely ineffectual that it could be of no importance whether he was trying to obey the commandments or not, and that as regards salvation, it would be just as well with him if he were leading a vicious life as a virtuous one; or even one step further, to the point of teaching that the practice of good works was actually a hindrance rather than a help towards the reception of saving faith? Such might indeed seem to be the legitimate consequences of the Lutheran position in its broadest statement. And to that bad extreme the doctrine was actually carried, at least by some who called themselves Lutherans. How far the great Reformer himself stopped short of that point has been a matter of controversy;[6] but it cannot

[6] See the late Archdeacon Hare's very able, but perhaps not always quite successful, *Vindication of Luther*, where many of the most objectionable expressions on the subject of good works will be found quoted. The following proposition, put forward first in 1516 for discussion in the University of Wittenberg, might seem to contain the very worst consequences that could be drawn from the doctrine of Free Grace: "Cum justitia fidelium sit in Deo abscondita, peccatum vero eorum manifestum in seipsis, verum est non nisi justos damnari, atque peccatores et meretrices salvari." But no doubt it would be hardly fair to judge a man's real opinion from propositions the object of which was to attract attention by paradox, without hearing the expla-

be disputed that if in his later writings he indignantly disowned the immoral consequences drawn by the sectaries, he used on different occasions many extremely rash expressions, which greatly need explanation to clear them of their apparently evil intention. Probably the truth may be that Luther at no time deliberately held, or meant to teach, Antinomianism—as the doctrine, that good works are contrary to grace, is called; but, being a man incapable of self-restraint, he delighted in using violent and exaggerated language; and having the greatest horror of all dependence on human merit, he sometimes forgot the obvious distinction that it may be possible to endeavour to do that which is right, and after all acknowledge oneself an unprofitable servant.

Were I to attempt, then, to balance the merits and defects of these opposing theories of justification—a task, however, which I am perhaps not called upon to attempt—I would say that while the Roman theory supplied a practical basis for action, and so far appealed to the common sense of mankind, it had become the occasion of enormous abuses which by all means called for speedy reformation. The Lutheran theory, on the other hand, while it crushed the pretensions of the priests, and cleared away every obstacle between the individual soul and its God, destroyed human responsibility, and left man utterly helpless in the hands of Omnipotence.

Be that, however, as it may, one thing is clear, that Luther had now, by the year 1516, or before it, come to

---

nation, which might have greatly modified their apparent meaning; and, as Mr. Hare observes, "every candid mind will make allowances for exaggerations in such apophthegmatically worded scholastic theses, which were the fashion of the day."—p. 63.

the same practical conclusions as Erasmus in regard to the crying evils of the time. What the one had learned from his shrewd common sense and sharp insight into human nature, as well as from his knowledge of Scripture and of the Fathers, had come home to the other, as if by revelation of God, through deep spiritual experience and the struggle of a soul intensely and terribly in earnest. Erasmus opposed himself to the superstitions of the monks, because he held them to be things of human device, contrary to Scripture, and not really sanctioned by his Church, as well as in themselves stupid and ridiculous. Luther came in time to see all this; but his first step was to adopt a principle involving consequences which he did not perhaps at first clearly perceive, but which, by rendering all the external means of salvation superfluous, shattered, as it were, at a single blow, the entire fabric of the Papacy. At first, he had no more thought of leaving the communion of Rome than Erasmus himself had, and, indeed, it was not until Rome cast him out, that he found himself compelled to set her at defiance. Armed, however, with this great weapon of the sufficiency of grace and salvation without works, he was prepared to throw all the weight of his unconquerable will and vigorous eloquence into the scale of spiritual freedom, and join heart and hand with Erasmus in denouncing the corruptions of the Church and accusing the wickedness and folly of the monks. In all other respects these two men were probably as different from one another as two men could well be. This we shall have ample opportunity of discovering hereafter.

The 31st of October, 1517, was the day, ever memorable in the annals of the Church, on which Luther posted up on the doors of the palace-church of Wittenberg those ninety-five propositions which led so swiftly to the disunion of Christendom. It was on the 10th of December, 1520, that he burned the Pope's bull of excommunication; and from that moment Germany was Protestant.

The story of the indulgences has been often told. Leo, finding the Papal treasury exhausted, and wanting money for the accomplishment of his ambitious designs and the enrichment of his family, resolved to have recourse, as his predecessors had before him, to another treasure, which did not indeed consist of silver or gold, but which consisted of what could easily be exchanged for German florins or English crowns. This was the treasure of the Church, and consisted of those merits of Christ which had not been required for the salvation of the world, and those merits of the saints which had remained in excess of what was demanded for their own salvation. The Jesuit Maimburg traces up the practice of issuing indulgences to the time when the Apostle Paul remitted the remainder of his punishment to the Corinthian fornicator; but the Protestant may be permitted to believe that the doctrine was of gradual growth, and that it attained its distinctest expression in the famous decretal *Unigenitus* of Clement VI., in the middle of the fourteenth century. According to that Pontiff, a single drop of Christ's blood would have sufficed for the redemption of the world; but as all his blood was shed, the Church possessed in this, together with the merits of the Virgin and the saints, a treasure which she could employ as she would; a treasure, moreover, which could never be consumed, both because Christ's merits were infinite, and because, inasmuch as others were made righteous by its application, the more it was drawn upon, the more it increased. Certainly the theory of the indulgence was, that it was simply a remission of temporal punishment, and perhaps originally of those punishments which were imposed by the Church, insomuch that in Switzerland the Pope's pardons were commonly known as "butter-letters," it being understood that their chief effect was to permit people to eat butter and eggs upon fast days. And logically they could be nothing more: for redemption from the eternal fire being already provided for, what more *could* the Church do than remove those barriers which she had herself placed in the way of a man at once completing his salvation by partaking of the Eucharist—in other words, dispense with the intervening sacrament? But then, it may be said, this virtually amounted to a complete pardon; and, indeed, so long as contrition and confession were put forward as conditions, it would not seem that the Church, in granting remissions of all sins, was exceeding the power which, from her own point of view, was her legitimate right. The real evil, no doubt, lay in that merely external method of looking at religion as if its whole operation were outside a man, and not within him, which the sacramental theory did so much to encourage. The worst abuse arose when, under the very thinnest disguise, the indulgences were exchanged for money.

It is true the indulgences were not sold; let any one draw the distinction who cares to do so. You only contributed so much, according to your means, to the building of St. Peter's Church, or any other pious object, and then received the document absolving you from all your sins, remitting the pains of purgatory, and guaranteeing you a sure entrance into Paradise upon your death. According to the instructions issued to the preachers, indeed, contrition and confession were essential preliminaries to the enjoyment of these privileges; and there were certain other conditions, such as visiting seven churches, repeating certain prayers, and so on, which had to be fulfilled.[7] But the Dominican friars to whose care the pardons were committed did not think of troubling the people with these conditions. What they preached was, on the payment of certain florins, pardon for all sins past and to come, and after death, salvation; or, if the object was to release the soul of a departed friend from purgatory, then that the moment the money rattled in the collector's box, the object was effected. So shameless were the preachers, that the pardons were sometimes actually put up to auction.[8]

Such a perversion of religion might well excite the indignation of all good men, of all who were not complete slaves to monkish superstition; and how many thousands were there through Germany whom the writings of Erasmus had taught to think for themselves and to despise the ignorance and vulgarity of the friars. Nor were the secular princes likely to look with much favour upon a proceeding which tended to drain their country of its resources and send their people's wealth beyond the Alps. The Dominicans had just sustained a great defeat in their attempt to destroy Reuchlin. They had been laughed almost to death in the "Letters of Obscure Men;" and it was not likely that they were now to be permitted to carry everything their own way.

---

[7] "Instructio Summaria ad Subcommissarios," *ap.* GERDES: *Hist. Ev. Ren.* vol. i. App. p. 83.

[8] SECKENDORF: *Hist. Luth.* lib. i. sect. 6.

Accordingly there was needed but a spark to set Germany in a flame, and so soon as Luther had posted up his ninety-five propositions against indulgences upon the church doors, the obscure monk became at once the acknowledged leader of German independence. Luther, however, was far from having any intention at this time of disowning the authority of Rome.[9] What he undertook was to interpret the mind of the Pope on the subject of the indulgences and to expose the scandalous perversions of the Dominican preachers. About the same time that he published his propositions he enclosed them to the Archbishop of Magdeburg and Maintz, to whom the distribution of the indulgences in Germany had been entrusted, and who indeed was to receive half their proceeds, hoping, no doubt, that he would at once interpose and issue some stricter injunctions for the guidance of the preachers; and in the following year he wrote to the Pope himself in most respectful terms, assuring him that he was ready to listen to his voice as to that of Jesus Christ Himself. Events, however, proved too strong for him. Had Leo understood the real position of affairs, had he known how rotten the foundations had become on which the power of the Church rested, he would have tried, and probably tried with success, the effect of conciliation. But how could he have supposed that there could be the slightest difficulty in crushing one poor monk setting himself in opposition to the interests of all the monkish orders? Happily for the world, he made the attempt, and so drove Luther himself, and all northern Germany with him, into open revolt.

[9] Luther's fifth proposition was: "Papa non vult nec potest ullas pœnas remittere, præter eas quas arbitrio vel suo vel Canonum imposuit."

Meantime, while the event was yet undecided, there was a question which must have presented itself to both sides, not indeed as one of the deepest interest, but still as sufficiently important to occasion some anxiety. What will Erasmus do? That his sympathies were heartily with Luther in his warfare with the monks there could be no doubt at all. So much at least was clear to every one who had ever read a line of his writings. But how far was he prepared to follow him? Should it come to a breach with the Papacy, as may have seemed to many from the first not improbable, will he throw the weight of his influence into the scale to help Germany to throw off once and for ever the spiritual yoke of Rome? Or will he, on the other hand, continue, as before, protesting against the abuses of the Church, while remaining true to her principles? Luther, at any rate, knew, if nobody else did, that there was a great gulf between himself and Erasmus. Writing just a year before the publication of the Wittenberg propositions, he finds fault with him for interpreting the righteousness of works, or of the law, or one's own righteousness, of the ceremonial law only; and for not allowing that St. Paul, in the fifth chapter of the Romans, speaks of original sin. And, again, the next year, in a letter to a friend, he remarks, "I am reading Erasmus, but he is losing credit with me every day. . . . I fear he will not much further the doctrine of Christ and of God's grace."[10] That it was simply impossible for Erasmus to join the Lutheran reformation will, I think, appear abundantly hereafter. Let these words be noted now as the first signs that it was so. Still it was obviously of considerable importance to draw over the

[10] *Apud* SECK. lib. i. sect. 8.

learning, the talents, the reputation of so distinguished a man to the side of the Reformation, and to separate them, if possible, from the cause of Rome. Accordingly, on the 28th of March, 1519, when matters were now ripening towards the final consummation, we find Luther writing to Erasmus, and indeed a little more in his own style than one would have expected. In this letter he tells him how much he has profited by his works, and remarks that it is monstrous they should not know one another, seeing how often he converses with him. He adds that he has heard from Capito that his name was known to him "through those trifles of his about the indulgences." This was the only overture which Luther ever made to the great chief of the literary republic, and it certainly shows no extraordinary confidence in his sympathy. His letter indeed has the tone of one writing at the suggestion of others, rather than from any strong individual impulse.[11]

Erasmus, on his part, was not long in appreciating the character of his new ally. It may be doubted indeed whether he ever did justice to the heroism of Luther's nature, but his faults he saw at the first glance. His violence, his dogmatism, his total want of moderation or self-restraint, were in direct antagonism to all that Erasmus had been preaching and practising throughout his life; and he saw clearly, or thought he saw, that such qualities were much more likely to injure than to help the cause in which he was interested. They might create disturbances amid which the voice of letters would be silenced; they would rouse the enemies of reformation to more violent opposition; they might even, instead of reforming the Church, lead

[11] cccxcix.

to a schism in it, which was a thing that he by no means desired. Accordingly, in reply to Luther's advances, he wrote him the following exceedingly kind letter, in which, while he expressed all the sympathy for him which he felt, he took occasion to give him the counsel of which he stood so much in need, but by which his own violent temper prevented him from profiting as he might :—

Erasmus *to* Martin Luther.[18]

"*Louvain, May* 30, 1519.

"My dearest brother in Christ,—Your letter, in which you show no less your truly Christian spirit than your great abilities, was extremely acceptable to me. I have no words to tell you what a sensation your writings have caused here. It is impossible to eradicate from people's minds the utterly false suspicion that I have had a hand in them, and that I am the ringleader of this 'faction,' as they call it. Some thought an opportunity had been given them for extinguishing literature, for which they cherish the most deadly hatred, because they are afraid it will cloud the *majesty* of their divinity, which many of them prize before Christianity ; and at the same time destroying myself because they fancy I have some influence in promoting the cause of learning. The only weapons which they use are vociferation, rash assertion, tricks, detraction, and calumny ; and had I not been present as a spectator—nay, had I not myself had experience of it—I should never have believed theologians could have gone to such extremes of madness. You would think it was a deadly contagion. And yet this poison began with a few ; it then spread more widely,

[18] *Ep.* ccccxxvii.

until a large part of this University, where there are so many students, was infected by the disease. I have assured them that you were quite a stranger to me, that I have never read your books, and that I therefore neither sanction nor condemn anything you have said. I have only advised them not to bellow so fiercely in public before reading your books, but to leave the matter to those whose judgment ought to have the greatest weight; also to consider whether it was expedient that such questions should be brought forward in mixed assemblies, and not rather be refuted in books, or discussed among learned men, especially when the author's life was universally well spoken of: but all to no purpose: such is the fury with which they carry on their ill-natured and calumnious disputes. How often have we agreed on terms of peace; how often have they, on the slightest suspicion, excited new disturbances! And these men, with such conduct as this, think themselves theologians.

"People who are in favour at Court—and that is a character which they impute to me—generally dislike this class of men. It is true I find all the bishops very kind to me, though they will not put their sentiments in writing. These men have no hope of victory but in slander and deceit, and these are arts which I despise, because I rely on my own conscious rectitude. Towards you they are becoming somewhat milder; perhaps their own evil conscience leads them to fear the pens of the learned; and I would certainly paint them in their own colours, as they deserve, did not the teaching as well as the example of Christ dissuade me. Wild beasts may be tamed by kindness, but if you do good to these men it only makes them more ferocious.

"You have friends in England, and among them men of the greatest eminence, who think most highly of your writings. Even here there are some who favour you, and one of these is a man of distinction. For myself, I am keeping such powers as I have to help the cause of the revival of letters. And more, I think, is gained by politeness and moderation than by violence. It was thus that Christ won the world to obedience to His authority. It was thus that Paul abrogated the Jewish law, putting an allegorical interpretation on its enactments. It is more expedient to declaim against those who abuse the Pope's authority than against the Popes themselves; and the same thing may be said of kings. Instead of holding the universities in contempt, we ought rather to endeavour to recall them to more sober studies; and regarding opinions which are too generally received to be rooted all at once from people's minds, it is better to reason upon them with close and convincing arguments than to deal in dogmatic assertions. The violent wranglings in which some persons delight we can afford to despise, and it is useless attempting to answer them. Let us be careful not to do or say anything savouring of arrogance and tending to encourage party feeling; thus only, in my judgment, will our conduct be acceptable to the Spirit of Christ. Meantime we must not permit our minds to be corrupted by anger, or hatred, or vain glory; for this last is an insidious enemy, and especially dangerous in the cultivation of the religious feelings. I do not, however, give you this advice because I think you need it, but in the hope that you will always go on as you have begun.

"I have skimmed through your 'Commentaries on the Psalms,' and I like them exceedingly, and hope they will be very useful. There is at Antwerp a prior of a monastery there, a man of a pure Christian life, who loves you immensely; he declares he was once a disciple of yours. He is almost the only one who preaches Christ; the rest generally preach either human fables or their own gain. I have written to Melancthon. The Lord Jesus give thee more abundantly of His Spirit every day, to His own glory and the good of the world. When I wrote this your letter had not reached me. Farewell."

Probably this letter confirmed Luther in his belief that there was very little real accord between himself and Erasmus, nor did any farther correspondence take place between them until they were engaged in open controversy with one another. As to the adherents of the Papal system, the men in authority, the great cardinals, the Pope himself, while they quite understood the importance of retaining a man like Erasmus in the service of the Church, they had probably little fear of his defection. Men of the world themselves, they were not likely to judge him by any but a worldly standard; and they well knew how many motives he had for keeping on good terms with them. Or if they had any doubts, he hastened, as we shall see presently, to reassure them. The monks, on the other hand, would willingly have been rid of him on any terms. They regarded him, not without reason, as their arch-enemy, as the prime mover of the revolt against the Church, and they would have thought he was only following out his own principles in joining heart and hand with the more open adversaries of Rome. Learning they detested, both because they had no taste for it and because they saw how fatal it was likely to prove to their own power. Their policy, therefore, was to confound the cause of letters with enmity to the Church, Erasmus with Luther, in the hope that both might perish together. Perhaps they were really stupid enough to believe that Luther had not written his own works, that Erasmus had written them for him, or at least lent his assistance; perhaps they had invented and disseminated this idle story from mere malice, and in the determination by any means to destroy so inveterate and so dangerous a foe. According to these foolish heads, no one could be a heretic but Erasmus; he must needs be the author of every book which contained a tolerant sentiment, or which levelled a sarcasm against priestly superstition. They ascribed to him the *Nemo* of Ulrich von Hutten, the reply which Bishop Fisher had written to Faber, even the "Utopia" of Sir Thomas More. They charged him with having assisted in the composition of the "Letters of Obscure Men." They ascribed to him, with more probability, the authorship of a satirical dialogue in which Julius II. is introduced, demanding admission to Paradise, but forbidden by St. Peter to enter, and in which the character of that warlike and ambitious priest is lashed with no sparing hand;[13] and notwithstanding the denials of Erasmus, who might have thought himself justified by personal danger in repudiating the work, the point may perhaps be considered doubtful. How far such representations might have been successful if they had remained unrefuted, we need not consider. Erasmus was keenly alive to his danger—indeed, as events showed, greatly overrated it. He remembered that the Dominicans—that powerful

[13] *Er. Op.* iii. 323, B—D.

order, of whom a Pope was known to say that he would rather quarrel with the greatest princes of Europe than offend one of its least members—who were now beginning to move in earnest against himself and Luther, had destroyed the noble-hearted Jerome Savonarola, and rendered the declining years of the learned and excellent Reuchlin miserable. Accordingly, he lost no time in avowing his warm attachment to the Holy See, and especially to Pope Leo X., to whose kindness, he said, he owed so much. At the same time he disclaimed all connection with Luther. He felt, as he had a right to feel, that it was very unjust that he should be made responsible for Luther's works, which he had not even read, or for Luther's extravagance, which he had rebuked. The letters which he wrote about this period are full of such protestations. Some of them are elaborate compositions, and are addressed to the highest dignitaries of the Church —to Campeggio, the Papal legate to England, to Wolsey, to Albert, the Cardinal Elector and Archbishop of Maintz and Magdeburg, to the Pope himself. The letter to Wolsey is an elegant composition, and the panegyric which Erasmus pronounces on him must have been gratifying to the vanity of the ambitious Cardinal.[14] "You have cleared England," he says, "of burglars, robbers, and idle vagabonds, so that the country is not more free from poisonous weeds or savage beasts than from evil men. You have composed the dissensions of the nobles, restored the ancient discipline of the monasteries, reformed the manners of the clergy, sustained the declining cause of liberal culture; polite letters, still struggling

[14] *Ep.* cccxvii. This letter is dated May 18, 1518, but the mention of Hutten's *Febris*, which appeared in Feb. 1519, would compel us to make it a year later, if there were no other reason for doing so.

with the patrons of the old ignorance, you support by your favour, protect by your authority, adorn by your splendour, cherish by your goodness, while you secure the aid of the most learned professors by the magnificent salaries which you offer. In establishing libraries, enriched with the best authors on every subject, you rival Ptolemy Philadelphus himself, who was more celebrated for this than even for his government." He then proceeds to say some severe things of the enemies of learning, and protests against the unfairness of confounding the cause of letters with the cause of Reuchlin and Luther, "seeing that they have nothing to do with one another. For my part," he continues, "I never cared for either the Cabbala or the Talmud; and I only once met Reuchlin at Frankfort, when I had no other intercourse with him than such a friendly interchange of civilities as there ought always to be among scholars. Nor, indeed, should I be ashamed to be connected with such a man; he has letters from me, in which I admonished him, when he was yet a stranger to me, to abstain from the open abuse in which he indulges, in German fashion, against his adversaries, so far am I from ever countenancing libellous compositions. Luther is a perfect stranger to me, nor have I ever had time to read more than two or three pages of his books; not that I have any objection to do so, but my own studies give me no time for it; and yet I hear some persons pretend that he was assisted by me." After some further notice of Luther, which, to avoid repetition, I omit, as a fuller account of him will presently be quoted from another letter, Erasmus goes on to speak of the many talented young Germans whose learning and eloquence he hoped would by-and-bye raise their country to the same height of glory which England already enjoyed. "Of these," he says, "I have no personal acquaintance with any but Eobanus, Hutten, and Beatus; they fight with all sorts of weapons against the enemies of languages and learning. . . . Whatever they publish is suspected to be mine, and this suspicion prevails even in your country, if your merchants who come over here tell true. . . . As if, forsooth, I must be responsible for whatever comes into their head to write, or as if I had not enough to do to defend my own writings! Why, they are Germans, they are young men, they are provided with pens, they are not wanting in abilities, and there are plenty of people to provoke and stir them up by their attacks. I have warned them all by my letters to keep their liberty within the bounds of moderation, and at any rate abstain from attacking the dignitaries of the Church, by whose patronage they stand against their enemies, and not put this additional stigma on the defenders of polite literature." Here is what he says here of the *Julius Exclusus*:—"Some months ago there was published a ridiculous book, which the argument proves clearly was written in the last schism, but by whom is uncertain, except that the book proves that, whoever he was, he was partial to the French. Suspicion has fixed itself on many, especially in Germany, for in this country the book is known under various titles. Well, some years ago, having found that this book was read on the sly, and having dipped into it—for I skimmed through it more truly than read it—many can testify how heartily I abused it, and what pains I took to have it buried in eternal darkness; which many will allow I did in the case of other books also. . . . I have never yet written any work, nor do I intend ever to write any, without putting my name to it. . . . All my labours hitherto have had for their object to aid useful studies and advance the religion of Christ. And from every quarter thanks are returned to me by all but a few monks and theologians who don't want to become either wiser or better." The letter (which was accompanied by a presentation copy of the second edition of the New Testament) concludes by expressing the writer's absolute devotion to the Holy See.

In his letter to Campeggio,[15] Erasmus says that the *Julius Exclusus* was ascribed by some to a certain Spaniard whose name was not mentioned, by some to the poet Faustus, and by others to Jerome Balbus. He expresses great surprise that any one should fix it upon himself, seeing that the style was so unlike his own; or if there was any resemblance, it was no great wonder, considering that everybody was reading his works. He had heard, he said, that Campeggio himself had been induced to entertain this suspicion regarding him, but he would never believe it; or if indeed it were so, he felt sure he could clear himself, if he had an opportunity of conversing with him. In an elegantly written and highly complimentary reply, Campeggio assured him that he had never affirmed or hinted to any one a suspicion that he was the author of the satire on Julius, but he admitted that he had thought so. He thanked him for the New Testament, of which a copy had been presented to him, and which he said he would "devour," and enclosed a ring of adamant, of which he begged his acceptance, in token of the high consideration in which he held him.[16]

[15] *Ep.* ccccxvi.   [16] *Ep.* cccclxiii.

One of those who sought thus to injure Erasmus by identifying him with works with which he had no direct concern, we need not be surprised to find was Hochstraten, the unscrupulous and bigoted leader of the persecution against Reuchlin. In the preface to a pamphlet which he had published, full of ignorant abuse of Reuchlin and the Jewish Cabbala, Hochstraten went out of his way to attack Erasmus, not, however, mentioning his name, but citing a passage from his notes on the New Testament with the evident object of rousing suspicion against him as a favourer of the Jews; and Erasmus thought it advisable to repel this indirect attack by a letter addressed to the inquisitor himself. He here takes Hochstraten severely to task for his treatment of Reuchlin. He had, indeed, he says, been exceedingly sorry to find that Reuchlin had indulged in such open abuse of his adversaries, but on the writings of the other side being put into his hands, he had found himself obliged to confess that the blame must be thrown on those who ought to have set an example of Christian moderation, but who had been the first to provoke, by their virulent attacks, the otherwise mild temper of Capnio. Hochstraten himself is thus pretty plainly described:—" As regards your own character, there were different opinions. Some said that you were of an easy temper enough, but were incited by others: but, on the other hand, a good number asserted that you had no advisers but your own ambition and avarice, your haughty and violent temper making you wish to take the lead of everybody, and your insatiable greed prompting you to long for the riches of the Jews." He then proceeds to notice his writings against Reuchlin's works on the Cabbala, and points out how much more becoming to him it would have been to have argued the question calmly and civilly, than to have made it the occasion for an outburst of such manifest personal hatred. His duties as an inquisitor, he urges, did not require him to do more than point out to his bishop any error which he might suppose would be injurious to the piety of Christians. "Had you not," he asks, "fully satisfied your duty, in following up for so many years an obscure book, which perhaps no one would ever have heard of if you had not made it famous? ... I would you had spent all that labour, time, and money on preaching Christ's gospel; if you had, either I am greatly deceived or James Hochstraten would be a greater man than he is now, and his name would be held in greater honour by those whose opinion is worth having, or at any rate would be less hated. ... The question which you, in your wisdom, had to consider, was this, whether that work of Capnio's contained anything that threatened serious danger to the Christian religion. Now the chief import of that book is the protection of the Jews against unjust treatment. To what purpose was it, then, to make such violent efforts to bring odium on the Jews? Is there any one among us who can be accused of lukewarmness in cursing that unhappy race? If it is the mark of a Christian to hate the Jews, we are all of us the very best of Christians in this quarter." Erasmus next proceeds to deal with the attack upon himself, and exclaims, "I trust Christ may love me as much as I hate the Cabbala!" The specific charge against him was that he had advocated divorce for other causes than the one allowed by Scripture, and, contrary to the law

of the Church, had pleaded for re-marriage after it; but
he had no difficulty in showing that, in merely expressing
a wish on the subject, he was neither showing his ignorance of the actual state of the case nor calling in
question the authority of the Church. "I am not," he
says, "in favour of divorce, but I do feel pity for those
who are on the brink of ruin, and Christian charity
often wishes for that which is impossible." The question is discussed at some length, but there is no need
to follow the discussion farther. Erasmus concludes
by exhorting Hochstraten to consult for the honour not
only of the Dominican order, but of the faculty of
divinity everywhere, by exerting his influence "to silence
those who in public and private harangues, in debates,
at dinners, at meetings, at conferences, and, what is
worst of all, in their sermons, pour out the most virulent
abuse of languages and polite letters, calling those who
study them anti-christs and heretics and other such
names."[17] This letter is dated from Antwerp, August 11,
1519. It seems to have called forth no reply. Erasmus says, at the beginning, he would not have written
it had he not been assured by the suffragan Bishop of
Cologne that his advice would be well taken. Possibly
Hochstraten was too much mortified by his defeat in
the affair of Reuchlin to be anxious to engage in further
controversy.

But the most elaborate statement of his position on
the part of Erasmus, and of the relations in which he
conceived himself to stand both to the Reformers and to
the Mother Church, is that contained in his letter to
Albert, the Archbishop of Maintz and Magdeburg.
This young prince, who, at the early age of four-and-

[17] *Ep.* cccclii.

twenty, had been elevated over the heads of all the bishops in Germany, was, as we have seen, deeply interested in the sale of the indulgences, having bargained with the Pope for half the profits. Otherwise his youth, his learning, and his German nature would have led him to sympathize with Luther; and, according to the testimony of Capito, long his chaplain and his counsellor, but afterwards well known as one of the most distinguished of the reformers, he did actually for a long time prevent the monks from attacking Luther.[18] Albert made no secret of his admiration for Erasmus. He had made the first advances towards him, and written inviting him to visit his court and expressing the highest appreciation of his literary labours.[19] Erasmus, not having found him at home either on his way to Basle—when he went thither to see the second edition of his New Testament through the press—nor on his return northwards, had not yet come into personal contact with him, but he had already twice written to him, first to introduce his friend Richard Pace, the King of England's ambassador to the Elector's court, and again on the occasion of the election of Charles V. as Emperor of Germany.[20] We have seen him dedicating to Albert his little treatise on the method of true theology, and in return Albert had sent him by the knight Ulrich von Hutten, who was then in his service, a richly carved gold cup of beautiful workmanship. This was the occasion which Erasmus took to enter at length upon his vindication of himself from all complicity with Luther; and as the letter is very important for enabling

---

[18] D'Aubigné's *History of the Reformation*, book iii. chap. iii.

[19] *Ep.* cccxxxiv.

[20] *Ep.* ccccxix. ccccviv.

us to understand his real sentiments, I reproduce it without abridgment.

ERASMUS *to* ALBERT, *Cardinal Archbishop of Maintz and Prince Elector.*[21]

"*Louvain, Nov.* 1, 1519.

"HONOURED Prelate and most illustrious Prince,—Your Highness's present has reached me, and most beautiful indeed it is, both in its workmanship and its material, and truly worthy of being sent by such a Prince; but whether Erasmus is worthy of receiving it I am not so sure, seeing that it were more fitting for him to drink from cups of glass or any common ware than from golden bowls. But if your cup were of glass, it would nevertheless be deposited among my favourite treasures, simply as having come from a person of such high distinction. Your present, however, which for its own sake was extremely acceptable, was recommended to me in no small degree by our friend Hutten, who informed me that it was called the cup of love, as being sacred to the Graces, I suppose, because when two people touch it with their lips, as if they were kissing it, they are made one; he adds that there is such virtue in it, that all who drink from it will be henceforth bound together by ties of the strongest kind. Wishing to try the experiment, when Cardinal William Croy within the last two or three days was visiting my library, I drank his health out of your cup, and he mine. He is a most fortunate young man, and his abilities, I think, are not unworthy of his great good fortune.

"I am sorry, however, that your present did not arrive sooner. For I had recently made peace with the

[21] *Ep.* ccclxxvii.

divines of Louvain on the understanding that they would silence the noisy tongues they had set a-going against me, and I, as far as I could, restrain the pens of my sympathizers. At the supper-party where the bargain was struck (for nothing can be done here without drinking), I would have produced your cup, if I had had it, and if they had drunk from it, perhaps our peace would have begun under better auspices; as it is, however, our friendship did not last long, a letter of mine, the meaning of which has been entirely misunderstood, having come to their knowledge, so that the short calm only made the storm which followed seem doubly furious. Nor do I doubt that this is owing to the arts of Satan, who hates nothing worse than concord among Christians, and on that account endeavours in every way he can to disturb the tranquillity of life and of letters; and this under the garb of religion, in order to do the greater hurt.

"On this subject I should be glad that your Highness, if your business permit it, should be informed of one or two facts, not merely for my sake, but, it may be, for your own—at any rate, in the interests of learning, which all right-minded people ought to support. In the first place, permit me to say that I have never had anything to do either with the affair of Reuchlin or with the cause of Luther. I have never taken any interest in the Cabbala or the Talmud. Those virulent contentions between Reuchlin and the party of Hochstraten have been extremely distasteful to me. Luther is a perfect stranger to me, and I have never had time to read his books beyond merely glancing over a few pages. If he has written well no praise is due to me; if not, it would be unjust to hold me responsible. This I know, that it is not the best judges who are most offended by his writings; not, indeed, that I suppose they approve of everything, but they read them in the spirit in which we read Cyprian or Jerome, or even Peter Lombard himself—that is to say, with considerable allowance. 'I was sorry when Luther's books were published; and when they began showing about some of his writings, I made every effort to prevent their publication, lest they should become the cause of any disturbance. Luther had written to me in a very Christian tone, as I thought; and I replied, advising him incidentally not to write anything of a factious or insulting nature against the Roman Pontiff, nor to encourage a proud or intolerant spirit, but to preach the Gospel out of a pure heart with all meekness. I did this in gentle language, in order to make the more impression; and I added that there were some here who sympathized with him, which has been very foolishly explained to mean that *I* sympathize with him; although my object evidently was to induce him to consult the judgment of others, and I am the only person who has written to give him advice. I am neither Luther's accuser, nor advocate, nor judge; his heart I would not presume to judge—for that is always a matter of extreme difficulty—still less would I condemn. And yet if I were to defend him, as a good man, which even his enemies admit him to be; as one put upon his trial, a duty which the laws permit even to sworn judges; as one persecuted—which would be only in accordance with the dictates of humanity—and trampled on by the bounden enemies of learning, who merely use him as a handle for the accomplishment of their designs, where would be the blame, so long as I abstained from mixing myself up with his cause? In short, I think it is my duty as a Christian to support Luther in this sense, that if he is innocent I should not wish him to be crushed by a set of malignant villains; if he is in error, I would rather see him put right than destroyed; for thus I should be acting in accordance with the example of Christ, who, as the prophet witnesseth, quencheth not the smoking flax, nor breaketh the bruised reed. I should wish that mind on which some bright sparks of evangelical doctrine seem to have fallen not to be extinguished, but to be corrected and taught to preach the glory of Christ. As it is, certain divines with whom I am acquainted neither warn Luther nor teach him; they merely traduce him before the people with insane clamours, and tear him to pieces with virulent abuse, while they have not a word on their lips save heresy, heretics, heresiarchs, schism, and antichrist.

"It cannot be denied that the most odious clamour has been raised against him here by persons who have never read a word he has written. It is certain that some have condemned what they did not understand. For example, Luther had written that we are not bound to confess mortal sins, unless they are manifest, meaning by that known to us when we confess. Some one interpreting that as if manifest meant openly perpetrated, raised a most astounding outcry, simply from not understanding the question. It is certain that some things have been condemned in the books of Luther as heretical, which in those of Bernard or Augustine are regarded as orthodox, if not even as truly religious. I advised these men at the first to abstain from such clamours, and to proceed rather by writings and by arguments. I urged in the first place that they should not publicly condemn that which they had not read—nay, which they had not considered—for I will not say which they did not understand; secondly, that it was unbecoming to divines, whose judgment ought ever to be most grave, to attempt to carry anything by tumult; finally, that one whose conduct was universally admitted to be blameless was no fit object for blind denunciation. Besides, I told them that it might not be altogether safe to touch upon such subjects before a mixed crowd in which there are many who have great objections to the confession of secret sins. Should such persons find that there are divines who deny the duty of confessing all crimes, they will eagerly seize the excuse for adopting so congenial an error. Though this was not merely my opinion, but the opinion of every sensible man, notwithstanding, in consequence of this friendly counsel they took up the suspicion that Luther's books were in a great measure mine, and written in Louvain, though in reality there is not a letter in them which is mine, or published with my knowledge or consent. And yet, relying upon this utterly false suspicion, without attempting any explanation with me, they have created frightful disturbances here, such as I have never seen in my life before. Besides, while it is the proper office of divines to teach, I find that many in our days are only for compulsion, for destroying and extinguishing; though Augustine did not approve of compulsion, unless teaching was combined with it, even against the Donatists, who were not merely heretics, but blood-thirsty robbers. Men who more than all others ought to be distinguished for their gentleness, seem absolutely to thirst for human blood, so eager are they for the capture and destruction of Luther. Such conduct is worthy of butchers, not of divines. If they want to prove themselves mighty theologians, let them convert the Jews, let them convert the heathen to Christianity, let them reform the public morals of Christendom, which are worse even than those of the Turks. How can it be just that he should be punished who at first merely proposed for debate questions which have always been subjects of discussion in all the schools of divinity? Why should he be persecuted who desires to be taught, who submits himself to the judgment of the Roman See, who commits his cause to the decision of the universities? But if he will not trust himself in the power of those who would rather see him destroyed than converted, it ought not to be thought very strange.

"Consider, first, the origin of this mischief. The world is weighed down with human constitutions, with scholastic opinions and dogmas, thanks to the encroachments of the begging friars, who, though they are dependents of the Roman See, yet have advanced to such a pitch of power and so increased in numbers, that the Roman Pontiff himself, and even the princes of the world, stand in awe of them. In their eyes the Pontiff is more than a god, when he acts as they desire; but if he does anything which conflicts with their interests, they value him no more than a dream. I am not condemning all, but there are a great many who will not scruple to ensnare the consciences of men if they can thereby increase their power or put money in their pockets. And such is their audacity, they had now begun to drop the name of Christ, and preach nothing but their own strange dogmas, which were becoming more shameless every day. They spoke of indulgences in such terms that even the most ignorant could no longer bear it. Owing to this and other similar causes, the true Gospel religion was gradually dying out, and it seemed probable that, while things thus got worse and worse, the fires of Christian piety, from whence only the flame of charity can be rekindled, would be altogether extinguished; in fact, religion was fast becoming a mere affair of worse than Jewish ceremonies. These things good men sigh over and deplore; they are acknowledged by all divines who are not monks, and in private conversation even by some who are. It was, I apprehend, such facts as these which drove Luther to raise his voice against the intolerable impudence of certain of the monks; for how can I form any more unworthy suspicion of one who neither courts honour nor covets wealth? I do not discuss the merits of those propositions of Luther's which are objected to; I speak only of the manner and occasion of publishing them. Luther had the presumption to call the indulgences in question; but then others had made the most impudent assertions regarding them. He presumed to speak disrespectfully of the power of the Roman Pontiff; but then his opponents had first written in extravagant terms respecting it, particularly those of the order of preaching friars, Alvarus, Sylvester, and the Cardinal di San Sisto. He presumed to despise the *ipse dixits* of St. Thomas; but then the Dominicans almost set them above the Gospels. He presumed to raise some scruples on the subject of confession; but then that is an institution which the monks employ for entangling the consciences of men. He presumed to neglect in some degree the doctrines of the schools;

but then they ascribe to them an extravagant authority, and, notwithstanding, differ about them among themselves, changing them from time to time, and introducing new ones while they abolish the old. This gave great offence to pious feelings, when it was found that in the universities there was scarcely ever a discourse upon evangelical doctrine, that those sacred authors to whom the Church from of old has given her sanction were now considered obsolete—nay, that even in sermons there was very little about Christ, but much about the power of the Pontiff and the opinions of recent writers. So evident was it that the sole object of preaching was to make money, to flatter, to rise in the world, and to paint over vice in false colours.

"These things, then, I think, should bear the blame, even if it be true that Luther has written somewhat intemperately. Whosoever favours Gospel doctrine is a friend to the Roman Pontiff, who is the chief herald of the Gospel, as other bishops are his heralds. All bishops are vicegerents of Christ, but among them the Roman Pontiff is pre-eminent. Such is the opinion we must entertain regarding him, because he desires nothing so much as the advancement of the glory of Christ, whose minister he boasts himself to be. They are his worst enemies who ascribe to him, in order to flatter him, an authority which he himself does not claim, and which it is not for the advantage of the Christian flock that he should possess. And yet some who are stirring up all this tumult are actuated by no zeal for the Pope; they merely abuse his power with a view to their own gain and the extension of their usurped authority. We have at present, as I judge, a pious Pontiff; but in such stormy times there must be many things of which he is ignorant, some things which he cannot control, even if he wished; but, as Maro says,—

Fertur equis auriga neque audit currus habenas.

He, therefore, helps the Pontiff in his pious designs, who exhorts to those things which are most worthy of Christ. It is no secret that there are some who are inciting the Pope against Luther, or rather, indeed, against all who presume to utter a whisper against their dogmas. But the authorities of the Church should look rather to the constant will of the Pontiff than to any good-natured compliance that may be extorted from him by dishonest representations.

"Now, as to the authors of this disturbance, I could most truly point them out, did I not fear to be thought a calumniator in my endeavours to tell the truth. I know many of them intimately; many of them have themselves declared what manner of men they are by their published books, in which their character and life are reflected as clearly as in a mirror. And would that they who assume the rod of censorship, with which they expel whom they will from the Christian fold, had deeply imbibed the doctrine and spirit of Christ! They have no right to wield it whose minds are not purified from the filth of this world's lusts. Whether they are thus pure may be easily proved by any one who will converse with them on a subject having to do with their own gain, or glory, or revenge. I wish I could instil into your Highness's mind what I know by experience and what I have learned on the authority of others respecting these matters. For it becomes me to remember the modesty of a Christian. What I have said I say the more freely because I have not the remotest connection with the cause of Reuchlin and

Luther. For I should not myself choose to write in that way, nor do I pretend to such learning as to have any wish to defend what others have written; but I cannot refrain from disclosing this mystery, that they have a far other aim than that which they pretend. They are angry that languages and literature are flourishing, and the old authors, who were formerly covered with dust and devoured with moths, reviving, and the world returning to the very fountains of truth. They are trembling for their money-boxes; they wish it to be thought that they know everything; they are afraid lest their *majesty* may suffer. This is the sore which they have long tried to conceal, but which has at last broken out, the pain being too great for them any longer to dissemble. Before Luther's books were published, they were making every effort they could for this end, especially the Dominicans and Carmelites, most of whom, I fear, are more wicked than ignorant. When Luther's books had come out, they seized the opportunity of confounding the cause of languages and literature—ay, and my cause too—with that of Capnio[22] and Luther, in which they showed themselves very bad logicians. For, in the first place, what connection have liberal studies with the question of faith; and, secondly, what have I to do with the cause of Capnio and Luther? But they have artfully mixed them together, in order that, by the odium they roused against both, they might crush all the students of letters.

"Moreover, that they are not sincere may be inferred from this fact, if from nothing else: as they themselves allow that there is no author, either ancient or modern,

---

[22] Capnio was the name, of Greek derivation (καπνός, *rauch*, smoke), by which Reuchlin was often called.

in whom errors may not be found, and even pronounce him a heretic who obstinately defends his errors, why do they pass over all others and make such vexatious inquiries into the opinions of one or two? They do not deny that Alvarus has committed many errors, or the Cardinal di San Sisto, or Sylvester Prieras; but nothing is said of them, because they are Dominicans. Against Capnio alone is a clamour raised because he knows the languages; against Luther, because they believe him to be learned in our sense of the word, though in reality he is so only to a small degree. In many things that Luther has written, he was improvident rather than impious, and what they are most angry at is that he does not pay much respect to Aquinas, that he has diminished the profits of the indulgences, that he does not pay much respect to the mendicant orders, that he shows less deference to the dogmas of the scholastics than to the Gospels, that he despises the ingenious subtleties invented by human disputants. These, forsooth, are intolerable heresies! But affecting not to notice such things, they go to the Pope with the most odious charges—those men, I say, who can be both peaceful and ingenuous whenever it is their object to inflict a wound. Formerly, too, a heretic was heard with respect, and absolved if he gave satisfaction; but if, after being convicted, he persisted in his errors, the extreme penalty was that he was not admitted to catholic and ecclesiastical communion. Now the charge of heresy is another thing, and yet for any light cause they take the cry on their lips, 'It is a heresy.' Formerly he was considered a heretic who dissented from the Gospels, from the Articles of Faith, or from those doctrines which enjoyed equal authority with them.

Now if any one dissents from Aquinas he is denounced as a heretic; nay, he is so if he dissents from any piece of reasoning which any sophist fabricated yesterday in the schools. Whatever they don't like, whatever they don't understand, is a heresy; to know Greek is a heresy; to speak with a good accent is a heresy; whatever they do not do themselves is a heresy. I confess it is a grave crime to corrupt the faith, but every subject ought not to be made a question of faith. And they who decide upon questions of faith ought to be free from all appearance of ambition, avarice, hatred, or revenge. But who is there that does not see what these men are aiming at? If the restraints on their cupidity shall be once relaxed, the life of no good or great man will be safe from their fury. They will at last threaten the bishops, and even the Roman Pontiff himself; and, indeed, if some of them are not doing so just now, I am willing to be accounted a false prophet. What the Dominican Order will adventure, Jerome Savonarola and the catastrophe of Berne—to quote no other instance —ought to admonish us. I am not reviving the infamy of the order; but I warn the world what it must expect if they are allowed to succeed in every rash attempt.

"Whatever I have said thus far has nothing to do with the cause of Luther; I am discussing only the means by which we may escape the danger we are in. The Roman Pope has taken Capnio's cause into his own hands. Luther's affair has been handed over to the universities, and far be it from me to question their judgment, whatever it may be. I have always been careful to avoid writing anything obscene, or seditious, or contrary to the doctrine of Christ; nor have I ever knowingly been either a teacher of error or an author of disturbance, and would submit to anything rather than excite sedition. Nevertheless, for certain reasons, I wished these things to be known to your Highness; not that I would presume to advise you, or anticipate your own judgment, but that, if the adversaries of polite letters should attempt to make use of your high rank for their own purposes, you may be able, with greater certainty, to determine concerning these matters what is best to be done; and, in my opinion, the more you abstain from this course, the more you will consult for your own peace. I have revised the 'Method of Theology,' which is dedicated to your Highness, and enlarged it with no small additions.

"May Christ, who is supreme in goodness and in power, preserve you safe and well to eternity."

Thus could Erasmus generously plead the cause of one in whom he saw much to admire, and whose earnest spirit he hoped might be of service, if only it could be kept within due bounds, in fighting the battle of pure religion and elegant learning against superstition and ignorance, at the very time that he was disclaiming all responsibility for the extravagances against which he felt bound to protest. He had indeed no sympathy with the doctrinal paradoxes of Luther. He felt, however, that he was in the main right, if somewhat needlessly violent, on the question of indulgences; and while fully resolved not to be confounded with him in any resistance to the Holy See, he was willing, nevertheless, to do all he could to protect him from the common enemies of both. Indeed, in this letter to the Cardinal Elector he had probably been carried in his praise of Luther farther than he had intended; and he soon found that it was made use of in a way which he had never contemplated. It had been entrusted to the care of Hutten, with instructions to deliver it if he thought it expedient to do so, but if not to suppress and destroy it. Hutten, it would seem, was so pleased with the letter that instead of delivering it to the Cardinal he had it printed, and, with a view to committing Erasmus still more decidedly to the opinions it expressed, he interpolated the word "our" before the first mention of Luther.[23] This was, of course, very annoying to Erasmus, who, though he must have hoped that his letter would have some influence with the Cardinal in disposing him to see that Luther had fair play in his battle with the monks, had certainly no thought of its publication; and we find him, not unnaturally, complaining, in writing to Mosellanus, the professor of Greek at Leipsic, in reference to this point, that "our enemies are wiser than we, for they keep everything secret, and conspire in the dark, while we conceal nothing."[24] But his letter to Luther, and a particular expression he had used in it, in which he had seemed to approve of Luther's conduct, were in danger of proving even more prejudicial to him than anything he had written to Albert. This will appear from a letter which he addressed to the Pope in the following year, shortly before the actual publication, in Germany, of the bull against Luther, but some months after its sanction by the Sacred College, and when it was well known at Louvain that Dr. Eck had returned in triumph from Rome, armed with the terrible weapon with which the Reformation was to be utterly crushed. Even then, it will be seen, Erasmus did not hesitate to speak favourably of Luther.

[23] *Er. Op.* iii. 584, D. 588, C.   [24] *Er. Op.* iii. 561, C.

ERASMUS *to the Most Blessed Father* LEO X.[25]

"*Louvain, Sept.* 13, 1520.

". . . . I have no acquaintance with Luther, nor have I ever read his books, except perhaps ten or twelve pages, and that only by snatches. From what I then saw, I judged him to be well qualified for expounding the Scriptures in the manner of the Fathers—a work greatly needed in an age like this, which is so excessively given to mere subtleties, to the neglect of really important questions. Accordingly, I have favoured his good, but not his bad qualities, or rather I have favoured Christ's glory in him. I was among the first to foresee the danger there was of this matter ending in violence, and no one ever hated violence more than I do. Indeed, I even went so far as to threaten John Froben the printer, to prevent him printing his books. I wrote frequently and industriously to my friends, begging that they would admonish this man to observe Christian meekness in his writings, and do nothing to disturb the peace of the Church. And when he himself wrote to me two years ago, I lovingly admonished him what I wished him to avoid, and I would he had followed my advice. This letter, I am informed, has been shown to your Holiness, I suppose in order to prejudice me, whereas it ought rather to conciliate your Holiness's favour towards me. For what do I omit there of which I ought to admonish him? I do this civilly, it is true, but I was more likely to succeed in that way than by severity; besides, I was writing to a stranger. Having prescribed to him a certain method of procedure, lest the freedom of my admonition might give offence, I added, 'I write this,

[25] *Ep.* dxxix.

not because I think you need my advice, but in the hope that you will always go on as you have begun,' implying of course that he was already acting of his own accord as I would have him act. If, however, I had really approved of the style which Luther at first adopted, what need was there for me to use so many words in suggesting a new one? And yet I hear that certain persons have impudently and calumniously twisted the sense of that passage; and even more that of the following words, that there are many here who sympathize with him. This was perfectly true. A great many here sympathized with what was good in him just as I did.

". . . . If any one has ever heard me defending Luther's dogmas even over the bottle, I shall not object to be called a Lutheran. But it is urged that I have not attacked him with my pen. In the first place, I could not refute him without reading his writings attentively and more than once. For this I had not time, being fully occupied with my own studies. In the second place, I believed the task to be too great for such moderate learning and ability as I possess. Besides, I was unwilling to rob the universities which had undertaken this office of the honour which was their due. Finally, I was afraid to provoke the hostility of so many powerful men, especially as no one had assigned me this province. Wherefore, if the enemies of learning in Rome calumniate me, my surest defence is in your wisdom and my own innocence. I am not so infatuated that I should think of resisting the supreme vicegerent of Christ, I, who would not oppose even my own bishop. . . . . I merely disapproved of the mode of attacking Luther, not because I was concerned for Luther, but for the authority of theologians. . . . . If they had first refuted Luther, and then burned his books, they might have destroyed him without throwing the world into tumult, if he indeed deserved what they say of him. . . ."

The Pope's bull, excommunicating Luther and commanding that his works should be burned, greatly alarmed Erasmus. He dreaded the consequences to himself and the cause of letters of such a victory on the part of the monks. "I greatly fear," he writes, "for the unhappy Luther. The conspiracy is so hot everywhere, the princes, and especially Pope Leo, are so exasperated against him. I would that Luther had followed my advice and abstained from those violent and opprobrious writings. More would have been gained and with less odium. The death of one man would be a small matter; but if the monks should succeed in this attempt, there will be no bearing their insolence. They will never rest till they have utterly abolished linguistic studies and all polite literature. They are now attacking Capnio again, merely from hatred of Luther, who, contrary to my advice, mixed up his name with his own business, and thus roused fresh hostility against Reuchlin, while he did himself no good at all. Eck challenged to a disputation; Hochstraten had promised I know not what syllogisms, to which all should be compelled to yield. The divines of Louvain were disputing and even writing. The judgment of the University of Paris was expected, and lo! suddenly all seems likely to end in a bull, and in smoke. A most formidable bull has been printed, but the Pope has forbidden its publication. I am afraid a terrible disturbance will follow. They who are instigating the Pope to this course give him advice, of the piety of which I will say nothing, but which, in my opinion, is certainly most dangerous. The whole affair sprang first from bad causes, and has been pushed on by equally bad methods. The tragedy originated in the stupidity of the monks and their hatred of learning. Then, by means of violent abuse and malicious conspiracies, it proceeded to the height of madness which it has now reached. What their aim is no one can doubt—namely, to suppress the literature of which they are ignorant, and then reign triumphant, they and their barbarism. I am taking no part in this tragedy, else I might have a bishopric if I would write against Luther. I am grieved to see the Gospel doctrine thus oppressed, and ourselves not taught, but compelled; or else taught things contrary to the Holy Scriptures and to common sense."[86]

The effects of the bull were indeed, as might have been anticipated, to lash the monks into fury. They considered their victory won, and if they had before muttered, they now fairly roared. At Antwerp so violent were the declamations against Luther that the civil power was compelled to interpose, though it would seem its interference was in vain.[87] A Dominican was heard to say, "I should like to fix my teeth in Luther's throat, and would never hesitate to approach Christ's body with his blood still red on my lips."[88] Everywhere the names of Luther and Erasmus were coupled, and at Louvain it was said that two or three monks had agreed over their cups that this should be so.[89]

[86] *Ep.* dxxviii.
[87] *Er. Op.* iii. 629, A.
[88] "Utinam mihi liceret dentibus meis demordere gulam Lutheri, nihil vererer ore adhuc cruento accedere ad corpus Christi."—*Ib.* 630, C, D.
[89] *Er. Op.* iii. 579, F.

Luther, it was said, was a pestilent fellow, but Erasmus was far worse, for it was from his breasts that Luther had sucked all the poison in his composition.[30] "Erasmus," cried others, "laid the egg, and Luther has hatched it." Everywhere they were preached against and prayed for. Prayers were offered that as Paul from a persecutor had become a teacher of the Church, even so Luther and Erasmus might be converted.[31] At Bruges a drunken Franciscan, in a public harangue, bellowed for hours against Luther and Erasmus, calling them beasts, asses, cranes, and clods. The same man, on another occasion, having asserted that there were heresies in Erasmus's books, and being asked to point out any, replied, "I haven't read his books; I tried to read his 'Paraphrases,' but the Latinity was too profound, and I am afraid he may fall into some heresy on account of his profound Latinity."[32]

Soon, however, it became evident to sensible people that all this violent abuse, as is usually the case when that abuse is entirely unfounded, did more good than harm to the persons attacked, and helped rather than hindered the cause against which it was directed. "Do you imagine," asks Erasmus, in a letter addressed to one of the most obstinate of his enemies, "that the people have no common sense? Do you form your opinion of all by yourself and the like of you? Even the common people have some sense, which they got by nature, by experience of the world, by intercourse with learned men, by the reading of books. What do you suppose they must think when they see a doctor of divinity, dressed in his clerical costume, in a sacred place, from the pulpit, from which they expect to hear the Gospel

[30] *Ib.* 628, D.   [31] *Ib.* 537, D.   [32] *Ib.* 580, B.

preached, railing, with violent hate and virulent tongue, against his neighbour's good name, his eyes all on fire, his lips foaming, in a tremendous voice, every movement of his body showing the envy and hatred which fill his soul? If all he said were true, still the people are not so stupid as not to see that such things are said in the wrong place, or that what is said in such a hostile spirit cannot proceed from a pious mind." [33]

It was at this time that Edward Lee was such a sharp thorn in the side of Erasmus, but having already noticed him in another connection, I need say no more about him here. [34]

The chief enemy of Erasmus at Louvain was an old Carmelite priest, very ignorant, very obstinate, and very violent, named Egmund. It is to him that the prayer above quoted must be credited, and we learn that in one of his pulpit harangues he had declared that Erasmus would fight out his battle with Faber in the depths of hell. Being asked what fault he had to find with Erasmus, he replied that he had written his New Testament. "And what then?" it was asked. "Why, then, our whole system is at an end." [35] This man had attacked the learned scholar so persistently and so furiously in his pulpit harangues, that he at length thought it necessary to appeal to the Rector of the University to know how long this was to be permitted. In the hope of making peace, the Rector invited them both to a conference at his house; and on their appearance, in case angry words should lead to blows —such is the expression of Erasmus himself, who gives this humorous account of the interview to his friend More

[33] *Er. Op.* iii. 626, A, B.
[34] See above, vol. i. pp. 327-335.
[35] "Ergo omnia nostra nihil sunt." —*Er. Op.* iii. 629, B, C, D.

—he took his seat between them. After a short prefatory statement from the Rector, Egmund, putting on a very grave face, began: "I have done no injury to any one," said he, "in my sermons; and if Erasmus thinks himself hurt, let him say how, and I am ready to answer him."

Erasmus then asked if he thought there could be any worse injury than to traduce and tell lies of an unoffending man in a public discourse.

At this Egmund became purple with rage. "And why," he exclaimed, "do you traduce *us* in your books of divinity?"

"Your name," replied Erasmus, "does not occur in my books."

"Nor has yours," retorted the other, "been ever mentioned in my sermons."

Erasmus answered that his books were not of the high character which Egmund ascribed to them, that much of them was of an amusing nature, but that this could not be pleaded for pulpit discourses. "Besides," he continued, "I have written far less concerning you than the facts warrant. You have lied publicly about me, affirming that I sympathize with Luther, whereas I never did so in the sense in which people interpret your words, and in which you yourself mean it."

"You lie!" roared Egmund, now fairly beside himself with passion; "it is you who are the author of all this commotion! You are the cunning rogue, the sly old fox, that turns everything inside out with his tail!" And so he went on, pouring forth in a torrent every epithet of abuse suggested by his fury.

Erasmus, too, now began to get warm. A contemptuous epithet escaped him, but he succeeded in repressing the speech which was about to follow it, and turning to the Rector with a smile, he said, "I might give evidence as to the insolence with which I have been treated; I might answer abuse with abuse. He calls me cunning, I might call him a fox; he calls me a double-dealer, I might call him a four-fold dealer; he says I turn everything inside out with my tail, I might say that he poisons everything with his tongue. But such language is not worthy of men, and scarcely even of women. Let us proceed to arguments. Imagine that I ——"

"I don't imagine," roared the monk, interrupting, "I won't imagine; that is your business: you poets imagine, and never tell anything but lies."

"If you won't imagine," replied Erasmus, now more inclined to laugh than be angry, "then grant."

"I won't grant," cried Egmund.

"Suppose that it is so."

"I won't suppose."

"Well, then, put the case."

"I won't put."

"Well," said Erasmus, "let it be."

"But it isn't," shrieked Egmund.

"What, then," said Erasmus, "do you want me to say?"

"Say it is," said the monk.

The Rector at length prevailed on him to permit Erasmus to speak. "Though it be true," he said, "that I have written some things in my books not exactly as I ought, nevertheless it was not right for you to abuse the authority implied in a sacred place and a discourse on sacred subjects, as well as the credulity of simple people, to gratify your own vengeance. You might have written against me, or you might have brought an action against me. As it is, you are doing an injury, not so much to me as to this whole University, the whole people, and the office of preaching, which is dedicated to far other purposes."

Not knowing what answer to make, Egmund twisted himself round, and exclaimed, "Ja! you and I would like to have the same authority."

"What," replied Erasmus, "of preaching?"

He assented.

"And yet," continued Erasmus, "I am a preacher of long standing, and I think I could preach better sermons than I ever hear from you."

"Why don't you do it, then?"

"Because," he continued, "I think I am doing more good in writing books; though I should find no fault with your employment, if you would only teach such things as contribute to good morals."

Here a phrase which Erasmus had made use of in his letter to the Rector, to the effect that having done no harm, or, rather, having rendered some good service, he ought not to be treated in this way, occurring to Egmund, he asked, "When have you rendered good service?"

"Most people," replied Erasmus, "allow that I have rendered no ill service to good letters."

"Ja!" cried Egmund, "so you call them; but they are bad letters."

"In sacred letters, too, I have restored a great deal."

"No, you have corrupted a great deal."

"Why, then, does the Roman Pontiff approve of my work in his brief?"

"Ja! your brief! Who has seen your brief?" asked the monk, meaning that it was forged.

"Do you require," rejoined Erasmus, "that I should carry the brief about with me, or exhibit it in the market-place? I showed it to Atensis, and Dorpius saw it."

"Ja! Dorpius!" cried Egmund, and was only restrained by a look from the Rector from uttering some term of reproach.

"You shall see it too, if you wish," said Erasmus.

"I don't want to see it," cried the other.

"Then why do you condemn it? Why does the Pope's authority weigh so much with you in condemning Luther, while in approving of my writings it is lighter than a feather?"

He then began to remind Erasmus what honours the divines of Louvain had paid to him before he had written against them. To which he replied that it was not his habit to make light of any kindness, but that he had not experienced very much from the divines.

By-and-bye, going off to another subject, he said he would never have done preaching against Luther till he had put an end to him.

Erasmus replied that he might vociferate against Luther till he burst, provided he did not bellow against himself; that he did not complain of what he had said against Luther, but of what he had said against himself. But if he pleased, let him go on; he would gain nothing by it, but become the laughing-stock of all good men; and, indeed, during his discourse, many had been seen to laugh.

"Ja!" cried Egmund, "they were your partisans."

"How that could be I don't know," answered Erasmus, "for most of them I had never seen before."

At length, after much more of the same kind, the Rector interposed, and observing that such recriminations were unworthy of theologians, said that he would gladly continue to listen if anything could be said tending towards peace.

Erasmus having asked Egmund what terms he proposed, he replied, "That you should restore my character, which you have injured."

"Where? In my letters?"

He nodded.

"As they have been already published," answered Erasmus, "what you ask is not in my power."

"Well, then," said the other, "make your recantation."

"What?"

"Write that there are good and sincere theologians at Louvain."

"That," said Erasmus, "I have never denied; but if those whom I have taxed will give me good materials for it, I will write grandly about them."

"And if you," retorted Egmund, "will give us materials for speaking well of you, we will speak well of you. You have a pen, we have tongues. You tax us behind our backs, but I have the courage to speak to you to your face."

"And no wonder, with your manners, if you had courage even to spit in the face of a good man."

Egmund said he would not be so rude; whereupon the Rector, again interrupting, desired them to speak of Luther, his cause being the real point in dispute between them.

"Well," exclaimed Egmund, "you have written in defence of Luther; now write against him."

Erasmus declared he had never written in his defence, but rather for the theologians against him, and pleaded his occupations, his inability, his fears, adding that he would consider it cruel to take up his pen to stab a man who was already down.

"But," rejoined Egmund, "this is just what we want you to write, that we have conquered Luther."

"There are enough," said Erasmus, "to raise this cry, though I hold my peace. Besides, it will be more proper for those who have gained the victory to celebrate it. But," he added, "there is no evidence that they have gained it, seeing that their books have not yet seen the light."

On this, Egmund turned to the Rector in despair, and said, "Did I not tell you it would be of no use? As long as he refuses to write against Luther, so long shall we account him a Lutheran."

"By this reasoning," retorted Erasmus, "you will be a Lutheran in my eyes, seeing that you have written nothing against him; and not only you, but a great many others besides."

Egmund, having no reply ready, here made a bow to the Rector, and without condescending to take further notice of his antagonist flung out of the room; and thus ended this somewhat grotesque attempt to bring an obstinate and angry man to reason.[36]

The tragedy is evidently not without its comic scenes. At Nuremberg a little incident occurred, which is amusingly narrated, in a letter to Erasmus, by his friend Bilibald Pirckheimer. At a large party, where there was present a fat and stolid mendicant friar, with great pretensions to sanctity, the conversation turned on

---

[36] *Ep.* dliv.

Erasmus, and much was said in his praise, to the evident annoyance of the monk, who all the time kept shaking his head and muttering inarticulately to himself. Pirckheimer, observing this, turned to him and asked what fault he had to find with Erasmus. With a face of portentous gravity, the monk replied that there were many faults in him which called for censure. Being pressed to name one, after long hesitation he at length replied, "Though I had resolved to be silent, lest it should be supposed that what I say is prompted by envy, still, as you urge me, this Erasmus of yours, whom you are all praising to the skies, is a great eater of fowls; and this I have not on mere hearsay, for when I was acquainted with him at Basle I saw it with these two eyes." "Indeed!" said Pirckheimer. "Pray, may I ask, were the fowls stolen or bought?" "Bought," said the monk. "Why, then," retorted Pirckheimer, "that vile fox is a much greater knave which comes into my yard every day and carries off a fowl without ever paying for it. But is it, then, a crime to eat fowls?" "Most assuredly," answered the monk; "for it is the sin of gluttony, and the more heinous when it is committed frequently and by men who have taken vows." "Perhaps," said Pirckheimer, "he eats them on fast-days?" "No," replied the monk, "but we ecclesiastics ought to abstain from all such delicacies." "And yet, my good father," exclaimed Pirckheimer, "unless I am much deceived, it was not by eating wheaten or barley bread that you got that huge paunch of yours; and if all the fowls with which you have stuffed it could now raise up their voice and cackle, they would drown the trumpets of an army!"[37]

[37] *Er. Op.* iii. 550, E.—551, A.

A little later Erasmus had another opportunity of speaking an effectual word for Luther; it was, perhaps, the most effectual he had spoken yet. Charles V. was crowned Emperor of Germany at Aix on the 22nd of October, 1520, and soon afterwards the court repaired to Cologne. The Elector Frederic of Saxony, being then undecided what course to pursue towards Luther, being urged by Aleander, the Papal nuncio, to take strong measures, and hearing that Erasmus was at Cologne, sent a message to him desiring that he would wait upon him. Erasmus accordingly came—this was on the 5th of December—and he and the Prince and Spalatine, to whom we are indebted for the anecdote, conversed together, standing by the fireside. The Elector proposed to Erasmus to speak in Dutch, but Erasmus—who we know had no affection for his native language — preferred speaking in Latin, which the Elector also understood, though he chose to answer through Spalatine. The Elector then desired Erasmus freely to give him his opinion of Luther. Erasmus, pressing his lips close together, stood musing and delaying to reply; while Frederic, as his manner was when he was discoursing earnestly with any one, fixed his eyes steadily upon him and stared him full in the face. At last Erasmus burst out with these words, "Luther has committed two sins; he has touched the Pope on the crown and the monks on the belly." The Elector smiled at the expression, and it is said called it to remembrance a little before his death.

On his return to his lodgings, Erasmus immediately sat down and wrote some axioms, as he called them, which he gave to Spalatine; but soon afterwards he sent him a letter, begging him to return the manuscript, lest

Aleander should see it and be provoked to do him an injury. The axioms, however, have been preserved, and are as follows:—

"That the source of all these dissensions was the hatred which some persons entertained for literature."

"That only two Universities had pretended to condemn Luther."

"That Luther made very reasonable demands by offering to dispute publicly once more."

"That being a man void of ambition, he was less to be suspected of heresy."

"That they who condemned him deserved to be condemned themselves for advancing propositions offensive to pious ears."

"That the Pope's unmerciful bull was disapproved of by all honest men." [38]

Erasmus, it was said, even went so far as to accuse Aleander of having forged the bull; but the only authority for the statement being the nuncio himself, this may be considered doubtful. At all events the position which he assumed, and his advocacy of Luther's cause, were never forgiven by Aleander, who from henceforth became his bitter enemy.[39]

If the dates of the letters may be trusted so far, Erasmus must have left Cologne immediately after the interview with Frederic, and returned to Louvain, whence, on the 6th of December, he wrote another long defence of himself to Cardinal Campeggio.[40] He begins this letter by saying he had intended to spend the winter in Rome, in order to avail himself of the advan-

---

[38] JORTIN, i. 226.
[39] Ib. 222.
[40] Ep. dxlvii. Perhaps, however, this letter was not written at Louvain, but at Cologne.—Conf. Ep. dxlix.

tages afforded by the Pontifical library, but had been prevented by their frequent royal congresses, from which it was not for his interest to be altogether absent. He hopes, however, to accomplish his purpose next year, and looks forward with pleasure to spending the remainder of his life in Rome, where learned men are not only permitted to pursue their studies in peace, but meet with honours and rewards. This intention he never fulfilled; perhaps it was never so serious with him as he wished his Italian correspondents to believe; but he had, no doubt, by this time made up his mind to leave Brabant. "This country," he remarks, "is becoming more civilized every day; still it cannot altogether divest itself of its rude manners, and ancient barbarism finds here some of her most indefatigable defenders." He is thus led to speak of the monks and their scandalous attacks on literature, and especially on himself as its representative, for which purpose they were not ashamed to make use of the pulpit, the purity of which, he remarks, is more essential to public morality than even that of the blessed Mass. Certain members of the order of St. Dominic—an order which contains many men of distinguished learning and piety, but among so many thousands it is no wonder if there are some of a very opposite character—together with some of the Carmelites, are the leaders of this party, and they pretend to regard him as their enemy, notwithstanding that there is no greater friend to true religion than himself. "I venerate and adore Christian piety," he exclaims, "in whatever garb it may appear, whatever frock it may put on, black or white, linen or woollen, yellow or brown, provided only there is evidence that it is genuine." The source and seed-bed, however, of all this commotion is the incurable hatred of languages and letters. "From time to time the scene is changed, new actors and new characters are introduced, but it is always the same play. Hence the storm let loose on John Reuchlin, under the pretext of defending the faith, when in reality the sole object was to gratify one man's revenge. This attempt having failed, on the unlucky publication of certain writings of Martin Luther's, their courage immediately rose, as they thought that a weapon was thus put into their hands by which they might at once destroy languages and polite letters, Reuchlin and Erasmus." He then proceeds to review once more at considerable length his connection with Luther, explains the suspected passages in his own letter to him, and advocates the use of mild remedies, maintaining that whatever be Luther's deserts, it would certainly be more humane to cure than to kill him. "I am surely a strange kind of Lutheran," he concludes; "I was the first to condemn Luther's books, because I thought they threatened disturbance, which I have always heartily abhorred; I was the first to oppose the publication of his writings; I am almost the only man that has never read his books; I alone have never attempted to defend anything he has said, not even over the bottle. I always exhorted those who could to dispute against Luther, and write against him. When this was begun at Louvain, I expressed my unhesitating approval, and I would they had set about it in a more rational way. Then there came out the judgment of the two Universities against Luther; a terrible bull was published in the name of the Roman Pontiff; Luther's books were burned; a popular clamour was raised, and there was an evident determination to take the severest possible measures. Everybody thought the bull more unmerciful than might have been expected from the mild character of Leo, and yet its severity was exaggerated in no small degree by those who were entrusted with the duty of putting it in execution. Meantime no one observed that Erasmus was either disquieted or graver than his wont. . . . I am not so impious as to dissent from the Catholic Church, nor so ungrateful as to differ from Leo, from whom I have experienced no common favour and kindness. . . . If the corrupt manners of the Roman court call for some great and immediate remedy, certainly it is not for me or the like of me to usurp this office. I prefer the present state of things, such as it is, rather than run the risk of exciting new commotions, which often turn out quite differently from what was intended. . . . Let others affect martyrdom ; I do not think myself worthy of such an honour. . . ." Erasmus then explains that his object in writing at such length was, in case any one should have attempted to raise suspicions against him, to assure his Eminence that he always had been, and always would be, the most devoted servant of the Holy See, to which he owed so many obligations, and so he brings his letter to a close.[41]

It was only a few days after this letter was written—namely, on the 10th of December—that Luther startled the world, and made the separation of Germany from Rome a fact never to be recalled, by throwing the decretals and the Pope's bull into the burning pile by the Holy Cross at Wittenberg. The next year was an eventful one in the annals of the Reformation. On the 28th of January the young Emperor, Charles V., opened

" *Ep.* dxlvii.

the Diet of Worms, amid the eager expectation of the German people on the one side, hoping that a bold front would be opposed to Roman usurpation and insolence, and yet trembling for the safety of their champion; and of the Papal party on the other, confident that this new heresy would now at once be extinguished, and this audacious blasphemer of the true Church meet with the fate he deserved. Luther's triumphal progress through Germany, and his entry into Worms on the 16th of April, his heroic appearance before the Diet the next day and the day following, the attempts made to induce Charles to violate his safe-conduct, happily unsuccessful, the imperial edict against Luther making it high treason to harbour him or give him food or drink and commanding his books to be burned, Luther's seizure and confinement in the Wartburg—these are the events, all-important in the history of human liberty, and possessed therefore of undying interest for all generations of men, which were passing in the world, while Erasmus was quietly pursuing his studies at Louvain or fighting his battles with his persecutors. They are brilliantly described in the pages of D'Aubigné, and here need only be recalled in order to preserve the connection of the life whose story we are reviewing with the general history of the times. At Louvain Erasmus remained till towards the end of the year, no unconcerned spectator of what was going on around him. If he had disapproved of Luther's violence before, he must have thought his open defiance of the Pope's power and his burning of the bull little short of madness. Yet he continued to preserve the same moderate language regarding him, condemning only what he looked upon as his intemperance and extravagance, but defending his character, and not sparing those who were crying for his blood. Once, indeed—and this was before either party had proceeded to extremities—he had broken out into a petulant expression, which was perhaps as nearly a curse as his principles and his gentle nature permitted. "It is clear," he said, "that the monks are thirsting for the blood of Luther, and, for my part, I don't care whether they eat him roast or boiled!"[42] Doubtless he thought it hard that his studies, which he believed were infinitely more important to the world than the question whether the Pope's pardons were worth the money paid for them or no, should be disturbed to satisfy the conscience of an obscure monk, and by a matter with which he had never mixed himself up. Generally, however, he kept his temper, and spoke of Luther as one who had great faults indeed, but for whom, nevertheless, he felt great respect. Peace was what Erasmus desired before all things—peace for himself, that he might pursue those studies which he loved, and which he hoped would of themselves, by the diffusion of knowledge and the overthrow of superstition, work out a real and lasting reformation, peace for the Church, because he held that no other state was in accordance with the spirit or purpose of Christ. And if he sometimes implies a doubt whether he ought not to have joined the side of Luther, whether he was not prevented by mere weakness from doing so, this was perhaps not so much because his reason was convinced, as because his sensitive nature and quick sympathies enabled him to see all round the question, and to feel how much good there was even on

---

[42] "Isti nihil aliud quam esuriunt Lutherum, nec mea refert, elixum malint, an assum."—*Er. Op.* iii. 544. C.

the side which he felt it impossible for him heartily to embrace. Erasmus was undoubtedly in a most difficult position. He went with the Reformers to a very great extent; but he quite sincerely believed that it was both possible and desirable, while clearing away abuses and asserting liberty of conscience, to maintain the unity of the Catholic Church under its visible head—the Bishop of Rome. He saw clearly the evils which the movement of Luther was producing, and was destined to produce, in the immediate future, but he failed to perceive that the good which he, in common with the Reformers, desired, was not attainable by the mild measures which alone he was willing to countenance. He failed to perceive that the spiritual despotism of Rome would never, of its own accord, change into the gentle paternal superintendence of which he dreamt as the result of his own labours. A few more characteristic passages from his letters will throw some further light on his opinions and feelings during this great crisis of the world's history, and will complete our review of his connection with the Reformation :—

ERASMUS *to a certain Influential Personage.*[a]

"*Louvain, January* 28, 1521.

" . . . . I AM very far from approving of the conduct of those who howl and shriek against the Roman Pontiff, or bespatter him with abuse. For if Peter justly blames those who speak evil of dignities—that is, of men entrusted with the exercise of power—how much less can it be right to attack him in whom almost all churches acknowledge that the supreme authority is invested? Nor do I now stop to ask from whom he

[a] *Ep.* dlxiii.

derives this authority; at any rate, as, in ancient times, of many equal presbyters, one was chosen Bishop, in order to prevent schism, so now, out of all the Bishops, it is expedient that one should be chosen Pontiff, not only to put an end to dissensions, but also to restrain the power of other Bishops in case any one should be inclined to abuse it, as well as that of the princes of the world. Nor, indeed, am I ignorant of the complaints that are commonly made about the Roman See; but as it would be folly to believe every popular rumour, it would surely be unjust to attribute to the Roman Pontiff everything that goes on at Rome. Much goes on there without his knowledge—for it is impossible for one man to take cognisance of everything—much, too, against his will, and in spite of his resistance. And in the present state of the world, if Peter himself were at the head of affairs in Rome, he would be compelled, I think, to wink at some things which he could by no means approve of in his heart. But, however that may be, far more would be effected by petitions expressed in moderate language, or by arguments or quiet complaints, than by violent attacks or bitter invectives. If, however, our crimes deserve that the world must be chastised with great disturbances, and if offences must needs come, I will at least take care that they do not come through me. No one shall find me either the teacher of error or the leader of disturbance.

". . . . On the publication of the bull, which, with all its terrors, has not succeeded in alienating the minds of the common people from Luther, certain persons conspired over their cups always to couple my name with his in their public harangues, thinking, of course, to take away my character at the same time;

for they think me their enemy, because I have somewhere spoken of the folly of those who are so much in love with Scotist subtleties that they never reach the sources of divine wisdom; because I sometimes dissent from St. Thomas in my Annotations; because I recommend that young men should not be enticed into taking on them the restraints of the monastic life before they know their own mind and understand the meaning of religion; because I maintain that true piety does not consist in ceremonies, but in the affections of the heart; because I defend polite learning, on which they have long ago declared war. When they are asked what heresy they have found in my books, they answer that they have not read them, but still that there must be danger in my obscure Latinity. These answers are made both by theologians and monks; both by men of the lowest character and sometimes by Bishops. By such brawlers is the Pontifical majesty defended and the Church upheld. But the people are beginning to learn wisdom, and unless they pursue some better method, I don't see what they are going to accomplish.

"As to your advice that I should join Luther, there will be no difficulty about that, should I find him on the side of the Catholic Church. Not that I pronounce him alienated from it, for it is not for me to condemn any one; to his own master he stands or falls. But if matters shall come to extremities, and a revolution take place, by which the Church shall be made to totter on her throne, I will in the meantime anchor myself to that solid rock until it shall become clear on the restoration of peace where the Church is, and wherever there is evangelical peace there will Erasmus be found."

Erasmus *to* Nicholas Beraldus.[+]

"*Louvain, Feb.* 16, 1521.

". . . . Such is the fury of certain monks here against polite letters that my studious hours are now become mere weariness. I am pelted every day with the abuse of the Dominicans, even in public assemblies, so that if I endured this for the faith I should be no whit behind the proto-martyr St. Stephen himself. He was stoned once, and that was the end of his sufferings; he was attacked too with stones only, while I am pelted again and again wherever I turn, besides being poisoned with lies and abuse; nor are they ashamed, while they act in this way, to come out and parade themselves before the multitude. By their own showing, indeed, their character is such that, if I had described it, no one would have believed me; but now they must be believed, since they speak for themselves. And yet such is their blindness that they desire to injure their neighbour even to their own hurt.

"Luther is bringing the greatest odium both upon me and on liberal studies. Everybody knew that the Church was oppressed by tyranny and burdened with ceremonies and human decrees invented to make money; and many were already wishing for or devising a remedy, but remedies unskilfully applied are often worse than the disease, and it generally happens that those who try to throw off the yoke, but fail in the attempt, are carried back into still more cruel slavery. I wish that man had either kept out of it altogether, or made the attempt more moderately and circumspectly. For Luther I do not trouble myself, but I feel con-

"*Ep.* dlxvi.

cerned for Christ's glory; for I see some are of such a temper that if they should succeed nothing will be left but to write the epitaph of the Gospel."

ERASMUS to JODOCUS JONAS.[45]

"Louvain, May 10, 1521.

".... At first Luther received more applause than I fancy has fallen to the lot of any mortal for several centuries past. For, as we easily believe what we desire very much, it was supposed that a man had arisen free from all the passions of this world, who could apply a remedy to the great evils under which we were groaning. Nor was I altogether without hope that it might be so, except that at my first glance into the works which had begun to appear in Luther's name, I feared that the matter would end in tumult and in a universal revolution. Accordingly I wrote letters, warning both Luther himself and friends of his, whose influence I thought was likely to weigh with him; what advice they may have given him I know not—this only is certain, that there is danger lest through want of skill in the use of remedies the mischief may be doubled. And I greatly wonder, my dear Jonas, what demon inspires Luther to inveigh as he does against the Roman Pontiff, all the Universities, philosophy itself, and the mendicant orders. Now, if all he says were true—which they who take it on them to criticise his writings say is by no means the case—what other issue could be expected by the provocation of so many than that which we actually see?

"Certain offensive passages, which were thought to have a close relationship with some of Luther's dogmas,

[45] *Ep.* dlxxii.

have been extracted from my books, which I wrote before I had the least idea that Luther would ever arise, and have been published in German. And the men who act thus wish to be regarded as my friends, though my deadliest enemy could not well do anything worse. Those who wished me most evil never displayed so much ingenuity in devising methods of hurting me. It is they who have put this weapon into the hands of my enemies, so that they can now declare in their sermons what are the points on which I agree with Luther; as if, forsooth, falsehood did not border upon truth on both sides if you never pass the boundary line. I somewhere recommend, it may be, that vows should not be made rashly, or I express my disapproval of the conduct of those who run away to the shrine of St. James, or to Jerusalem, where they have no business whatever, leaving at home their wife and children, whose maintenance and protection from evil ought to have been their first care. I recommend that young men should not be enticed into submitting to the restraints of religious vows, before they know their own mind, and understand the meaning of the word religion. Luther, it is said, condemns all vows without restriction. I complain somewhere that the duty of confession is made doubly onerous by the subtleties with which it is frequently complicated. Luther, it is said, teaches that confession should be altogether abandoned as dangerous. I have somewhere taught that the best authors should be read first of all, adding that so much profit cannot be gained from the works of Dionysius as the titles seem to promise. Luther, I understand, calls this author a fool, and not deserving of being read at all. A fine agreement truly, if somebody else must corrupt and carry to

the most extravagant lengths what I have said incidentally and with strict regard to truth and modesty!
... Yet, to speak candidly, if I had foreseen that such times as these were coming, I would either have not written some things which I have written, or I would have written them in a different spirit. For my desire is to do good to all in such a way as, if possible, to injure no one.

"What other result, I should like to know, has been produced by so many abusive pamphlets, so much fire and smoke, so many terrific threats, and so much turgid talk, but that what before was debated in the Universities as a probable opinion must hereafter become an article of faith, and even now it is unsafe to teach the Gospel, the passions of men being roused to fury, and calumny laying hold of and perverting every word that may be spoken. Luther might have taught the philosophy of the Gospel with great advantage to the Christian flock, and benefited the world by writing books, if he had abstained from what could not but end in disturbance. He has taken from my lucubrations too a great part of the good they might have done. Even the debates in the Universities, which used to be perfectly untrammelled, are no longer free. If it were permissible to hate any one on account of private offences, there is no one who has been more injured by the Lutherans than I have, and yet, if it could be done without taking Luther's life, I should wish that this dissension, which is by far the most dangerous that has ever yet been, might be composed, and composed in such a manner that there might be no fear it would again break out with still more serious danger hereafter, as wounds when badly dressed are apt to do."

ERASMUS *to* LOUIS BERUS, *Provost of St. Peter's College at Basle, and a most accomplished theologian.*[46]

"*Louvain, May* 14, 1521.

"WE are greatly indebted to Luther, most learned sir, for having put into the hands of certain bitter enemies of learning the very weapon they would themselves most desire wherewith to attack polite letters, and all who in simplicity of heart favour Gospel truth. Either I am greatly mistaken, or he is acting his part very badly, however excellent that part may be in itself. A worthy defender of Gospel liberty, which he has vindicated in such fashion that I am afraid we may find ourselves compelled to bear two yokes instead of one, and so experience the fate of those who, after trying unsuccessfully to escape from prison, have their chains doubled, or of those who by the misapplication of drugs only make their disease worse! He is perhaps safe enough himself, but all the more fiercely do these fanatical beasts and devoted enemies of learning attack every sensible man. For they think that whoever favours Gospel truth or polite literature belongs to Luther's faction. I am so pelted with their abuse, in their sermons, at their supper-parties, in their conversation, that I think Stephen himself scarcely endured more. He was crushed to death at once, and there his sufferings ended, while I am stoned without end by such crowds of brawlers, whom nevertheless I have done all I could to serve.

"By the bitterness of the Lutherans, and the stupidity of some who show more zeal than wisdom in their endeavours to heal our present disorders, things

[46] *Ep.* dlxxiii.

have been brought to this pass that I, for one, can see no issue but in the turning upside down of the whole world. What evil spirit can have sown this poisonous seed in human affairs? When I was at Cologne, I made every effort that Luther might have the glory of obedience and the Pope of clemency, and some of the sovereigns approved of this advice. But lo and behold! the burning of the Decretals, the 'Babylonish Captivity,' those propositions of Luther's, so much stronger than they need be, have made the evil, it seems, incurable. Luther seems to me to act as if he set no value on his life, while, on the other hand, some of the opposite party speak of the matter so foolishly in public, as if they were in collusion with Luther, and only pretended to be on the side of the Pope. The only thing that remains to us, my dear Berus, is to pray that Christ, supreme in goodness and in power, may turn all to good, for He alone can do so. For a long time past I have been thinking of coming to you, but there were, and there still are, some things which keep me here. I hope, however, I shall be with you next autumn; and meanwhile Christ keep you safe, with all your family."

ERASMUS *to* NICHOLAS EVERARD, *Governor of Holland.*[47]

"*Mechlin,* ——, 1521.

"IF Luther had written more moderately, even though he had written freely, he would both have been more honoured himself and done more good to the world; but fate has decreed otherwise. I only wonder that the man is still alive. . . . They say that an edict is in

[47] *Ep.* cccxvii. App.

readiness far more severe than the Pope's Bull; but from fear, or some other reason, it has not yet been published. I am surprised that the Pope should employ such agents, some of them illiterate men, and all of them certainly headstrong and haughty, for the transaction of such important affairs. Nothing can exceed the pride or violent temper of Cardinal Cajetan, of Charles Miltitz, of Marinus, of Aleander. They all act upon the principle of the young king who said, 'My little finger is thicker than my father's loins.' As to Aleander, he is a complete maniac—a bad, foolish man. . . . I hear they are now using poison, and at Paris some who were open defenders of Luther were suddenly put out of the way. Perhaps it is part of their commission, that since the enemies of the Roman See (for so they are called who are not absolutely devoted to those harpies) cannot be overcome by other means, they are to be removed by poison with the Pope's blessing. This is an art in which Aleander has great skill; at Cologne he used to invite me to breakfast very urgently, but the more he pressed the more persistent was I in excusing myself. Against the indulgences there is this remedy, if everybody abstains from purchasing, until a more favourable opportunity presents itself for putting a stop to this blasphemous merchandise. I have thus, my dear sir, written very freely to you. Pray take care that this letter does not find its way into the hands of many persons, for the Germans publish whatever they get hold of."

The edict here referred to was that drawn up by Aleander and signed by Charles at Worms, after many of the princes had left the Diet, and which, in order to conceal this fact, was antedated May 8, 1521.[46] It was certainly well for Erasmus that the above letter did not fall into the hands of an enemy.

ERASMUS *to* RICHARD PACE.[49]

"*Brussels, July 5,* 1521.

". . . . I FEAR the Dominicans and some of the divines will use their victory intemperately, especially those of Louvain, who have some private grudge against me, and have found in Jerome Aleander an instrument most admirably adapted to this purpose. This man is mad enough naturally, without any one to instigate him; but, as it is, he has instigators who might drive even the most moderate to madness. The most virulent pamphlets are flying about on all sides, and Aleander ascribes them all to me, though I was ignorant of the existence of many of them before I heard of them from him. Luther has acknowledged his own books in the presence of the Emperor, and yet the 'Babylonian Captivity,' which is one of them, is ascribed to me. A prolific author indeed I must be, seeing that I was able to write so many pamphlets, while meantime I was emending the text of the New Testament with the utmost labour, and editing the works of Augustine, not to speak of other studies. May I be lost if in all Luther's works there is a single syllable of mine, or if any calumnious book was ever published of which I was the author; on the contrary, I do all I can to deter others. Now, however, they are adopting a new course, and asserting that Luther has

[46] D'AUBIGNÉ's *History of the Reformation*, book vii. chap. xi.
[49] *Ep.* dlxxxii.

borrowed some of his doctrines from my works, as if he had not borrowed more from Paul's Epistles. I now, at last, see clearly that it was the policy of the Germans to implicate me whether I would or not in Luther's business ; a most impolitic piece of policy indeed, for nothing would sooner have alienated me from them. Or what aid could I have given to Luther if I had associated myself with him in his danger? The only result would have been that two must perish instead of one. I can never sufficiently wonder at the violent spirit he has displayed in his writings, by which he has certainly brought immense odium on all the friends of polite literature. Many indeed of his doctrines and exhortations are excellent, and I wish he had not vitiated the good in his writings by intolerable faults. If, however, he had always written in the most reverent spirit, still, I had no inclination to risk my life for the truth. It is not everybody who has strength for martyrdom, and I am afraid that if any outbreak should take place I should imitate St. Peter. When the Popes and the Emperors decree what is right, I obey, which is the course of true piety; but when they command what is wrong, I submit, and that is the safe course. I think also that good men are justified in acting thus if there is no hope of success. They are again trying to fix on me the authorship of the book on Julius, so determined are they to leave nothing untried to injure both myself and the cause of letters, which they cannot bear to see prospering. . . ."

Erasmus *to* Peter Barbirius.[50]

"*Bruges, August* 13, 1521.

". . . . But you will tell me I have not yet written anything against Luther. The two principal reasons why I have not done so are want of leisure and the consciousness of my own inability. I am so overburdened by my own studies, that my health is often endangered by my excessive toils. I saw, too, that it is a very different thing to encourage the pursuit of learning, to recommend a moral life, to write annotations on the Scriptures and the Fathers, and to treat of matters of faith with the whole world as an audience. I saw that both sides were so inflamed with zeal that the one could not be satisfied unless they were allowed to shriek and bellow at the very pitch of their voice, while the other was so well provided both as to numbers and with brochures of the sharpest edge, that I would rather be exposed to the lances of the Swiss than run through with their pens; for they have many whose writings seem likely to go down to posterity.

"And yet I admit that in the cause of the faith we ought to despise even life itself, if the prospect of success justifies our good intentions. . . . I have never ceased dissuading all I could, both in conversation and by letters, from having anything to do with that faction. No entreaties have had any effect in inducing me to give it even the smallest countenance; and this, I think, has done more to break the strength of that faction than the tumults which some have stirred up. Germany is so well aware of these facts, that now, for a whole year past, none of those who are believed to favour Luther

[50] *Ep.* dlxxxvii.

have written a word to me, no one has called upon me or saluted me, while formerly they almost killed me with such attentions. . . .

"In truth, I am well rewarded for all my labours by being pelted on both sides! Among ourselves I am most falsely accused of being a Lutheran, while among the Germans I am evil spoken of as an adversary of the Lutheran faction. I would, however, gladly give up not only my good name, but my life itself, to calm this most disastrous storm! I see no end to it unless Christ himself, by a miracle, will bring these miserable doings to a happy issue."

ERASMUS *to* RICHARD PACE.[51]

"*Bruges, August* 23, 1521.

". . . THE book which the King's Majesty has written against Luther, I have myself seen in the hands of Marinus the apostolic nuncio. I long greatly to read it; for I have no doubt it is worthy of those brilliant talents which appear to succeed so wonderfully in everything they attempt. In former times it was considered an act of extraordinary piety, and one that entitled its author to a place on the roll of saints, if a prince had saved the necks of Christians from a foreign yoke by force of arms; but Henry VIII. uses his talents and his pen in defence of the Spouse of Christ, thus clearly proving what he could do, if the occasion should call for arms. Meantime, what he is doing now is, in my opinion, not only much more difficult, but will obtain for him far more solid and more enviable praise. For the praise of warlike success is divided by fortune

[51] *Ep.* dlxxxix.

among a number, and often she claims no small portion for herself, whereas in this field, seeing that everything depends on mental powers, whatever praise there is, is fairly due to Henry alone. We who cultivate and love polite letters should be most ungrateful, did we not recognize with the utmost joy and veneration those talents which are such an ornament and recommendation to our own studies. I trust, moreover, that this bright and unfortunately very rare example will provoke many other sovereigns to emulate it. Surely priests, monks, and bishops will be ashamed hereafter to know nothing of theology, when they see so great a king, notwithstanding his youth and the distraction of affairs of state, yet such a proficient in the study of sacred literature as to be able to come to the rescue, by his own writings, of the imperilled Christian faith. Nor do I doubt that he has succeeded considerably better than some who have previously tried their strength in the same department. But I will write more positively on this subject when I have devoured the book, which I am extremely anxious to read; for the Cardinal of York promised to lend it to me. It was very annoying that you were not present at that interview; I should have taken it more patiently, however, if you had visited us even by a letter. Remember, my dear Pace, who it is to whose place you have succeeded and what you have promised us; for I expect that you will give me no reason greatly to regret Colet. You have promised something even more precious; but you will amply satisfy both my own wishes and your promises, if you will help me to recover the trifles I left in your charge at Ferrara."

ERASMUS *to the most learned* PAUL BOMBASIUS.[52]

"*Anderlecht, Sept.* 23, 1521.

"WHAT do you tell me, Bombasius? Pope Leo—the great Leo—has read that careless and familiar letter which you received from me? What can have induced him to trouble himself with such trifles, or even to look at them? And he has not only read it, but asked for it a second time, in order to show it to the learned men of his court? And not read only that which I wrote to you, but also those which I wrote to other friends? I am accustomed, indeed, to pour into the bosom of such friends, with the utmost freedom and carelessness, all my troubles, as well as my less serious thoughts, whatever they may be. I am undone if you tell me true, especially as I don't know myself what gossip I may have indulged in, in such letters.

". . . The fortune you have amassed at Rome, and which you owe exclusively to your own industry, falls far short of your deserts; but notwithstanding, as times now go, I congratulate you on your good fortune in having relieved yourself of the intolerable burden of poverty. I see you are now looking round for some independent, quiet employment, in which you may find a secure haven of rest. And yet I am afraid you may prove the truth of the story Horace tells of the weasel, which had crept, in a half-starved state, into a corn-store, but when he had grown fat on the corn, found it impossible to escape; still I think you must make the effort. But where can you hope for this if not at Rome?
. . . Yet you are aware that our friend Scipio Carteromachus failed to find liberty, which he loved beyond all other men, even at Rome. For my own

[52] *Ep.* dxciv.

part, though my income is less than yours, I have ceased to complain of Mercury. I have as much as enables me to live respectably, and I can sometimes even afford a guinea for a needy friend; so little am I compelled to be a burden to any one. I do not covet honours, especially when they cost so dear; but had they been offered to me gratuitously, or at least at no great expense, and had they been offered in time, I should not have been inclined absolutely to reject them, if for no other reason, at least on this account, that they secure one against the contempt of evil men. In this indeed, as in everything else, More has shown himself farther-sighted than I; for he received from his most excellent sovereign the honour of knighthood, and he is now his Privy Councillor and Lord of the Treasury, both of which offices are tolerably independent, as well as honourable in the first degree, so that he is now more beloved by the good and more dreaded by the bad. For these are times in which not even such extraordinary natural goodness, such unheard-of sweetness of character, can entirely escape envy. . . .

"I am neither ignorant nor do I forget, my dear Bombasius, how much I owe to Leo's kindness to me, of which I have now had so many proofs. Nor have I been so silent in his cause as you suppose. In the first place, I tried to prevent this disturbance arising; then to allay it, when it had arisen; and, finally, when the conflagration had spread far and wide, to check it with the least possible interruption of the public tranquillity. For I thought that it very much concerned the dignity of the Pope, besides being the most effectual way of ending this tragedy, that the mischief, having been once checked, should not again break loose. When, however, this plan was thwarted by the agency of certain persons who look to their private interests rather than to the public good, I prevented many, partly by my letters, partly by conversation, from mixing themselves with this business. But for my not having heretofore engaged in a written controversy with Luther, there are a great many reasons, which I need not here rehearse, but the principal one was that I had no time at all to read what Luther has written. I am too much engaged with revising my own writings, and you see how very prolific he is. Besides, he is not alone; he has a hundred hands. Nor would it be sufficient to read his books once; I should be obliged to go through them again and again; and even that would not suffice: many are publishing books against him in various parts of the world, and I should have to inspect every one of these if I wished adequately to fulfil the duty I undertook. . . . It is a task full of danger, and I have had more experience in another field of study. Moreover, after having published so many works, I might fairly expect to be released from labour, and be permitted for the future to pursue my studies in peace. This was demanded by my increasing years, and earned by the labours I had undergone in promoting literature among the public. This business is of such a kind that, once I enter upon it, I shall be compelled to devote myself to it for the rest of my life. O my dear Bombasius, it is easy to say, 'Write against Luther;' but for this more things are needed, as Hesiod says, than for making a waggon. I know well how fickle and how ill-natured are the judgments of men, especially in this age, which is the most intolerant that has ever been. In many articles the Cisalpine dissent from the Transalpine universities;

and even theologians of the same university give utterance to different sentiments in their public discussions and their writings from what they do in their confidential conversations. Besides, it is extremely difficult to regulate one's style in such a way as to observe the dignity of men without injuring the glory of Christ, or to please human sovereigns without displeasing Christ our heavenly King. If, however, the present mischief can be overcome by pamphlets, swarms of books are appearing every day, so that there is no need of Erasmus; or, if vociferations are likely to prove more effectual, Stentors are not wanting. There have been plenty of fires on all sides. In the edicts that have been published no element of terror has been omitted. I am afraid, however, lest by these means the mischief may be repressed for a time rather than extinguished, and that it will presently burst out with greater danger; a result from which I shrink in horror, and which I desire before all things may be avoided.

"No country more heartily supports the Papal dignity than my own; but the odious patronage of certain persons has done it a great deal of injury. If those men had never acted in such a mad way, the thing would never have gone the length it has. Nay, if they would even now hold their peace for three months, Luther and his books would absolutely cease to interest, and not even the smallest change would take place in the world on his account. I am quite taken up in revising my New Testament and some of my other lucubrations, like a bear, licking into shape the rude offspring of my brain. I hope, however, I shall have more leisure in a short time. I have been diligent in begging from Jerome Aleander permission to read

Luther's writings, for every place is full at present of informers. He assured me that he could not grant it unless he were to obtain it in express words from the Pope. First, then, I wish you would procure me this permission by a brief; for I should not wish a handle to be given to the wicked, who want nothing else. Very few have ever been more heartily in favour of maintaining public tranquillity than I am, and to establish Gospel truth I would gladly give my life. Nor am I ignorant how much I owe, even in my private capacity, to the Pope's unheard-of goodness to me; and if I shall have the good fortune to live three or four years more, I will either die in my efforts or I will give him good reason to say that I have not been altogether ungrateful. His extraordinary goodness deserves to be celebrated in the writings of all the learned, and if I can believe that others will be more successful, I am sure none will be more zealous; and though nature deny me eloquence, warmth and passion will be mine in abundance. Some think that his interests are best taken care of by making him as formidable as possible, but my effort will be to make the world love Leo rather than fear him. Unless, however, he will himself interpose to preserve me for this office, I do not see how I can escape with my life, with such dire hatred and certain accursed scoundrels conspiring against me. They shriek against me by name in their public lectures and their sermons, they traduce me before the people, they bring up my name in the presence of kings. They suborn men to take my character to pieces by the publication of calumnious books—nay, they threaten daggers and poison. Nor is it any secret what they are ready to attempt.

" . . . I had quite made up my mind to set out on my journey, with the intention, after finishing my work at Basle, of removing to Rome for good, there to spend the remainder of my life among its learned men and its rich libraries. And I had already made my preparations for the journey, for rusticating here through the summer has made me a good deal stronger, but a bloody war, which is growing more desperate every day, prevented me. And yet I am still longing, and, perhaps, shall at length have courage to cast the die, especially as I am invited to do so by Aleander, whose wisdom in the transaction of affairs I value no less than his judgment in literature. Meantime enjoy your fortune, and expect me to share it with you, if only the quarrels among our rulers here can be composed."

ERASMUS *to* WILLIAM MOUNTJOY.[53]

"*Anderlecht*, ——, 1521.

" . . . You tell me that a report has been spread in your country that I not only sympathize with the Lutheran party, but that I am an aider and abettor, and all but its author; and you urge me to clear myself by publishing a work against Luther. To show you that this is as impudent a lie as to say that Erasmus had wings, I will explain in two or three words the source in which this rumour originated. There are some here who hate me mortally, because I am believed to have imported the languages and polite letters into what they regard as their own dominions. These men, even before the world had heard of Luther's name, were looking everywhere for a weapon with which to take vengeance for this outrage on their feelings. Accord-

[53] *Ep.* dcvi.

ingly, they who had been the first to originate this report, had not yet succeeded in persuading themselves of that of which they tried to convince others. They endeavoured to provoke against me by the most extraordinary lies Jerome Aleander, the apostolic nuncio, a man of great learning, and with whom I was connected by the ties of an old and very agreeable acquaintance. Libellous pamphlets were flying about on every side, and certain Germans, in order to avert suspicion from themselves, charged me with their authorship. In short, they persuaded Aleander, who is a far-sighted and simple-minded but credulous man, that my sentiments and language regarding him were not very friendly; and if there were any signs of a reconciliation between us, there were always plenty to renew the breach by every now and then bringing up new accusations. Of this, however, be assured, as a fact more certain than if it was written on the Sibyl's leaf, that in all the works of Luther and the Lutherans not a single syllable is mine, or written with my knowledge . . .

" . . . As to your statement that it is in my power to put an end to all this disturbance, I would that what your Highness says were true. Had it been, this tragedy would never even have begun. They say here that I have lost my pen. I have a pen, indeed, but there are a great many reasons which dissuade me from using it in this way. To call Luther a mushroom is very easy, but to defend the cause of the true faith by appropriate arguments I, at least, find exceedingly difficult. And, so far, others have not succeeded very well. Still, I would gladly gird up my loins for this task if I were assured that certain persons, who, under the pretext of defending the faith, are really pleading the cause of the world, would use their victory for the good of the Christian religion. Nevertheless I will go to Basle with the resolution that, after finishing the work I have on hand, I will undertake something which may tend to allay this strife; or, at any rate, I will give evidence of my own feelings on the subject."

CHAPTER XIV.

ERASMUS THINKS OF LEAVING LOUVAIN—MEETING WITH ALEANDER—STARTS FOR BASLE—TAKEN ILL AT WORMS—ARRIVAL AT BASLE—VISIT TO CONSTANCE—ACCESSION OF ADRIAN VI.—ERASMUS'S ADVICE TO HIM—ULRICH VON HUTTEN—ERASMUS DECLINES AN INTERVIEW—LETTER TO LAURINUS—HUTTEN'S EXPOSTULATION—ERASMUS'S SPONGE—HUTTEN'S DEATH—JUDGMENT ON THE CONTROVERSY.

ERASMUS had been now for some years resident at Louvain. As I have already remarked, it was the natural place for him to reside as long as he was one of the Emperor's councillors, and anywhere out of Charles's dominions he would have run the risk of losing his pension, as, indeed, he found to his cost on his final removal to Basle. The healthiness of the climate, too, and the amenity of the situation, we find him mentioning as special recommendations of Louvain, and in a letter to his friend Vives he goes so far as to say that these were the only considerations which had induced him to settle there.[1] He had, indeed, had a hard time of it, battling with the monks. Still, he might have supposed he would be in a more favourable position for meeting their attacks when living in one of their strongholds than if he had merely heard of them from a distance, or he hoped to conciliate their favour by frank and friendly dealing; and, meantime, he had found

[1] *Er. Op.* iii. 689, F.

many warm friends and admirers, and time to pursue his favourite studies. Great changes, however, had taken place in the world since Erasmus went to Louvain, and the immediate effect of these changes had not been to encourage learning. The defenders of the "old ignorance" had been roused to fury by the audacities of Luther and his followers, and had gained strength by the accession of many timid men, who would have rejoiced to see learning triumphant, but dreaded any disturbance in the Church. Thus, some who had welcomed Erasmus to Louvain—among them the Chancellor Atensis—had become his enemies, or, at any rate, cold and distant; while he was in danger, on the other hand, of being equally persecuted by the Lutherans, amongst whom he persistently refused to number himself. But what he most dreaded, so long as he remained in the Emperor's dominions, was lest the influence of the court should be used to compel him to write against Luther.[2] Nothing could be more likely; for Charles had shown himself determined to put down the heretics and maintain the authority of the Roman See, and the most effectual way in which Erasmus could prove his often-professed devotion to the Pope would be to enter boldly into this great controversy, which was threatening to rend the Church, throw in the weight of his learning and influence against the Reformers, and, as it might be supposed he would have no difficulty in doing, refute the heresies of Luther. Determined to avoid, if possible, a task so distasteful

---

[2] Erasmus himself acknowledges as much :—"Ergo si quid erat quod hic metuebam, nihil aliud erat, quam ne cum Lutheranis conflictandi negotium ab eo mihi delegaretur, cui negare fas non fuisset."—*Er. Op.* iii. 753, C.

to him, and weary of the vexatious persecutions of the monks of Louvain, it is not strange if he now thought of seeking some more congenial place of residence.

He left Louvain in the spring of the year 1521, and we find him in April at Antwerp, whence he writes to the Governor of Holland, sending a leaden statue of himself and his two replies to Lee, and promising a visit to that country in the course of the summer.[3] From Antwerp he went to Anderlecht, a village in the neighbourhood of Brussels, whither he carried his whole library with him, and where he remained for three months with great benefit to his health, now much broken by severe study, constant fatigue, and the diseases from which he suffered.[4] He was also, in the course of the summer, at Bruges, where the Emperor was holding his court, and where he met his old friends Tonstall, More, and Mountjoy. It was then, he tells us, that he first saw Henry VIII.'s book on the "Seven Sacraments," in answer to Luther. He was waiting to pay his respects to Cardinal Wolsey, who was then at Bruges negotiating peace between the Emperor and the French King, when the Apostolic Nuncio, Marinus Caracciola, entered the room, carrying a book in his hand. Erasmus asked if he might look at it. The nuncio assented, and Erasmus, having glanced at the title, and noticed the King of England's autograph at the foot of the first page, returned it with a smile, observing that he envied Luther such an adversary. This somewhat equivocal remark was answered by the nuncio with a sound that resembled a growl rather than a laugh; but on Erasmus explaining himself more clearly, he rejoined, "And I congratulate the Pope on such a

[3] *Er. Op.* iii. 676, A. 1697, A—D.   [4] *Ep.* cccxv. App.

defender."[5] This little incident is related by Erasmus to refute the charge brought against him by some of the Lutherans of having been himself the author of Henry's book. Absurdly enough, he was afterwards suspected by the opposite party of having written Luther's reply.[6]

If there was nothing else to induce Erasmus to fix on Basle for his future residence, Froben's press, and the advantages it offered for publishing the results of his labours, might have done so. At Louvain he had not been idle, nor had he permitted his controversies with the monks to take up all his time. Besides the great work on which he was engaged—the "Paraphrase of the New Testament"—and the other lesser labours which have been already mentioned, he had prepared an edition of Cicero's "Offices," which was printed by Froben and published in September, 1519. It was accompanied by brief annotations, and a dedicatory letter to his old friend James Tutor of Orleans, in which he bursts out into the warmest praise of the great Roman orator and philosopher, as so much superior to those who, "being Christians, teach the mysteries of the Christian faith, and discuss the very same subjects as Cicero does, with great subtlety it may be, but without the slightest warmth."[7] He had also studied with greater care than ever before the works of Cyprian, and had prepared an edition of that Father, in whose favour he was now almost inclined to retract his verdict formerly pronounced in favour of Jerome, as ranking first among orthodox writers of Latin. The "Cyprian" was dedicated to Cardinal Lorenzo Pucci, in a letter

[5] *Er. Op.* iii. 762, D, E.   [6] *Er. Op.* iii. 771, C.
[7] *Ep.* cccclvii.

dated July 31, 1519.[8] The third edition of the Greek Testament was also in preparation, and by the autumn of 1521 had been for some time in the printer's hands.

Erasmus would by no means allow that his departure from Louvain was a flight, nor that he was actuated by any desire to conceal himself. These were the malicious and utterly groundless rumours spread by his enemies, and in order to confute them he wrote about a year and a half afterwards a long letter, intended, of course, for publication, to his friend Marcus Laurinus, now dean of the convent of St. Donatian at Bruges. As to his hiding himself at Anderlecht, the thing was perfectly absurd. After the Emperor's return to Brussels, there was scarcely a day that he might not have been seen there riding through the market-place and past the court; and, in fact, he lived at Brussels more than at Anderlecht. His journey to Basle, he assures us, was undertaken for precisely the same reason as his former journey thither — namely, to superintend the printing of his New Testament, of which the third edition was then in Froben's hands: the first volume was already printed, but the second, containing his annotations, was awaiting his revision, and he was anxious to be present in order to make some necessary alterations and additions. This cause, he remarks, may appear a slight one to those who would think nothing of travelling all the way to Basle on foot for a sumptuous banquet, but to him it was of no less importance than the conquest of Milan to the King of France. It had been known perfectly well for six months previously that he intended going to Basle, and on this very ground the Emperor's treasurer had permitted him to draw his pension before

[8] *Ep.* ccccxlviii.

it was due. While waiting for a safe-conduct and for the purpose of getting some money that was owing him, he spent six days at Louvain, "hiding himself," as he says ironically, in an inn, where it so happened that Aleander was also staying, and with him he spent some pleasant evenings—he had forgotten, it would seem, his fear lest the Nuncio should poison him—their conversation being prolonged till midnight. It was on his birthday, the 28th of October, at two o'clock, that Erasmus mounted his horse to start for Basle. As far as Spire he had the escort of a large party of soldiers, both horse and foot, who were transporting their plunder and their sick and wounded in waggons. At Worms, where he met his friend Hermann Busch, he was taken ill, having remained too long in a room heated with a stove, a thing which never agreed with him. He was able, however, to push on to Spire, and after resting there for two days, he was sufficiently recovered to finish his journey by easy stages to Basle. There he was received with hearty welcome, the good old Bishop Christopher and the civic authorities vying with the learned men in doing him honour.

Through the whole of this winter Erasmus suffered tortures from the stone. His health was sufficiently good until it became too cold to dispense with the use of stoves; but having permitted one to be lighted in his room, he was seized with a stomach complaint, which he thought would have ended him. This was succeeded by his old enemy the stone, and there was not a day that he was free from pain. He was worn to a mere skeleton, and his tortures were so excessive that he felt he need no longer be afraid of death. Yet his spirit was unbroken. He was even able to make a jest out of his sufferings, and speaking of the invitations he was receiving from different sovereigns to reside in their territory, he adds, "but I am afraid King Stone will shortly send me to another world."[9] And meantime his pen was flying as fast as ever. He had finished his annotations for the third edition of his New Testament, and this winter he began and completed, within about two months, his "Paraphrase of St. Matthew," which was sent to the Emperor and received with great favour.

A question which was under hot discussion in Switzerland just about this time was the duty of observing the fasts of the Church; and upon this subject also Erasmus completed a short treatise, in the form of a letter to the friendly Bishop of Basle,[10] which, as was usual with his writings, was not likely to give satisfaction to either party. Fasting, he here maintains, serves two purposes, either to subdue the flesh or to appease the wrath of God. He thinks, however, that Christ imposed no rules, but that Christians, though left quite free, abstained of their own accord, and that afterwards, when people's love waxed cold, the authority of the bishop, and finally of the Pope, intervened. Fasting, therefore, and the choice of meats, he thinks, should not be altogether condemned, and he cites Jesus and Paul to show that we ought to comply with customs not bad in themselves rather than cause our brother to offend. On this principle he condemns the Lutherans for the extremes to which they run on the plea of evangelical liberty, and complains that they are doing harm by compelling the magistrates to impose

---

[9] "At vereor ne rex calculus me brevi transmittat in alterum mundum."—*Er. Op.* iii. 744, C.

[10] *Desiderii Erasmi Epistola Apologetica de interdicto esu carnium.*—*Er. Op.* ix. 1197, *sqq.*

severe penalties. By-and-bye, falling into his own humorous vein, Erasmus proceeds to show what nice questions are raised by the prohibition of flesh-meat. What is included under that name? "The sea contains many animals, not very unlike land animals, such as seals and sea-dogs; and there are also amphibious animals, such as the beaver. Again, there may be a question about cockles, tortoises, frogs, and snakes. On some days eggs and milk are permitted, on others milk only. And on some again even this may not be touched. There are some days on which everything is forbidden which has ever lived. Do sponges fall under this rule?" Again, he complains that fasting often in reality ministers to luxury, and that there are no days on which the kitchens are busier, or the expense greater, than the fish-days. "Thus it happens that the poor starve, while the rich live more delicately than usual. For who would not rather have a sturgeon, or a trout, or a lamprey than smoked ham or leg of mutton?" In the sequel this treatise assumes, to some extent, the form of a personal explanation; and Erasmus informs his readers that if he ever violates the fasts of the Church it is with him simply a matter of necessity. If he could preserve his life on a vegetable diet, he would never desire fish or flesh. Though, on account of his weak health and his abhorrence of fish, he was in danger every Lent, he yet never obeyed the physician who advised him to eat meat, except once in Italy, when he was assured his life was in danger. And now he does it for some days in Lent, for which he has a dispensation from the Pope, which he has never before used.

In the course of this composition he complains of the great multiplication of holidays, and recommends that they should all be abolished except Sundays. Referring to the celibacy of the priests, he thinks it might be better if that were abolished too. "There are now," he observes, "innumerable priests, but how few who live chastely!" His advice is therefore that marriage should be permitted; but at the same time he does not defend the priests who have married without the Pope's authority.

It is probable enough that Erasmus, in going to Basle, had formed no very settled plan for the future. He intended, of course, to pass the winter there, and we have seen that he spoke of going on to Rome. At any rate it may be considered certain that while his strength lasted he would not have remained very long in any one place. We have his own authority for saying that he actually set out on his return to Brabant, and indeed nothing is more likely than that as soon as he found himself settled in Basle, especially after his health broke down, he began to think he might be better off in his old quarters. At Schelestadt, however, his strength failed him, and after recruiting for a day or two at the house of his friend Beatus, he was compelled to return to Basle, whence he was fully resolved to start afresh, as soon as he felt equal to the journey, provided he should learn that the Emperor was still at Brussels. The Emperor, he ascertained by a servant whom he had despatched for the purpose, was to embark for Spain on the 1st of May; and as it would be hopeless for him to attempt to see him before he left, that day being now at hand, he gave up all thoughts of returning.

It is, perhaps, more difficult to believe that Erasmus entertained any serious intention of going to Rome.

And yet why not? He would have taken care to give no offence to those in authority, and there were many inducements which might have led him to think of it. He would have ample opportunities of study and of intercourse with learned men. Many old friends were there ready to welcome him; but, in particular, the Cardinal of Sion had written to him very urgently, offering him, besides a handsome board, the liberal sum of five hundred ducats yearly.[11] This was certainly no small temptation. On the other hand, he would require to keep his tongue and his pen under strict control, as it would be impossible for him any longer to avoid making himself a partisan against the Lutherans. As, however, he had set out for Brabant, so also he set out for Rome. He never got beyond Constance, whither he was accompanied by Beatus and a young man named Henry Eppendorf, of whom we shall hear again, and where he spent three weeks, hoping to be well enough to proceed. He has left us a pleasing account of his visit to this city. The broad and beautiful lake in which the Rhine, wearied with its tumblings amid the precipices of the Alps, sleeps peacefully awhile before it plunges over the falls at Schaffhausen; the mountains, near and distant, whose fir-clad sides lend an additional charm to the scene; the island, with its nunnery, formed, as if in mere wantonness, by the river; the immense trout drawn from the lake, and presented to the visitors by the learned and eloquent abbot of the Dominican convent; the tall and kindly Bishop Hugo, who offered his hospitality, and took no offence when it was gratefully declined—all are described by Erasmus in a way that shows how vividly

[11] *Er. Op.* iii. 719, A.

they had impressed themselves on his memory; nor does he forget his host, Botzemus Abstemius, the canon of the place, and his elegant mansion, adorned with so many pictures and statues and works of art that ten days would scarcely have sufficed to examine them all. His enjoyment of these things, however, was sadly marred by the pain he was suffering—a violent access of his disease having completely disabled him on his arrival at Constance. Notwithstanding he was determined to go on, and would have persisted, in spite of the dissuasions of his friends, had not the more forcible rhetoric of his disease persuaded him to return to Basle. On reaching home it occurred to him to try some Burgundy which had been given to him as a present some time before, and the relief he experienced was wonderful. He was thus confirmed in an opinion he had long held that the stone was due to the use of bad and sour wines, and to the chalk, alum, resin, sulphur, and salt with which they were adulterated. Such wines, he declared, were fit only to be drunk by heretics. He was now almost ready to go and live in France, for the sake of its wine; and this was the only one of the many reports spread by his enemies which he could admit had any truth in it.[16] He does not say that he thought of packing up a few dozens of Burgundy and again starting for Rome.

Meantime a new Pope had been called to the chair of St. Peter. Leo X., struck down suddenly in the height of his glory, in a moment of brilliant success, and at a time of life when he might have looked forward to many years of fame and power, had died on the 1st of December, 1521. Quite unexpectedly Adrian

[16] *Ep.* del.

of Utrecht, whom we have already met as a professor at Louvain, where Erasmus was sometimes a hearer of his lectures in divinity, was proposed to the Conclave, and the cardinals, unable otherwise to come to an agreement, allowed themselves to be surprised into accepting the nomination of this learned and, for their wishes, too upright and conscientious foreigner. Adrian, who had been tutor to Prince Charles and ambassador to the court of King Ferdinand of Aragon, after the death of that monarch had shared the regency with Cardinal Ximenes. He was now Governor of Spain, and was unable at once to answer the summons which called him to Rome. He arrived there on the 30th of August, 1522.

This appointment must have been very gratifying to Erasmus. Adrian VI.—as Pope he retained his own name—was an old acquaintance; he was also an upright, pious, and learned man; a supporter, it is true, of the scholastic divinity, but no enemy of good Latin or polite studies. Something might be expected from him in the way of reform; at any rate he would attempt to deal firmly with the gross abuses to which the Church had given no real sanction, and would not permit learning to be hunted down by mere bigotry and ignorance. Erasmus, having now at least abandoned all intention of going to Rome, wrote to the new Pope, with his congratulations, which, however, he observed, were due to the public rather than to Adrian, who, he was well aware, had accepted with reluctance the honour so unexpectedly conferred upon him. The state of the world, he added, required just such a ruler. He then took occasion to warn the Pope against any malicious reports that might have come to his ears respecting himself, and begged him, if any such had reached him, not to listen to them, or at least to suspend his judgment, as he had no doubt that if he had the opportunity he would be able abundantly to refute all such calumnies. The letter was accompanied by a copy of Arnobius on the Psalms, with a dedicatory epistle, in which the identity of this author, notwithstanding his numerous solecisms, with the Arnobius who wrote the eloquent treatise *Adversus Gentes*, is defended, on the rather untenable plea that this work was purposely written in the bad Latin which would be intelligible to the vulgar. Both the letter and the dedication bear the same date, August 1, 1522; and the latter concludes with an eloquent appeal to the Pope to unite princes and people in the bonds of Christian love, and put an end to the fatal contests about forms of doctrine.[13]

December came without bringing any answer from his Holiness, and on the 22nd of that month Erasmus wrote again, sending another copy of the Arnobius, in case the first had not reached him. In this letter he again dwells on the turbulence of the times, and offers, if the Pope desires it, to impart secretly his own advice as to the best means of extirpating the evil so completely that it will not again break out. "For it is of no use," he remarks, "to put it down by brute force, if it is to break out again worse than ever, like a wound which has been badly dressed." "In great tempests," he modestly and confidentially adds, "the most skilful pilots are willing to receive advice from any one. . . . If what I recommend shall meet your approval, you will have it in your power to avail yourself of it; but if not,

[13] *Ep.* dcxxxii. dcxxxiii.

as no one will know anything about it but our two selves, it can be forgotten and no harm done." [14]

Meantime the Pope had written on the 1st of December in reply to his first letter. Regarding any whispers against his character, implying that he favoured the Lutheran faction, he might set his mind at rest, for, although his name had certainly been mentioned to him in this connection, it was not his habit to lend a ready ear to reports affecting the character of good or learned men, who were always more exposed to calumny in proportion to their greater excellence. There was one way, however, it was hinted, in which Erasmus might effectually silence all such malicious rumours, if he would take up his pen against "those new heresies"—a task which he might well suppose had been specially assigned him by Providence. For this task he was eminently qualified by his splendid talents, his great and varied learning, his facility in writing, and above all by the authority and favour he possessed with those nations in which this evil had its origin. With great earnestness the Pope presses upon him the task of refuting the stale and malignant heresies of Luther, " which are subverting every day the souls of so many of your brethren, and filling the world with confusion," assuring him that he will never again have such an opportunity of doing God service or conferring a benefit on Christendom. "Arise," he exclaims at length, "arise, and aid the cause of God, and use in His honour, as you have done hitherto, those splendid talents which He has bestowed on you!" He concludes by pressing him to come to Rome as soon as the winter is over, promising him plenty of books and frequent conversations on the

[14] *Ep.* dcxli.

subject of the letter both with himself and with many other learned and pious men.[15]

His Holiness also replied most graciously to Erasmus's second letter, and cordially accepted his offer of advice.[16]

Thus encouraged he wrote as follows :—

Erasmus *to* Adrian VI.[17]

"Most blessed Father,—The bearer of this, whom I heard of quite unexpectedly this afternoon, will leave by daylight to-morrow morning. Accordingly I was almost disposed to think it better not to write at all to so great a sovereign on a matter of such moment than to write hastily. Nevertheless, since your Holiness in both missives (for I have received both) urges, beseeches, and all but adjures me to impart what counsel I have towards putting an end to these troubles, compelled by your authority and relying on your truly pontifical meekness, I will write, though it must be in haste, hoping to do so at greater length so soon as I shall have leisure and a messenger in whom I can place more trust. It would be safer indeed and more convenient to discuss these matters face to face, and it was my full intention to anticipate the very kind invitation of your Holiness by going to Rome. I am compelled, however, to obey the decrees of a most cruel tyrant, one far worse than Mezentius or Phalaris. You will wonder who I mean ;—his name is Stone. It is true in your city the pestilence has abated, the winter is over, but the journey is long, and it would be scarcely safe for me to run the

---

[15] *Ep.* dcxxxix. [16] *Ep.* dcxlviii.
[17] *Ep.* dcxlix. This letter has no date, but it evidently belongs to the early part of 1523.

gauntlet of the snowy Alps, those horrid stoves the very smell of which makes me faint, of dirty and uncomfortable inns, and sour wines whose taste puts me in danger of my life. . . .

"I would I had the gifts which you ascribe to me to put an end to this dissension; I should not hesitate to give up my own life if I could thereby heal the public malady. In the first place, there are many who surpass me in powers of composition, and it is not thus that this business will be settled. My learning is far below mediocrity, and, such as it is, it is derived from the study of the old authors, and is more adapted for teaching than for controversy. As to my authority, what authority can be possessed by an humble individual like myself? Can the authority of Erasmus avail with those in whose eyes that of so many universities, so many monarchs, and, lastly, of the supreme Pontiff weighs nothing? If I ever enjoyed any favour it has either lost its freshness, or has quite died away, or has even been converted into hatred. And I, who formerly used to be described in hundreds of letters as thrice-greatest hero, prince of letters, star of Germany, sun of learning, high-priest of the *belles-lettres*, defender of sound theology, am now either passed in silence or painted in very different colours. I regard not at all these empty titles, which were only a burden to me. Look at the abuse with which I am now overwhelmed, the bitter attacks which are made upon me through the press, the threats with which they try to frighten me. There have been those even who declared they would take my life if I stirred. Meantime others cry out that I am in league with the Lutherans, cry out that I write nothing against Luther, while the strong partisans of

Luther protest that I attack him often, and more bitterly than is becoming. . . .

". . . . But your Holiness points out a remedy for these evils. 'Come to Rome,' you say; 'or write as fiercely as you can against Luther; declare war upon all Lutherans.' In the first place, when I am told to come to Rome, it is much like telling a crab to fly. The crab answers, 'Give me a pair of wings.' And I will answer, Restore my youth, restore my health. I could wish that this excuse were less well-grounded than it is. It would be tedious to mention the causes which have persuaded me hitherto to remain at Basle; this I would most solemnly affirm, that if I knew of anything that could advance the cause of Christ I would do it, even at the risk of my life. I never wanted the inclination to act, but only the hope of doing good. Now what greater folly could there be than to touch an evil which was happily quiescent if you expected no result but some worse trouble? Suffer, I earnestly beg of you, one of your flock to speak thus freely with his shepherd. Though my health permitted me, what good should I do at Rome? I should be free from all association with the Lutherans. That I am already, for I have no correspondence with them whatever. Accordingly, I need apprehend no danger from them, as regards my own conversion. On the other hand, as regards their correction, I shall do more good when living near them than if I were removed to a distance; for of what use can a physician be to his patients if he runs away from them? When the rumour was spread here that I was summoned to Rome, the cry was immediately raised that I was going off to seize my booty. What weight, then, will be attached to anything I may write from thence, if people are persuaded that I am corrupted with bribes? I should live there, or write, it may be, in greater safety, but that would be to consult for myself, not for the cause. Should I write temperately and civilly against Luther, I shall be thought to be in collusion with him; but if I imitate his style and provoke the Lutherans to war, I shall only succeed in stirring up a nest of hornets. Thus far, I confess, I have cultivated as far as I could the friendship of learned men; for in this way I think I do more good.

"But so far, you will say, I have done nothing but pour out complaints, and you are waiting for my advice. All that I have yet said is part of my advice. However, to proceed: I see many are of opinion that the evil of the times may be cured by severity, but I am afraid the issue may hereafter prove this to be bad policy. For I foresee more danger than I could wish that the end may be slaughter and bloodshed. I do not now dispute what those sectaries may deserve, but what is for the interest of the public peace. This disease has spread too far to be healed by amputation or burning. By this means, I admit, the sect of the Wickliffites was formerly put down in England by the power of the kings, but it was put down rather than extinguished. And I am not sure that what was possible at that time, and in that kingdom, the whole of which is under one sovereign, would be possible here in so vast a territory, divided among so many monarchs; at least if it is determined to stamp out this plague by means of imprisonment, scourging, confiscations, exile, severe sentences, and death, there can be no need of my counsel. I perceive, however, that your gentle temper would prefer a different policy, and that you would rather cure than punish. This would not be very difficult if all were animated by the same spirit as you, and if, as you say, they would put aside their private feelings and consult honestly for the glory of Christ and the salvation of the Christian people. But if every one is intent on his own private advantage, if the divines demand that their authority shall be maintained intact, if the monks will suffer nothing to be taken from their privileges, if the princes keep firm hold of all their rights, it will be extremely difficult to consult for the common good. The first thing will be to discover the sources whence this evil springs up again and again; these must before all things be healed. Then, however, it will be well that pardon be offered to all who have erred by the persuasion or the impulse of others, or rather an amnesty for all past misdoings, which seem to have come about by some fatality. If God deals thus with us every day, forgetting all our sins, as often as the sinner groans, why should not the vicar of God do the same? And yet in the meantime innovations which make very little for piety, but a great deal for sedition, are checked by the magistrates and sovereigns. I could wish, if it were possible, that the licence of publishing pamphlets should be under some restraint. Besides, let hope be given to the world that some grievances of which it justly complains will be removed. At the sweet name of liberty all will breathe again. The interests of liberty will be consulted in every way, as far as may be without injury to religion; measures will be taken for relieving the conscience of the people, but at the same time the dignity of princes and bishops will be no less considered. But this dignity must be estimated by those things in which their dignity truly consists, as the liberty of the people must also be estimated. Your Holiness will ask, 'What are those sources, or what are the grievances which must be removed?' To consider these questions, I think there should be summoned from every country men of incorruptible integrity, grave, mild, gracious, unimpassioned, whose opinion——"

But there, in consequence, it may be supposed, of the sudden departure of the messenger who was to carry it,[18] the letter breaks off, not, however, before we have clearly sketched for us the plan which the writer proposed to impart with so much mystery to his old friend, the former professor of Louvain. It was excellent advice. Deal gently with errors; pardon past misdoings; reform abuses; and call a general council from which all but moderate men shall be carefully excluded. Excellent advice, and—one would have supposed, though we are informed that it was not acceptable [19]—very much in accordance with the spirit of the conscientious and well-meaning Adrian; but it was too late now to save the unity of the Church. The Germans had taken reform pretty effectually into their own hands. With the Emperor and the King of France at war, and with the Turks threatening Christendom, the times were by no means adapted to the calling of a general council. Adrian, a stranger in Rome, and little versed in the politics of the Papal court, was too un-

---

[18] "Erasmus, when he printed this letter, thought proper to suppress the secret advice which he had given to the Pope; and that is the reason for which the epistle breaks off abruptly."—JORTIN, vol. i. p. 288. But it is not easy to think what Erasmus could have added that he would wish suppressed. He says himself, in reference to his proffered advice, "Misi partem, sed displicuit."—(*Er. Op.* iii. 819, C.) The explanation in the text is suggested by the opening sentences of the letter itself.

[19] See the preceding note.

popular, and he reigned too short a time, to be able to accomplish much. As Protestants we may rejoice that conciliation was impossible. By a voluntary and internal reform, indeed, some of the immediate evils—the strife and the bloodshed—which followed on the divisions in the Church might have been avoided, but it is doubtful whether the more distant blessings—liberty of conscience and the freedom of the press—which indirectly resulted from them, would have been so effectually obtained. Still we may commend the wisdom of Erasmus, which suggested the only measure in which there was any hope for the peace of the world and the unity of Christendom.

The reform party might, by this time, have been convinced that Erasmus would never commit himself to an open contest with the Papacy; but a fresh attempt which was made in the course of the coming winter to gain him over, led to one of the most bitter controversies in which he was ever engaged, the history of which we must now follow.

Ulrich von Hutten, whom we have already met with more than once, was one of the young Germans to whom Erasmus had chiefly looked as likely to succeed himself in advancing the cause of sound learning, and who he hoped would eclipse his own fame. Born in the year 1488, at his ancestral seat of Steckelberg, of a noble family, he had been early placed in the monastery of Fulda, from which, however, he managed to escape without taking any vow. He afterwards studied at Cologne, and at Frankfort-on-the-Oder, where he took his degree of Master of Arts. After this he led a life of wild adventure mingled with hard study, and soon gained a great name in literature, being crowned Poet

Laureate by the Emperor Maximilian, from whom also he received the honour of knighthood. A determined enemy of the Papacy, he espoused the cause of Reuchlin with enthusiastic ardour, and wrote in his defence, besides the famous "Letters of Obscure Men," which were called forth by the same controversy, a poem entitled "Reuchlin's Triumph," which, however, he suppressed for two years, by the advice of Erasmus, lest if published prematurely it should do more harm than good.[20] So bitter were his satires on the Roman Court, that Leo X. gave orders to have him sent bound to Rome, but in the temper of the German people at that time such a command was more easily issued than executed. Nevertheless Hutten had to fly for safety, and on his way to the castle of Ebernburg, where he took refuge with Franz von Sickingen, it is said that meeting Hochstraten, he drew his sword upon him and threatened to kill him, but on the cowardly monk throwing himself at his feet and begging for mercy, spared his life, remarking that he would not pollute his sword with the blood of such a scoundrel.[21]

Hutten had early conceived a very great esteem for Erasmus,[22] from whose works no doubt he derived much of his own inspiration; but there was at no time any great degree of intercourse between them. He had first met him at Maintz, and afterwards at Louvain, where he had requested a secret interview with him, and this being granted, had begun to speak of declaring war upon the Romans. Erasmus at first thought he was

---

[20] *Er. Op.* x. 1638, E; 1668, E.
[21] *Ott. Brunfelsii Resp. ad Spong. Erasmi.*—*Hut. Op.* vol. iv. p. 523.
[22] "Qui te et tua prædicatione et mea conscientia aliter non quam veluti religione quadam contactus, reverentissime semper colui."—*Exp. Hut. Op.* iv. p. 344.

joking, but seeing he was in earnest he warned him that he would find it a dangerous business, and presently cut the conversation short by telling him that he did not want to hear more of the matter, which lay altogether outside his province, and by advising him not to mix himself up in any such foolish and rash proceedings.[83] He had before counselled him by letter to restrain the liberty of his pen, and to keep on good terms with the ruling powers, and this advice was taken in very good part; but the more the cause of the Reformation advanced, and the more warmly he himself became interested in it, the less could Hutten understand how it was possible for Erasmus to stand apart and refuse to identify himself with Luther; and the more determined did he become to separate him, by main force if necessary, from all connection with the Papal party. We have seen already how, with this view, he surreptitiously printed, and even altered, the letter to the Elector of Maintz,[84] with which he had been entrusted, and we must now notice his further proceedings for the same object.

If it was not by Hutten's advice that Erasmus had removed from Louvain to Basle, at any rate it would seem that he had advised it. On the 15th of August, 1520, he had written to him from Steckelberg, pretty freely taking him to task for weakness and indecision in regard to Reuchlin and Luther, and begging him, if he could not commend his own conduct, to be altogether silent, rather than say anything disparaging, seeing how much weight would be attached to a single unfavourable word from him. And just three months afterwards, on the 13th of November of the same year,

[83] *Er. Op.* x. 1668, C.   [84] See above, p. 46.

he wrote to him again from Ebernburg, asking him what he meant by staying in places where the greatest hatred prevailed against their party, and the Pope's mandates were strictly executed. Did he think himself safe where Luther's books were burned? He must now see that the attempt which he had persevered in so long to win over the Pope and his adherents by flattery and praise, had failed. Let him fly then ere it be too late. The outbreak he and Franz are contemplating will render his position still more critical, and he will have to fear not only open attack, but poison and the dagger. He advises him therefore to exchange Louvain for Basle where he is loved and honoured, where men's minds are naturally free, and now besides stirred by Luther's writings, and a poem in German of his own composition.[23]

It was about two years after this letter that Hutten, cast off by his friends, exiled from his country, overwhelmed with debt, reduced to the last extreme of poverty, bearing the scars of ancient wounds, eaten up with a vile disease, and breathing out contagion, made his appearance in Basle. On his way thither he had stopped at Schelestadt, and had borrowed money from his acquaintances all round, or perhaps only tried to borrow it. He had there met Beatus Rhenanus, and, as he was preceding him to Basle, he sent a message by him to Erasmus to the effect that he had noticed in him one serious failing, meaning, as was supposed, his timidity, but that *he* was coming to see him and would soon

---

[23] STRAUSS, *Ulrich von Hutten*, II. Buch, x. Kapitel, pp. 259 *sqq*. *Hutteni Opp*. ed. Münch, iv. p. 49 *sqq*. The second letter is addressed by Hutten to "his adorable friend, Erasmus of Rotterdam, the most Christian of divines, at Maintz, Cologne, or wherever he may be."

put some courage into him."[86] This message Beatus did not think it necessary to deliver.

It is not at all difficult to understand that Erasmus might have very strong objections to meeting this hot-headed knight. Hutten, it was known, wished to expostulate with him on two or three points in his conduct, and his expostulations were not likely to be very agreeable to listen to. Besides, if he once received him into his house he did not know when he should get him out again, or what other unpleasant consequences might ensue. He afterwards wrote to Melancthon that he was afraid Hutten, if once admitted, might quarter himself upon him for the winter, and that he should be compelled to entertain not only the knight himself, but also the troop of evangelicals, as they were pleased to be called, though they were anything but evangelical in character, with whom he consorted.[87] He resolved, accordingly, to avoid an interview if possible, and as soon as he heard of Hutten's arrival, he sent him a civil message to say that if he wished merely to pay him a visit of compliment, he would rather he did not come to see him, as his doing so might be very damaging to him in the position in which he was placed, and in which he had already a great deal of odium to bear, and could be of no advantage to Hutten himself; he added that he still entertained towards him all his old feelings of affection, and that if he could render him any service he would be most

---

[86] "Se mox Basileam aditurum, mihique plus satis meticuloso additurum animum."—*Er. Op.* x. 1636, A.

[87] "Erat mihi gloriosus ille miles cum sua scabie in ædes recipiendus, simulque recipiendus ille chorus titulo Evangelicorum, sed titulo duntaxat. Sletstadii mulctavit omnes amicos suos aliqua pecunia."—*Er. Op.* iii. 817, B.

happy to do so.[28] The person by whom he sent this
message, and who had first informed him of Hutten's
arrival, was a young German student, previously known
to him at Louvain, who called himself Henry of Eppendorf. But although he pretended to nobility, and talked
much of his father's castle and estates, Eppendorf was
in reality of plebeian origin, being the son, so at least it
was affirmed, of a small public-house keeper in the
village from which he took his name. He had, however, the advantage of a prepossessing exterior, and
being a young man of more than common abilities and
of very agreeable manners, he had no difficulty in acting
the part which he was pleased to assume.[29] It would
appear that he led a fast life, and was much given to
gambling and other kinds of dissipation, insomuch that
Erasmus, some time afterwards, felt himself called on
to write to George, Duke of Saxony, whose *protégé* he
was, advising that he should be recalled home and put
to some honourable occupation.[30] At this time, however, he was on the most friendly terms with Erasmus,
and being also intimate with Hutten, in whom he found
a congenial companion, it was natural that he should be
employed as a messenger between them. Eppendorf
undertook to deliver the message entrusted to him,
affirmed that he had done so with the utmost civility,
and when asked a day or two afterwards how Hutten
had taken the refusal, replied that he had smiled good-
humouredly, and had taken it in very good part. Erasmus

[28] *Er. Op.* x. 1632, D.
[29] "Rara indole juvenis, et ipsa fronte generis sui nobilitatem præ se ferens."—*Er. Op.* iii. 560, D. "Moribus suavissimis."—*Ib.* 754, B. "Ita scilicet est noster Hen-ricus à Epphendorf, fortassis ob cauponam cerevisiariam ab illius majoribus administratam." — *Ib.* 1732, D.
[30] *Ep.* dccclviii.

had reason afterwards to believe that this was a falsehood, but he again expressed his regard for Hutten, and his willingness to render him any service in his power; and some days after he begged Eppendorf once more to tell him honestly whether Hutten had taken the refusal in the same spirit in which it was meant, or had shown any sign of being offended. Eppendorf declared that he had observed no symptoms of that kind, but added on leaving, "I think he would like to see you." When asked if he had said so, he replied that he had not; but again added, "I think there is something he would like to talk to you about." "Well," replied Erasmus, "though I certainly wished to save myself from the odium that such an interview may bring upon me, still, I don't care about it so much that I would refuse to see him if he has really anything very important to say to me; or, if for any other reason he has set his heart upon it, I would myself call upon him, if I could only bear the heat of his stove. That, however, is a thing which, considering the nature of his trouble, he can probably not do without; but if he can bear the cold of this room, I am ready to talk to him till he is tired, and we will take care to have a bright fire on the hearth." To this Eppendorf replied that Hutten's malady was so severe as to make it quite out of the question for him to leave the stove. The last civil message of Erasmus was certainly never delivered, and shortly afterwards, the protection of the city being withdrawn from him by the magistrates, at the instigation of the clergy, who, not without reason, feared his turbulent spirit, Hutten departed to Mülhausen.[31]

He left Basle on the 19th of January in the follow-

[31] *Er. Op.* x. 1632.

ing year,[32] accompanied by Eppendorf, who by-and-bye returned to Erasmus, bringing word that Hutten was very angry with him, and was busy writing a ferocious attack on his character. The treachery of Eppendorf was now suspected, and was afterwards established beyond doubt.[33] Hutten, so far from taking the refusal of Erasmus to see him in good part, as Eppendorf had represented, was, in reality, as, indeed, might naturally be supposed, transported with rage; and Eppendorf, instead of endeavouring to soothe him, had done all he could to exasperate him, by omitting the civil words of Erasmus, and reporting in the worst sense any unfavourable remarks regarding Hutten that might chance to drop from him in conversation. Of this Erasmus mentions an instance, which throws some light on the character of Hutten as well as on the state of the times. Having asked how it was that Hutten had written, and intended to publish, an invective against the Count Palatine, Eppendorf replied that it was because the Count had put to death one of his most faithful servants, and a most innocent man. "An innocent man," replied Erasmus, "who attacked and robbed three Abbots in open day!" "True," said the other, "but he did it by his master's orders." "Would such an excuse," asked Erasmus, smiling, "acquit my servants, if they were caught committing a theft, and said they were acting by my orders?" Eppendorf

---

[32] STRAUSS *ubi supra*, p. 266.

[33] "Multis conjecturis adducor, ut credam Henricum Epphendorpium hujus fabulæ artificem; adeo ille subito factus Huttenianus."—*Er. Op.* iii. 721, D. The date of this is July 19, 1523. Some years afterwards Erasmus writes, in reference to Eppendorf's statement, that Hutten had taken the excuse for not seeing him in good part—"ex Heresbacchio et Hutteni litteris deprehendi rem secus habere."—*Ib.* 1734, F.

merely smiled in reply; but he took care to report the remark to Hutten, who flew into a violent passion on hearing a deed of knightly valour, for which he himself was responsible, compared with a base plebeian theft.[34] This was before he had left Basle; but after his departure for Mülhausen, Eppendorf continued to go back and forwards, carrying false reports and making mischief. Meantime, Hutten, in spite of his anger, may have been secretly not ill-pleased to have the opportunity of expostulating before the public with his pen, rather than in the privacy of a conference; and if he wanted any fresh provocation, or had any difficulty in finding a convenient basis for his attack without making it turn too much on a mere private affront, it so happened that Erasmus now furnished him with both, by the publication of an apologetic letter, intended to be a complete defence of himself against the suspicion of Lutheranism, and in which he gave a representation of his conduct towards Hutten, which appeared to the latter to be entirely false, and which, it must be confessed, seems to be not altogether in accordance with the facts of the case.

This is the letter, addressed to Marcus Laurinus, from which I have already taken some particulars, and which bears date February 1, 1523.[35] Its ostensible object was to contradict certain rumours by which his friend's mind had been disturbed, to the effect, apparently, that he had avowed himself a Lutheran, and was now in hiding to escape destruction; but it became in reality a complete defence of his conduct, and a vindication of his title to be considered a faithful son of the Church. With this view a sketch was drawn of his life

[34] *Er. Op.* iii. 1735, A. [35] *Ep.* del. See above, pp. 94, 95, and 98-100.

since his departure from Louvain, especial prominence being given to his interview with Aleander, and every other circumstance being mentioned which showed how high he still stood in the favour of the leaders of the Papal party, and even of the Pope himself. In regard to Luther, he declared, as he had always done, that he was no partisan of his, that he admired a great deal in him, but strongly disapproved of his intemperance and arrogance, and if Luther himself, he said, were to come to Basle, he would gladly converse with him, and freely tell him of his faults. On Luther's doctrines he had never ventured to pronounce an opinion; but whatever their truth might be, he was certainly neither their author nor their defender, as had been falsely alleged, and if there was great merit in promoting this cause, as every Lutheran must confess, seeing that he embarked in it at the risk not only of his own life, but of the lives of others, it would surely be the height of arrogance in him if he claimed to have any part in it. Still, he had never set himself in opposition to Luther, nor could he understand what ground the Lutherans had for regarding him as their enemy. It is true that, in one of his letters, he had expressed the hope that, if he could find time, he might do something for the peace of the Christian world and the dignity of the Apostolic See; but there was surely nothing in that which could be regarded as adverse to Luther? If it was asked, was not the Pope the enemy of God, the extirpator of gospel truth, and the seducer of the whole Christian people? he had never given any countenance to a Pope of that description; and yet, if there were such, it was not his business to hurl them from the throne: Christ still lives, and is armed with his scourge to drive out such robbers from his temple. Again, if, in his paraphrase on the ninth of Romans, he had ascribed a certain very small degree of efficacy to Free Will, he had only followed the authority of Origen and Jerome, and other Fathers. Moreover, his Paraphrase appeared before the publication of Luther's dogma that whatever good or evil we do is of absolute necessity. He had written, therefore, in ignorance that there was any one who totally denied free will, and even if he had held that doctrine, while quite admitting the danger of trusting to our own works, he would have been unwilling to disseminate it, on account of its dangerous consequences. "It may be, indeed," he continued, "that, not holding Luther's doctrines, I sometimes dash my foot against a stone; but if so, must his friends at once raise an outcry against me? There are such numbers in all parts of the world denouncing Luther's doctrine, and publishing books against him, and may I not even open my mouth if anything displeases me? Let a timid and unlearned man, as they truly call me, to whose judgment in such matters no weight can be assigned, at least be permitted to subscribe to the opinion of so many acknowledged authorities, and in so dangerous a crisis quietly embrace the opinion of those whose authority the Christian world has followed for so many centuries. If there is any one who cannot love Erasmus as a weak Christian, he must even feel towards him how he will; I cannot be other than I am. If there is any one to whom Christ has given greater gifts of the Spirit, and he has confidence in himself, let him use them to Christ's glory. Meantime, I prefer to follow an humbler and a safer course. I cannot help hating dissension, I cannot but love peace and concord, I could wish that all should unite their efforts for the promotion of evangelical concord all the world over, and for the establishment on sound principles, but without revolution, of the priestly office on the one hand, and the liberty of the people on the other—of that people whom the Lord Jesus wishes to be free. For those who are moving in that direction, Erasmus will do all in his power; but if any one likes better to throw the world into confusion, he must not expect me, at least, either as a leader or a follower. They pretend, indeed, the operation of the Spirit. Let those then dance and welcome among the prophets, whom the Spirit of the Lord hath possessed. That Spirit has not yet taken hold of me; when it does, perchance I, too, may be called a Saul among the Prophets."

In the course of this long letter, of which I have not given even an abstract, Erasmus introduced the name of Hutten, as it were, incidentally, but with the evident design of showing that, while he wished to be on friendly terms with him, he had no complicity in any of his plans against the peace of the Church. There were those, he said, who were determined to make him a Lutheran, by stratagem or even by force, whether he would or not, and for this purpose the most baseless rumours were put in circulation. Thus, it was reported that Hochstraten had burned his books at Cologne, in the hope that, roused by this indignity, he would use language which would have the effect of setting him irreconcilably at variance with the Papists, and compel him to join their adversaries. Again, it was said that his writings had been condemned at Rome, in the expectation that he would abuse the Pope. Finally, the story went that numbers of Lutherans were visiting him at Basle, and that Luther himself was in hiding there. Now, the fact was, that among the many who certainly came to see him, no one had ever avowed himself a Lutheran, and yet it would greatly please him if all the Lutherans and Anti-Lutherans, too, would come and ask his advice and follow it; if they would do so it would be for the good of the world. No doubt some had come to Basle who were suspected of holding Luther's opinions, but not one by his invitation, and how could he prevent them coming, seeing that he did not carry the keys of the city, nor hold any office in it? He then continued thus: "Hutten was here seeking protection for a few days, but during that time neither of us called upon the other; and yet, if he had sought an interview with me, I would not have refused to see an old friend, whom even now I cannot help loving for his great talents and his admirable wit. For whatever business else he has here, with that I have nothing to do. But as, owing to his bad health, he could not do without the heat of a stove, and that is a thing I cannot bear, it so turned out that we did not see one another."

These few sentences have not certainly much sting in them, but the whole letter, forwarded to Hutten by his friend in Basle as soon as it was in type, added to the indignity under which he was already smarting, and seeming, as it must have seemed from his point of view, to establish beyond question the treachery of Erasmus, and his determination to abandon the cause of reform, roused his fiery spirit to the utmost. It was then, apparently, that Hutten began his "Expostulation," and it was shortly afterwards that Eppendorf brought the tidings to Erasmus. A consultation, at which Beatus Rhenanus was present, was immediately held, to consider what steps should be taken to meet or avert the attack. His two friends recommended that before the appearance of Hutten's book a letter should be sent him with the view of soothing his anger, but Erasmus thought it better to take no notice, observing that spirits like his only became more exasperated by attempts to tranquillise them. As, however, the point was pressed, he consented, and wrote a letter to Hutten, in which he assured him of his continued regard, protested that in declining to see him he had intended no offence, and warned him that it would be impossible for him to do anything that would be more acceptable to Hochstraten, Egmund, and others, or more disastrous to the cause of letters, of which he professed himself the champion, than by attacking Erasmus. Let him, then, before open war be declared between them, at least tell him by private letter what it was he complained of in his conduct, for as for himself he could not divine, and, unless Hutten were greatly changed, he had no doubt he could satisfy him. Erasmus, however, either from anger or from mere insensibility, did not conclude without some cruel allusions to Hutten's position. If nothing else will move him, he said, let him consider how this matter will affect his own character. "It is probable there will be those who, considering the present state of your fortunes, will suspect that your object in resorting to such practices is plunder, and it is to be feared that this conjecture regarding one who is an exile, in debt, and reduced to extreme poverty, will stick in the minds of many."[36] As Erasmus anticipated, and as might be anticipated from the tone of the last remark, this letter called forth an angry reply, in which the following offences were laid

[36] *Ep.* delxxii.

to his charge: He had put Capito above Reuchlin as a Hebrew scholar; he had been severe on Hutten himself in a letter to Hochstraten; he had attempted to fix on Reuchlin a charge of treachery; he had flattered the divines of Louvain and other places; lastly—and this was the sum of all his offences—he had deserted the cause of the Gospel, and was exerting all his power to undermine it. The book itself in which these charges were to be enforced at length, he promised he would send in the course of a few days by a servant.[37] This, however, was not done, and Erasmus first heard from others that Hutten had written against him. He answered to the charges which were made in Hutten's letter, and Hutten then replied in somewhat gentler terms, telling him that the book was now in the hands of the printer, but if he would be silent friendship might still be preserved between them. At last a copy reached him, but without seal or cover. Some of his friends were urgent with him to send a bribe to Hutten to suppress it—this being no longer in his power—but Erasmus constantly replied that it had been best if such a book had never been written, but once it was put into circulation, the sooner it was printed and published the better.

"Ulrich von Hutten's Expostulation with Erasmus of Rotterdam, Priest and Divine,"[38] was printed in Strasburg, at the press of John Schott, and published in July, 1523. Hutten begins by denouncing the state-

[37] *Er. Op.* x. 1633, D. E. Of this letter we have only the abstract of Erasmus in the *Spongia*. To it, no doubt, also belong, as Strauss has remarked, the following words, which are subsequently quoted:—"Nemo instigat Huttenum, nec ille sustinet a quoquam instigari."

[38] *Ulrichi ab Hutten cum Erasmo Roterodamo, Presbytero, Theologo Expostulatio.*

ment of Erasmus regarding him in the letter to Laurinus as an entire figment. He was not only a few days, but more than fifty days, in Basle, and so far was it from the truth that he could not leave his stove that he was often for three hours together talking with his friends in the market-place, and even after the refusal of Erasmus to see him he had frequently walked up and down past his windows, hoping he would change his mind, and doubted not that he had seen him. He had left Basle sooner than he intended, but he continued to hear from his friends what Erasmus was saying every day against Luther, and how he was threatening to take up his pen against himself and to write whole volumes to strike terror into that "sect," as he called it. He restrained himself, however, until at length the letter to Laurinus reached him, and as soon as he recovered from the astonishment into which he was thrown by that letter, so full as it was of violent abuse, and giving such clear evidence of a totally altered mind, that he began to consider, in sorrow and anger, how it was that one who was lately for "calling the Pope to order," who used to denounce Rome as a sink of wickedness, who detested indulgences, condemned ceremonies, and, in one word, chastised with the utmost severity the universal hypocrisy of the Church, was now quite of a contrary opinion, and was for making terms with the opposite party. Several different ways of accounting for this change occurred to him. First, that insatiable thirst for fame, that greed of applause which will not endure merit in another. Secondly, his cowardice and infirmity of purpose. Neither of these, however, seemed satisfactory, and then it occurred to him that he must have been bribed; and his boasts of the splendid offers that had been made him if he would go to Rome confirmed him in this suspicion. Still, it was difficult to understand how one of his years, and who already had abundance for his wants, could permit himself to receive a bribe, but he thought it might have happened in this way: Erasmus, through natural timidity and littleness of mind, may have despaired of the cause, and then seeing the German Princes uniting against the Reformers, he may have thought it the best policy to go over to the other side. Thus he was ready to undertake the task so often pressed upon him of writing against Luther, and he hoped by threats to terrify the Reformers into submission.

Hutten then proceeds to enlarge on the charges which he had already laid against Erasmus in his preliminary letter. He is particularly hard upon him for his avowed friendship for Aleander, whom he had once described as the vilest of mankind, a man born for intrigue and deceit, ever faithless and treacherous, ever malignant and maleficent, who used his learning for no other purpose than to injure learning. He had it on the best authority, he said, that when Aleander was the Pope's Legate at the Diet of Worms, Erasmus had declared that he would be compelled to doubt whether there were free men in Germany if he was permitted to depart alive. Yet now he was hand-and-glove with this man, talking with him till midnight, and even arranging with him that they should go to Rome together; this, though it was perfectly well known that Aleander had come expressly to seize Erasmus as the author of all the disturbances in Germany and the ringleader of sedition everywhere, and forbore only because he thought it more politic to proceed by stratagem, and endeavour to gain his services for the Papal party. That Adrian, too, was hostile to him was no fiction of the Lutherans, for it was reported, on the best authority, that while Cardinal in Spain, he had written a letter to Rome reproaching those in power there with wasting their time in disputing with Luther when they ought rather to lay hold of Erasmus, the fountain-head of the evil, and the promoter of rebellion, who was schooling Germany to renounce the authority of the Pope. Yet now he was heaping the most extravagant praises upon this Pope, even before he had held the office long enough to show his real character. And in the same way he praised many of the bitterest opponents of the Reformation, such as Sylvester Prieras and Eck, and even Latomus, Egmund, and Atensis—men whose names would never have been heard of in Germany if it had not been for his invectives against them; and now it seems that Lee, too, must be delivered out of the hands of the Reformers and apologised for. Thus could Erasmus blow hot and cold, condemn and acquit, flatter and abuse, according as his caprice or his interest might suggest.

Hutten now, warming with his work, launches forth into a long and indignant denunciation of the inconsistency of Erasmus and his subserviency to the Holy See, charging him with abandoning, through cowardice and vainglory, if not for actual bribes, the cause of Reform, but assuring him, at the same time, that if he is determined not to retrace his steps they can endure his loss, and that even without his consent they will still have on their side auxiliaries furnished by himself—namely, his books, which will continue to fight for those whom he has so basely deserted. As to the charge that any Lutheran had endeavoured to bring him over to their side by stratagem, he repelled it with scorn. Let him, then, live secure among people of influence, who offer bribes and have bishoprics ready to bestow upon him, and other splendid ecclesiastical offices, if he will but write against Luther. "As for me," he continues, "I will remain here in the midst of danger, where there are honest, grave, truthful, and candid men, sincere, constant, and free, whom neither bribes move, nor honours change, nor dangers terrify; who respect justice, observe faith, value religion, and adhere firmly to the truth." [39] Hutten concludes his invective in a strain of impassioned eloquence, asking Erasmus on what possible pretext he can oppose that party, the destruction of which, he must himself admit, will be ruinous to Gospel truth and liberty, warning him of the danger to which he is exposing his own reputation,[40] and pointing out that the enemies of the Reformation are simply making use of him as a tool for carrying out their own purposes. Finally, he urges him to fulfil the hopes of his new friends, and prepare himself for the conflict. He will find his adversaries ready, but, in truth, his battle

---

[39] "Tu illic securus agas, ubi potentes viri sunt, qui munera offerunt, et paratos habent, si in Lutherum scribere vis, Episcopatus tibi, ac sacerdotia cedunt haud contemnenda. Ego hic periclitor, ubi integri, graves, veri, candidi, sinceri, constantes, et liberi homines sunt, quos neque munera movent, neque honores mutant, neque pericula terrent; quibus æquitas colitur, fides servatur, religio curæ est, veritas non deseritur."—*Hut. Op.* vol. iv. pp. 375-6.

[40] "Iterum responde mihi, quo honestatis prætextu speras te oppugnaturum eas partes, quas sentis ipse, si devinci unquam contigerit, magnam Evangelicæ veritatis ac libertatis ruinam secum abstracturas? ... Ut ne istud pensi habeas, quanto cum dispendio famæ et existimationis tuæ in illorum te dignationem insinues, cum hoc ætatis per æqua, per iniqua, potentissimorum hominum favorem captas."—*Ib.* p. 389.

will be less with them than with his own spirit and his own books.

Hutten's expostulation, on which he concentrated all his powers of eloquence, sarcasm, and irony, appears to have really alarmed Erasmus,—indeed, by exhibiting him as the prime mover in the attack on Rome, it was calculated to injure him as much with the Papists as the Reformers, and on the 10th of August we find him addressing a letter to the town-council of Zürich, whither Hutten had now removed, in which, after calling attention to his own services to literature, he appeals for protection against this man whom he had never injured by word or deed. He had, he said, published a book against him, full of palpable lies and calumnies, in which, moreover, he had attacked other good men, and spared neither Pope nor Emperor. He does not, however, ask that they would refuse him permission to reside in their city, but only that they would not allow him to abuse their kindness by such publications, which must be injurious to the cause of the Gospel, to letters, and even to common morality. The appeal called forth a rejoinder from Hutten, in which he expresses his confidence that his "dear Friends and Masters" will not permit him to be slandered without giving him the opportunity of defending himself, and begs that if any documents affecting his character be forwarded to them, either by Erasmus or any one else, they will furnish him with copies. For himself, it had always been his ambition, even from his boyish years, to lead a life of virtue and piety, as became a noble knight, and he knew how to defend his honour; and so he begged them to have confidence in him, as he had also good will to them, and to the Confederation.⁴¹ That any action was taken in consequence of the application of Erasmus, is not probable; indeed Hutten had already left Zürich, and was now in the neighbouring island of Ufnau, on the Lake of Zürich.

It was not long before Erasmus was ready with his reply to the "Expostulation." He dashed it off in six days, but owing to the pre-occupation of Froben's press, it was not out of the printer's hands till the 3rd of September. He called it a "Sponge to wipe away Hutten's Aspersions,"⁴² and promised that he would not retort upon his adversary any of his accusations, but would answer briefly and civilly. Nevertheless, the reply, if somewhat less vehement in tone, was considerably longer than the attack. Erasmus, in the first place, gives his own version of his refusal to see Hutten. It has already been laid before the reader, and there is no reason to doubt its substantial correctness, though it is of course obvious to remark that all his friendly messages may not have been accurately delivered to Hutten. He then goes on to deal at some length with the specific charges against him, and so far as these referred to his treatment of individuals, he has no difficulty in disposing of them. The allegation that he had referred offensively to Hutten in his writings was founded on a sentence in his letter to Hochstraten, to the effect that he could never have approved of the bitterness with which Hutten, Reuchlin, and others had attacked him, had he not first read the writings by which they were

---

⁴¹ *Hutteni Opp.* iv. pp. 397—400.

⁴² *Spongia Erasmi adversus Aspergines Hutteni.* Basiliæ, per Jo. Frobenium, an. M.D.XXIII. mense Septembri.—*Er. Op.* x. 1631. Two more editions, if not three more—the fourth seems to be without date—were called for before the end of the year. See *Hut. Op.* Münch, iv. 331-33.

provoked to such intemperance: but every one whose judgment is not utterly perverted must see that there is nothing here to offend any one but Hochstraten himself, on whom he retorts his own charge. But Hutten was still more indignant with him for having added that he had read these attacks with pain, because he feared impartial men might think that the object of such bitter reproaches deserved them. This Hutten thought far too mild; but it was surely only common sense to use gentle terms. If Hochstraten could be cured at all, civility was the most appropriate remedy, but if not he would suffer more in the eyes of sensible people from the moderation of his accuser than if he had attacked him with violence. It was rather late, too, for Hutten to find out this offence just now, after the book containing the words in question had been so long before the world, and considering that none of the other persons referred to had ever complained. He denies positively that he had ever praised Hochstraten, and challenges Hutten to produce a single passage from his writings where he had done so: on the other hand, he had not called him "a pest sent down in wrath from heaven to destroy literature and all men of superior talents."[43] This was clearly Hutten's language, not his, and at any rate it was too bad to bring up against him every expression which might have escaped from him in friendly conversation, or when the wine was freely circulated.

The next charge against him was, that he had

[43] "Fortasse sic me volebat Huttenus scribere: 'Spurcissima latrina, tun' audes viros heroas tuis merdosis libellis aspergere?' Forsitan sic decebat scribere Huttenum, at non decebat Erasmum. Si sanabilis erat Hochstratus, erat apta civilitas: sin erat insanabilis, magis illum apud bonos gravabat mea modestia, quam gravasset procacia."—*Er. Op.* x. 1638, C.

remarked in one of his letters that Capito was a more learned Hebraist than Reuchlin, and if he had poisoned Reuchlin, Hutten could not well have been more enraged. The answer to this charge was a very simple one. Reuchlin was admitted on all hands to have been the first to revive the study of Hebrew in Germany, and it could surely be no disgrace to him if he was succeeded by some one more learned than himself. That was his opinion of Capito at the time when he wrote, and those who were learned in Hebrew had since subscribed to his judgment. But his motive for this preference, according to Hutten, was jealousy, because some called Reuchlin Germany's other eye; and Erasmus could bear no rival near the throne. This was a likely charge indeed, that one who had always been such a friend to learning could not endure another engaged in precisely the same pursuits! The remark about Germany's other eye he confessed he could not read without laughter, as if he would have wished, by the exclusion of Reuchlin, to leave Germany one-eyed. Had he not always been a most constant friend to Reuchlin? But he must exalt Capito, it seems, because he had praised his New Testament. In reality he had merely cited the judgment of Berus and Capito, two theologians, in order to silence the clamours of other theologians, who thought that nothing should be read unless stamped with their approval.

But he now comes to that horrible and atrocious crime for which Hutten declared he could never forgive him. It was that in a letter to the Bishop of Rochester he had charged Reuchlin with treachery. The passage referred to is worth quoting:—"The case, if report tell true, was this: when there was reason to apprehend that the Duke of Würtemberg would recover Stuttgard, Reuchlin advised some of the citizens to remove elsewhere, telling them he would accompany them. They acted on his advice, but after their precipitate flight, Reuchlin changed his plans and remained behind to look after his furniture. Then again, on the defeat of the Duke, by the intercession of some friends, the victorious army was prevented from plundering Reuchlin's house, but the citizens, whom he had misled, returned and gave the old man some trouble. He has now, however, got away all his property in safety, and is living quietly at Ingoldstadt." All this he had of course written with the most friendly intention, simply to let the Bishop of Rochester know through what perils Reuchlin, in whom he took the greatest possible interest, had passed, and that he was now safe. Hutten thought Erasmus must have invented this story, but he had received the information from Dr. John Salius, at Louvain.

Another crime laid to his charge was that, whereas in conversation with his friends he had severely condemned the Universities of Cologne and Louvain, he now speaks honourably of them in his letters. In answer to this charge, Erasmus protests that he never had a quarrel with any university; he had friends at both those named, and at both there were some who opposed the progress of learning. Nor was it true that he dissented from those universities when they condemned certain articles of Luther's; he had never either approved or disapproved of those articles. So, too, he was accused of having been formerly hostile to the order of preaching friars, whereas now he would persuade the world that he had never wished them ill.

He had never been so mad as to wish ill to any order, and if it was right to hate all Dominicans because there are many bad men among them, it would follow that we must hate all orders, as there is none in which there are not a great many bad men. And on the same principle we must hate all Christians, as among them the bad are more numerous than the good. Here, therefore, was no inconsistency, but his constant sentiment as expressed both in his acts and his writings. As to Aleander, he had never spoken of him to Hutten at all, for he was still at Rome when the latter was in Brabant; and therefore what Hutten says of him is mere rumour, which no sensible man would trust. He then gives a true account of his intercourse with Aleander, observing that he was his friend before Luther's name was heard of, and if he had ever become his enemy, it was owing to the evil tongues of his valiant German friends who had spread such false reports concerning him. Whether what Hutten writes about the reigning Pontiff is true, Erasmus doesn't know; but no such report has ever reached his ears. He had certainly never said that he would turn out a bad Pope. This and other stories were mere lies which Hutten had picked up from some of his bottle companions. As to Latomus, Atensis, and Egmund, he confessed that he had sometimes complained in letters to his friends that certain persons seemed to have entered into a determined conspiracy against culture, but he had always opposed such men in a spirit which proved that he was ready to be at peace with them, if it were possible, and accordingly he had always spared Latomus, hoping he would desist of his own accord; he had never flattered Egmund, and as for Atensis, he was a good man, and no enemy of learning, but of an irritable temper, and this had been taken advantage of by certain monks and theologians, who, in thrusting him forward to play so odious a part, had brought him to his grave. Hutten was afraid he might even make friends with Lee. And why not, when the contest between them was at an end? He had met him accidentally at Calais, and had shaken hands with him, and had never been so violent as his German friends, who declared they would tear Lee in pieces, but whom he had urged to use arguments rather than abuse.

These, then, were the crimes which had brought down Hutten's wrath upon his head, and there was certainly nothing in them which need have interfered with the most common-place friendship. He now comes to the last grand count in the indictment against him, which covers all the rest, and is the head and front of his offending. This consisted of the union of two utter and palpable falsehoods, namely, that he had formerly been a member of the Lutheran party, and that he was now exerting all his strength to resist the cause of the Gospel. We need not follow him minutely through all the steps of his defence, but a brief abstract, taking in the most prominent points, will be necessary to enable us to understand his position. He had, he said, constantly declared in his letters, in his works, in every possible way, that he did not choose to belong to any party, and three years ago he had distinctly stated that he was not and never would be a partisan of Luther's. By a partisan he meant one who had bound himself to accept whatever Luther had written or would write hereafter, while he had never condemned anything he thought true from dislike of Luther, and would never, for love of him, sanction anything which he thought to be untrue. At the same time it was quite false—as Hutten might have learned from his friend Eppendorf—that he had given up all his other studies to attack Luther. He was, in fact, wholly engaged with his Paraphrase on Luke, when this champion of the Gospel appeared in the field. But "he had promised that he would write three dialogues against Luther." This was not true; he had not said "against Luther," but "on the Lutheran question;" and yet, if he were to write against Luther, he would be justified in doing so, seeing that he was never in league with him, but, on the contrary, had always dissuaded him from his undertaking. And supposing he had at one time been a supporter of Luther's, did it follow that he must approve of everything he should ever write? What if Luther should write against the Articles of Faith? Must he then be forbidden to write against him? And why should Hutten be so angry with those who write against Luther? If Luther's doctrine is true, it will acquire new brilliancy by contradiction, like gold purified by fire; but if it is false, it is well that all should oppose it. Will it subvert the entire Gospel to dispute with Luther whether every Christian is a priest, or whether all the works of the saints are sins? Not that he has any desire to enter into conflict with Luther, but he must answer Hutten's calumnies. On the contrary, he had resorted to every expedient, he had done and suffered everything; he had left the Emperor's dominions, and had refused the emoluments offered to him, in order to escape being drawn into this "gladiatorial arena." If Hutten would prove him inconstant, let him show that he has changed his principles. He cannot do so, for he is still engaged in those pursuits to which he has ever been attached—advancing the cause of letters, and advocating a purer and more simple system of divinity, and this he will continue to do, whether Luther, —who, after all, is but a fallible man,—be friendly or the reverse. " Luther will pass away with the rest of us, but Christ abideth for ever."⁴⁴ But he is ungrateful, it seems, in not returning the esteem in which he himself is held by Luther. Little cause indeed has he for gratitude, seeing that Luther has brought so much odium on himself and his books, has ruptured nearly all his old friendships, and done so much mischief to the cause of learning! And yet he has not said a single word against Luther; he has never charged him with heresy, nor called him a heretic; he had certainly spoken of his movement as a disturbance, but that word might be applied to the spread of the Gospel itself. But Hutten, having falsely charged him with hostility to Luther, was obliged to invent a cause for it, and the reason he assigned was jealousy of Luther's fame, because his works were now more widely read than those of Erasmus. He did not envy Luther's fame, and he would rather be obscurer than any dog than enjoy such a reputation as his.

Neither had Erasmus uttered an uncertain sound regarding the Roman See. Her tyranny, rapacity, and other vices, which are an old theme of complaint among all good men, he had never approved.

⁴⁴ "Verum ipsa res indicat, me perpetuo hoc agere, quod olim institui. Proveho bonas literas, ac sinceriorem et simpliciorem theologiam pro viribus instauro, idque quoad vivam facturus sum, sive amico sive inimico Luthero, quem ego pro homine habeo, et puto falli posse et fallere. Lutherus cum cæteris transibit, Christus manet in æternum."—*Er. Op.* x. 1653, B.

He had nowhere entirely condemned indulgences, however much he abhorred the shameless way in which they were bought and sold. What his opinion was about ceremonies was clear from many passages in his works: but when had he ever execrated the canon law and the pontifical decrees? What Hutten might mean by "calling the Pope to order," he did not very well know; and here Erasmus gives his own view of the Papal supremacy, a very intelligible one no doubt, as it was eminently moderate, but for that very reason not likely to be acceptable to the majority of Papists. It is well worth quoting. "In the first place, he will admit, I suppose, that there is a Church at Rome. For a preponderance of bad people does not invalidate its character as a true Church; otherwise we should have no churches whatever. I presume too it is orthodox; for in whatever proportion the impious may be mingled with the faithful, nevertheless the Church remains in the hands of the latter. Now, I suppose, he will set a bishop over this Church. This bishop he will allow to be a Metropolitan; seeing there are so many Archbishops in countries where no Apostle has ever been, while Rome has both Peter and Paul, beyond dispute two of the greatest. Now among Metropolitans what absurdity is there, if the first place be assigned to the Roman Pontiff? For as to the extravagant power which they have usurped for some centuries past, no one has ever heard me defend it." It is true, as Hutten says, and would it were possible to deny it, that Rome has been for many years the source of great evils to the world, but we have now a Pope from whom the best things may be expected, and if Hutten has declared war not on men, but on error, let him hasten to Rome and help this excellent Pope in his efforts for reform. "But Hutten has declared war on the Roman Pope and all his adherents." Has he declared war even on a good Pope? But what will he do to those who adhere to the Pope even against their will? What will he do to the Emperor, who is the Pope's closest ally? If he calls it war to lay waste territory, to sack cities, to pillage and rob, he has hitherto only cursed the Pope, and has not hurt so much as a Roman fly, unless he thinks that none at whom he has hurled an abusive epithet will ever rise again.

Erasmus would be glad to know whom Hutten means when he speaks of "us" and "we;" for among those who support Luther and wish evil to the Pope, there are men of very opposite characters. For his own part he wished to have nothing to do with the violent men on either side, but would gladly be friends with the moderate of both sides. Before Luther was heard of he was on friendly terms with nearly all the learned. Some of these had since become partisans of Luther, but he had not on that account renounced their friendship, and why then must he declare war on all who had written against Luther? It was utterly untrue that he was preparing to take flight to the victorious party. All he desired was tranquillity to do good as he had opportunity. Again, he was found fault with for praising the reigning Pope. He had, in fact, done so very sparingly, and why must Hutten be enraged at this, seeing that he himself was so often and so highly praised in his writings, and even in such a serious work as the "Annotations on the New Testament." He was certainly very glad to have the two briefs from the Pope, because many had promised themselves that on his election Erasmus would be undone, and they were disappointed. He had indeed promised to support the dignity of the Roman See, but he did not thereby undertake to defend the tyranny, rapacity, and other crimes which Hutten laid to its charge.

It was strange, Erasmus thought, that Hutten should be angry with him for saying that if he were compelled to enter into controversy with Luther he would abstain from abuse and endeavour to refute him by solid arguments and scriptural proofs, seeing that he himself had complained that hitherto there had been nothing but abuse and clamour. What most offended him in Luther's writings was his abusive language and his arrogance, nor can Hutten deny that he wants moderation and gentleness. He cannot persuade himself that the meek spirit of Christ dwells in that bosom from which flows so much bitterness. What right had he to say, for example, in his book in reply to the King of England, "Come, Master Henry, and I will teach you?" The King's book was in good Latin and contained marks of erudition; yet some thought such insolence wonderfully funny. Hutten had challenged Erasmus to name any one who had endeavoured by force or fraud to entangle him in Luther's cause; let him rather answer what was the object of those who had published his first letter to Luther, or of those who had collected from his books a number of the most damaging passages, translated them into German, and published them, or of those who had published his secret letter to the Cardinal of Maintz, and had not delivered it to the cardinal.

Erasmus had somewhere written that the truth should not be told on all occasions, and that the manner of telling it made a great difference, and this sentiment had excited the fury of Hutten, who declared that it ought to be thrust down his own throat. He defended it, however, by the example of Christ, who, when he first sent forth the apostles to preach the Gospel, forbade them to make it known that he was the Christ; of Peter, who, in his first discourses, called Christ a man but said nothing of his Godhead; and of Paul, who calls the apostles stewards of the mysteries of God, for a steward uses his discretion in what he will produce and what he will withhold. Why were not all the mysteries of the Christian religion made known at once to catechumens? Because they were not yet able to understand them. And yet he was not speaking of the Articles of the Faith, but of the paradoxes of Luther and of his scurrilous attacks upon the Pope. If he had to plead the cause of an innocent man before a powerful tyrant, should he tell the whole truth, and so betray the innocent cause, or should he be silent on many points? Hutten, no doubt, if he were asking a wicked Pope for an ecclesiastical office on behalf of some good man, would write thus: 'Wicked Antichrist, exterminator of the Gospel, oppressor of public liberty, flatterer of princes, thou basely givest to the base, and dost still more basely sell the offices of the Church: give this office to this good man, that all thy appointments may not be bad.' Such is the way in which these men plead the cause of the Gospel.

Having thus dwelt at great length on his relations to Luther and the Pope, he now proceeds to defend his character, which Hutten had declared he would constantly expose, however much wiser it would be in him if he studied to hide his own faults rather than expose other people's. How impudent in Hutten to attempt to censure the character of Erasmus, seeing he had never enjoyed his intimacy, and only once, or at most twice, been his guest. "He approves of my studies, but disapproves of my character, and would dissuade the Germans from copying it. Come, then, be this service divided between us. Let the German youth follow my example in their studies, but let them take Hutten as a pattern for their morals." He had never boasted of his morals; on the contrary, quarrelled with them every day, even now that he is an old man; still, he was glad to think he was free from those faults which Hutten so liberally ascribed to him. In the first place, he made him such a coward that he would almost be afraid of his own shadow. But Hutten should remember that there is a great difference between courage and rashness. Hutten is no doubt a very formidable personage, but when he was at Brussels, he had not the courage to remain there, but fled from Hochstraten, who was at that time neither Prior nor Inquisitor, nor provided with any bulls or edicts. Yet he must be called a coward if he refuses to provoke by foolish insults so many enemies who wish ill both to himself and Luther, and who are now fully armed with edicts and bulls, and have besides an army at their back. But Hutten thinks that even life ought to be risked for the sake of the truth. Certainly; but he had no mind to die for Luther and his paradoxes. "I am ready," says Erasmus, and the words may fairly be balanced against a previous declaration of which it will naturally remind us, "I am ready to be a martyr for Christ, if he will give me strength to be so, but I have no wish to be a martyr for Luther." [46]

[46] "Optarem esse Christi martyr, si vires ipse suppeditet; Lutheri martyr esse nolim."—*Er. Op.* x. 1663, B. See above, p. 64.

Hutten had also charged Erasmus with cunning; had he himself, when he left Basle, gone to Mülhausen by the high-road, or had he departed from Mülhausen by daylight? He had everywhere made him a most shameless liar, though the fact was that from his boyhood he had hated liars by a kind of instinct, even before he knew what a lie was; and now he trembled all over at the mere sight of men of that character. He had accused him of incivility, though he spent more than half his time in writing letters to his friends, and of treachery, a crime which his worst enemy had never yet laid to his charge. This last accusation Erasmus retorts upon Hutten by recounting fully the particulars of the publication of his letter to the Archbishop of Maintz—an act which had cost him the friendship of the Elector, but for which he had scarcely uttered a word of reproach, uncivil man that he was! Again he was accused of an insatiable thirst for glory. If that were true, he would long ago have attached himself to the court of Rome or that of the Emperor; he would have accepted the honours and emoluments offered to him. As it was, he had obstinately refused them all and preferred the inglorious tranquillity of his studies. And how could Hutten call him jealous of the fame of others. His writings were full of the laudations both of his predecessors and his contemporaries. Had he envied the rising fame of Hutten? So far from it that he alone had bestowed more praises on him than all his friends, while "he, who calls himself my friend, has heaped on me more accusations than all my enemies heretofore, or than he has ever charged upon his enemy; and yet in his letters to me he calls this a very mild expostulation, compared with the atrocity of my conduct." But Erasmus, it seems, was a flatterer. This charge did not seem very judicious in so strenuous an advocate of Germany, for as the works of Erasmus were filled with the praises of Germans, if he was a flatterer, his praise must be comparatively worthless. "He spoke too smoothly in addressing the great." It was true that he did so, and by that means kings and queens, who before were accustomed to read nothing better than fabulous histories, had the Gospels in their hands and were enabled to become acquainted with the mysteries of the Christian religion. Let Hutten say what good his cursing had ever done. If he had sought favours from the great, his smooth speaking might be justly suspected. But he had never sought any favours, or if he had, they were not for himself, but for the public good. He had, indeed, according to the established custom among the learned, dedicated his works partly to private friends, partly to men in authority. From his friends he would not even receive thanks, so far was he from extorting any acknowledgment. From the great he had never begged for anything, nor would it be believed how few had given him a present on this account. "And yet," he adds with caustic severity, "if any one were to avail himself of the generosity of the great, in return for honest industry, seeing that human life has many wants, he would act more excusably than those who borrow from their friends what they never return, who buy what they never pay, and extort money by threats from those who have done them no wrong." Erasmus is at a loss to understand how Hutten should have come to publish such an atrocious attack upon him, contrary to the advice of his own friends, and after all his charges had been answered, and is inclined to accept as probable the supposition entertained by some, that he was bribed by Hochstraten and Egmund, or some of their associates. Certainly no book could have been published more damaging to the cause of Luther, or more fitted to infuse joy into the hearts of the devoted enemies of learning. "Methinks I can already see them leaping and dancing, and congratulating one another, as they accompany Hutten's triumph: they clap their hands and cry, 'Bravo, Sir Knight! Strike home! Finish that fellow Erasmus, who by the importation of new languages and letters has undermined our power.'" Happy Hutten, when congratulatory letters, presents, and immense rewards shall come pouring in upon him from these new friends! If he was not bribed, for what object did he write? Was it for amusement? Was it to improve his style? Or did he wish, as some one had said, to leave behind to posterity a perfect specimen of eloquence, like the Philippics of Cicero? In any case, he ought to have chosen another subject. But there were some who affirmed that Hutten, being no longer able to mount his horse, was compelled to sit at home and write for money, and that his profits were derived from two sources, inasmuch as he was paid both by his employers and by those whom he attacked, who bribed him not to publish what he had written: and this suspicion, Erasmus thought, must have something in it. If so, and if his fortunes had reached so low a point, he pitied Hutten, although an enemy.

But it is time to have done with Hutten. Erasmus thinks he has now used the sponge sufficiently, and he accordingly concludes with a general exhortation to temperance, moderation, peace, and mutual forbearance. Let there be an end of wrangling about points of doctrine. It is sad that the world should be turned upside down for the sake of paradoxes, some of which are absolutely unintelligible, others of such a nature that either side may be taken indifferently, and others again not calculated for the improvement of life. Let each side then yield something to the other. Such is the advice of one who is devoted to neither party, but wishes well to both. As for himself, he was preparing for that day on which he must stand before the judgment seat of Christ; and therefore he turned from those contentions in which it is scarcely possible to engage without losing somewhat of the tranquillity of the Christian spirit, to the pursuits which compose the passions of the heart and tranquillize the conscience. "I feel," he concludes, "that I am deriving great advantage from my Paraphrases in this respect. Wherefore I am the more grieved that in this quarrel, in reading Hutten's calumnies and wiping away his aspersions, I have lost six entire days. Farewell, whosoever thou art, courteous reader."

The solemn reference to his own end, with which Erasmus concluded his defence, would have been more appropriate on the lips of his antagonist; for by the time the "Sponge" was through the press Hutten was already out of reach of the chastisement intended for him. He had retired, as we have seen, to the little island of Ufnau, in the Lake of Zürich, to seek aid from a priest who combined with his sacerdotal office considerable skill in the medical art. The remedies of the worthy pastor, however, proved of no avail, and the disease from which Hutten had so long suffered, and which at one time he believed he had succeeded in curing by the use of guaiacum, breakin...

out with new violence, he died somewhat suddenly on the 29th of August. Erasmus was afterwards very unjustly blamed for having published the "Sponge" after Hutten's decease, as though he had wished to fight with the dead; for, as he himself explains in an address to the reader, which in the fourth edition was substituted for the original dedication to Zwingle, he had written his answer in July, and the news of Hutten's death had only just reached him, when, on the 3rd of September, his book was out of Froben's hands. He acted, however, less magnanimously than his admirers might wish, in attempting to procure the punishment of the printer Schott, who had published the "Expostulation," by means of a letter addressed to the magistrates of Strasburg,[46] and in painting the character of his antagonist in darker colours than he had ventured to use while Hutten was alive. It is true that he claims credit for *not* having mentioned in the "Sponge" any of Hutten's vices, and implies that the omission was the result of forbearance and not fear. "I will appeal," he says, "to the conscience of those who knew Hutten intimately, though it is well known, even by those who had no familiarity with him, that his whole life was that of a soldier, to use no harsher phrase; and yet in the whole of my 'Sponge' I nowhere bring against him his luxury, of which not even the miserable disease from which he suffered could cure him, nor his fondness for gambling and women, his profuse extravagance, his debts, and his duns." But Erasmus must have known that the letter in which those words were written would be as widely read as the "Sponge" itself, and the charge, which, however, it is to be

[46] *Ep.* dclxxiv.

feared was too true, was not the less cruel for being indirect.

The impression made by Hutten's "Expostulation" was on the whole not a favourable one. It expressed, no doubt, the general sense of the Reformers, but in too violent a manner, and they did not hesitate to condemn its publication. They foresaw that it would do their cause more harm than good, that it would delight the enemies of culture, and stir up Erasmus to bitter hostility against their party. They could not but feel too that something was due to the years and fame of one who had rendered such good service to letters in his day, and who was so much older than any of them. This sentiment was expressed by the gentle Melancthon. Luther wrote that he could wish Hutten had not expostulated, but he was still less satisfied with the manner in which Erasmus had attempted to wipe away his aspersions. "If this," he asked, "is to use a sponge, what would be reviling and abuse?"[47]. That Hutten would have felt himself bound in honour, had he survived, to continue the contest, is probable, but now that the master's hand was cold his defence was taken up by others, who were but poorly qualified for the task. Eppendorf wrote some letters which have not been preserved. Hermann von Busch, indeed, who meditated a reply, might have produced something worthy of the occasion, but he was prevented from proceeding by Melancthon.[48] The only reply which we have to the "Sponge" is one by Otto von Brunfels, formerly a Carthusian friar, but now a warm supporter of Hutten's, and an earnest student of languages and

---

[47] STRAUSS *ubi supra*, p. 298, notes.

[48] *Epistola Secretissima ad M. Conradum Goclenium.—Er. Op.* i.

of medicine. It is in the form of a dialogue, one side
consisting of sentences taken from the "Sponge," to
which Otto replies in his own name, and contains some
spirited passages. There is also a "Judgment" by one
Erasmus Alberus, court-preacher at Brandenburg, who
sums up his opinion in the declaration that there is more
sound evangelical doctrine in Luther's little finger than
in the entire brain of Erasmus. Both these compositions Erasmus treated with supreme contempt, declaring that he had made up his mind for the future to
take no notice of such silly attacks.[49]

And thus ended the controversy with Hutten—a
memorable example of the misconstructions from which
the moderate man is sure to suffer at the hands of the
extreme partisans by whose violence he refuses to be
carried away. It is impossible, indeed, not to sympathize with the fervour and earnestness of Hutten, nor
need we attach much importance to the unworthy
insinuation of Erasmus that he had been bribed by the
Papists, nor even perhaps to the suspicion, more deliberately expressed, that his principal object in writing the
"Expostulation" was to extort money for its suppression. If there can be no doubt that such an attempt
was actually made—and Erasmus affirms it with the
most circumstantial details,[50] Eppendorf alone may
have been responsible. Or even admitting that Hutten

---

[49] "Post hunc (Huttenum) exortus est alius illo tum indoctior, tum rabiosior, cui nondum respondimus."—*Er. Op.* 792, E. "Othonis libellus rursus exiit, per auctorem recognitus, et, ni fallor, auctus: nondum vidi. Exiit et epistola Alberti (? Alberi) omnium stultissima. . . . Posthac non est animus talibus næniis respondere.—*Ib.* 803, C. D.

[50] *Er. Op.* iii. 1735, C, D, E, F. Further on, in the same letter, Erasmus says: "Jam si quis legat Huttenicas ad me epistolas, quas per Epphendorpium misit, nihil spirant nisi praedam;" but Strauss's

may have had the secondary object of raising money, which would not be wonderful, considering his distress, at any rate he honestly believed Erasmus to be a half-hearted coward, and a traitor to the cause of Reform, who deserved the very worst he had said of him; and in fact he has only expressed that view of his character and conduct which has been held by ultra-Protestants ever since. On the other hand, it may be contended that that view is an unjust one. Erasmus was not conscious to himself of any inconsistency. He was still pursuing the same objects which he had always pursued, by the same means which he had always employed. He had not abandoned one of his principles, nor changed in the smallest degree his tactics in the great warfare against superstition. In the "Sponge" itself he speaks as freely of the Papacy as in almost any of his works. But he had never been a Lutheran, and would not be frightened by Hutten's "noble rage" into declaring himself a Lutheran. His only fault, if it was one, was that he had not moved with the times: that he believed, however vainly, in the possibility of reforming the old system, and still strove to combine liberty of conscience with some kind of outward recognition of the Pope as the visible Head of Christ's Church.

question, why he has not produced those letters, is much to the point. It is noteworthy that Erasmus makes it a special charge against Hutten that, having failed to extort money from himself and his friends, he tried to get something out of the printer, who, as in other cases, was also the publisher. This, in those days, was thought at least questionable, while the legitimate reward of an author came from some wealthy patron, whom he had flattered extravagantly in a dedication. It is a change for the better, as Strauss remarks, that in our days this way of regarding the matter is reversed. —STRAUSS *ubi supra*, p. 296.

CHAPTER XV.

"THE FAMILIAR COLLOQUIES"— ORIGIN OF THE WORK — THE MAID THAT WOULD NOT MARRY—THE PENITENT MAIDEN—THE SOLDIER AND THE FRIAR — THE SHIPWRECK —GERMAN INNS—THE INQUISITION OF FAITH—THE OLD MEN'S COLLOQUY — THE POOR RICH MEN — THE ABBOT AND THE LADY — ICHTHYOPHAGIA — CHARON— THE SERAPHIC OBSEQUIES—SUCCESS OF THE WORK —THE ST. HILARY — ACCESSION OF CLEMENT VII. — ERASMUS AND THE REFORMERS— FAREL— THE DOCTRINE OF FREE-WILL —CORRESPONDENCE OF ERASMUS AND LUTHER—THE "DE LIBERO ARBITRIO"—RECEPTION OF THE WORK—LETTER TO FISHER—TO MELANCTHON—LUTHER'S REPLY—THE "HYPERASPISTES."

ERASMUS had assuredly not thrown himself into the arms of the extreme Papists, as any one judging him by Hutten's denunciation might easily be led to suppose. He was all this time—there can be no doubt of it—the same Erasmus he had ever been; as wise, as witty, as sarcastic, as full of irony, as keen to observe, and as powerful to expose the weaknesses and follies and the superstitions of mankind, especially of monastic mankind, as he had been in his best days, if indeed those were not his best days which he was now living at Basle by the banks of the green Rhine. At the very time that he was corresponding with Pope Adrian, at the very time that he was smarting under Hutten's keenest strokes, he was engaged in composing by far his most popular, his best known, and after the *Moria* his most characteristic work—the "Familiar Colloquies"—

a book once literally known to every school-boy, inasmuch as it was universally used as a Latin lesson-book, and which will always continue to be read by all lovers of excellent humour, as well as by every one who would understand the spirit and recall the manners of the early part of the sixteenth century. This work, to which we may now appropriately turn our attention, was in progress from the year 1519, when the first edition which had the sanction of the author appeared,—a mere pamphlet too small to be published separately—till 1530, or later, when by successive additions it had swelled to a considerable bulk. The origin of the work was as follows. About the end of the year 1518 there appeared at Basle a little book containing forms for familiar conversation, purporting to be by Erasmus,[1] and with a Preface by Beatus Rhenanus, in which he stated that the book was written at Paris by Erasmus some twenty years previously, by way of amusement for one of his pupils. This was followed, about a month later, by another edition, published at Louvain, in which Erasmus disclaims the authorship of the former one, but admits that he had dictated some trifling matters, more than twenty years ago, to the pupil in question, who, from his notes, and from other works which were then in progress, had put together the present volume, adding, however, some things of his own, so as to betray the ass in the lion's skin. And with these trifles he had imposed on some thick-skulled persons in order to replenish his purse. No further edition seems to have been published till 1522, when the work was reprinted by Froben with considerable additions, and with a dedication to Froben's son,

[1] *Familiarium Colloquiorum Formulæ et alia quædam, per Des. Erasmum Roterodamum.* Beatus's Preface bears date x. Cal. Dec. 1518.

Erasmius.² It was clearly his interest in this boy that suggested the pleasing dialogue entitled "Youthful Piety," which has already been referred to in an early part of this work.³ The death of John Reuchlin, on the 22nd of June in the same year, gave occasion to the dialogue called "Reuchlin's Apotheosis," in which one of the interlocutors describes a vision, showing how that accomplished scholar and high-minded man was welcomed to the other world by St. Jerome, translated with him in a pillar of fire, and without leave asked of the Pope, enrolled in the number of the saints: while the "Religious Banquet," leading in its sequel to the discussion of various texts of Scripture, and the topics they suggest, in its earlier part evidently enlarges and embellishes the hints furnished by the elegant mansion of Botzemus at Constance, with its curiosities, which would have required ten days to inspect. These are all of the more elaborate pieces which this edition contains; but in the smaller dialogues there are some sharp passages touching on the superstitions of the times.

It is not my intention to trace further the various editions of the "Colloquies," but rather to give some idea of the complete work. As it now lies before us,⁴ it consists of a large number of conversations on a great variety of subjects, whose easy flow and natural, graceful manner are not the least of their charms, full of delicate humour, keen irony, biting satire, elegant criticism, and

---

² *Familiarium Colloquiorum Formulæ, per D. Erasmum Roterodamum, multis adjectis non tantum ad linguam puerilem expoliendam utiles, verum etiam ad vitam instituendam.* —*Basil. Frob.* 1522.

³ Vol. i. p. 11.

⁴ *Er. Op.* i. 629 *sqq.* There is a neat edition of the "Colloquies" and the *Encomium Moriæ* by Tauchnitz (1829), to which, as easily accessible, my references will be made.

lively description, wherein now a text of Scripture, now a passage from the classics, is made the subject of discussion, now some folly turned into ridicule, now some superstition exposed, while occasional autobiographical touches or allusions to contemporaneous persons or events lend a great additional interest. The humanism of Erasmus comes out in his enthusiasm for Cicero— a far more rational admiration than that of the slavish imitators of the style of the great Roman philosopher and orator;—and there is little of either evangelical or popish narrowness in his declaration that "probably the spirit of Christ is more widely diffused than, in our mode of interpreting Scripture, we are accustomed to suppose."[5] It is in the "Religious Banquet" that this sentence occurs, and he adds the confession that "he can never read Cicero on Old Age or Friendship, or the 'Offices,' or the 'Tusculan Questions,' without pausing now and then to kiss the page, and pay homage to that holy soul whom God's Spirit has so manifestly possessed."[6] A little further on in the same conversation, referring to a beautiful saying of Socrates,—"Whether God will approve of our deeds I know not; but at least it has been our constant effort to please Him"—one of the speakers says, "When I read such passages as these, I can scarcely keep myself from saying, '*Sancte Socrates, ora pro nobis.*'"

In the *Virgo* Μισόγαμος, or "Maiden that would not

[5] "Et fortasse latius se fundit spiritus Christi quam nos interpretamur."—*Coll. Fam.* (Tauchnitz, 1829) vol. i. p. 122.

[6] "Fateor affectum meum apud amicos: non possum legere librum Ciceronis de Senectute, de Amicitia, de Officiis, de Tusculanis Quæstionibus, quin aliquoties exosculer codicem, ac venerer sanctum illud pectus afflatum cœlesti numine."—*Ib.* p. 123.

Marry," Eubulus woos a young lady who has no other objection to his suit but that she has resolved on entering a convent. Being asked how she had come to form such a resolution, she explains that when very young she had been taken to visit a nunnery, and that, having been there quite captivated by the splendour of the chapel, the beauty of the gardens, and the sweet faces and coaxing manners of the nuns, she had ever since longed for a convent life. Eubulus tries to induce her to change her mind, and advises her to marry, but, being assured that she would rather die than give up her virginity, admits that virginity is an excellent thing if it be pure, but contends that she may keep it more safely at home with her parents than "among those coarse, over-fed monks." "For," he adds, with a freedom which the manners of the time may have permitted, "you must not fancy they are eunuchs. They are called 'fathers,' and they often do all they can to deserve the name." Catherine complains that at home she is often compelled to hear things ill-suited to a maiden's ears; "but perhaps," rejoins Eubulus, "when you look a little closer, everything may not look so bright and beautiful in the convent as you think. Believe me, all are not virgins who wear the veil. CATH. Don't say that. EU. Why shall I not say what is true? unless there are many in our days who share what we used to think was the peculiar privilege of the Virgin Mary, of being a virgin after child-birth." Eubulus then goes on to show that whoever entered a convent, thereby became a slave, as was clear from the change of dress and name, and that there were even greater advantages for following a religious life outside a convent than in one, the only things peculiar to the monastic life being a veil, a linen dress, and certain ceremonies which, taken by themselves, have nothing to do with religion; adding that every maiden who has been baptized is already thereby married to Christ, whom, therefore, it is superfluous to marry a second time by taking vows. The severity of these strictures is not much relieved by the remark that there was no intention absolutely to condemn the conventual life, but merely to warn young maidens not to commit themselves thoughtlessly or hastily to irrevocable vows. Catherine admits the force of her lover's arguments, but refuses, nevertheless, to be convinced by them.

The "Repentant Virgin," which follows, shows how Catherine, when too late, acknowledged the wisdom of the advice she had rejected. The resistance of her parents had been overcome with difficulty—her mother's by her own entreaties, her father's by the importunities of the monks, who threatened him with a bad end if he refused His bride to Christ. Meantime every precaution was taken to prevent Catherine's mind from wavering; she was shut up at home, none of her companions allowed to come near her, and at last she was visited by a horrible spectre, with a hooked nose, long horns, sharp claws, and an immense tail—such, she was told, was often the experience of those who consecrated themselves to Christ, but if the tempter was overcome at the first encounter all would then be well. She had not been twelve days in the nunnery before she entreated her parents to take her home. At first they refused, but, on being assured it was the only way to save her life, consented, the irrevocable vow not yet having been taken. What had changed her purpose she cannot be persuaded to reveal, but the warnings of her lover in the former conversation make it too probable that in that short time she has been robbed of the treasure she had so anxiously sought to preserve.

In the "Soldier and the Carthusian" the author's hatred of war gets the better of his hatred of monasticism, and the friar not only successfully defends himself against the jeers of the warrior, but draws from the latter the confession that his life has been one of reckless extravagance, debauchery, and wickedness. In reply to the soldier's jest, that he wondered the friar, from being obliged to live so constantly on fish, had not turned into a fish himself, the Carthusian points to his own portly person, and asks which of them can boast the better habit of body—"*you*, who live on partridges, pheasants, and capons, or I who live on fish?" "At any rate," retorts the soldier, "you lead a Jewish life. CAR. Nay; we at least follow, if we do not attain, the Christian life. SOL. You put your trust in dress, meat, prayers, and other ceremonies, while you neglect the culture of evangelical piety. CAR. What others do, it is not mine to judge. I by no means trust in these things, and set very little value on them, but I do put my trust in purity of mind and in Christ. SOL. Why, then, do you observe them? CAR. That I may be at peace with my brethren, and give no offence to any one." He then calls on the soldier to give an account of himself, and asks him which he thinks the more unhappy fate—to cut the throat of a Christian who has never done you any wrong, or to doom yourself, body and soul, to everlasting destruction? "SOL. It is lawful to kill an enemy. CAR. Perhaps it is, if he invades your country. In that case it may be deemed pious to fight for wife and children, for parents and friends, for the altar and the hearth, and for the public peace. But what is there of all this in your mercenary service? If you had perished in the late war, I wouldn't have given a bad nut to save your life." The soldier's dress proves that he is not carrying home any great sum of money, and he admits that he is not only reduced to his last farthing, but is also deep in debt, having squandered in drinking, gambling, and debauchery, whatever he had gained by plunder, rapine, and sacrilege. He is, moreover, covered with disease, and has come to ask the monk, who is his brother, for something to help him on his way.

It would have been more generous in Erasmus if he had not taken his revenge on Hutten in these Colloquies; but the temptation was irresistible, and there can be no doubt that the deceased Reformer stood for the portrait of the soldier. He returns to the subject in a subsequent Dialogue, called the "Unequal Marriage," in which he paints Hutten in the most odious colours, describing him as an abandoned *roué*, a drunkard, a liar, a gambler, a robber, and a spendthrift. The subject is the union of a young and beautiful lady with a wretch, whose bad breath, sunken eyes, and hands covered with scabs, showed that he was the victim of a disease which, though called by many names, had as yet none of its own; and that there may be no mistake about the person referred to, it is added that his sole recommendation is the empty name of knight.

The "Shipwreck" gives an amusing account of some of the superstitions of sailors, and especially ridicules the prayers and vows which persons in danger at sea were accustomed to address to the Virgin and the saints. On such occasions, the Virgin was addressed as Star of the Sea, Queen of Heaven, Mistress of the World, Harbour of Safety, and "by many other titles which the Scriptures nowhere ascribe to her." "What," asks one of the speakers, "has she to do with the sea? She never made a voyage that I am aware of." To which the other answers, "In former days Venus had the charge of sailors, because she was believed to be born of the sea; but after she resigned office, the Virgin-Mother succeeded the mother who was no virgin." The various vows evoked by the storm are thus amusingly recounted: "There was an Englishman who promised mountains of gold to the Virgin of Walsingham if he should ever reach land alive. Some vowed many offerings to the wood of the true cross which was in such a place; others again to that which was in such another place. The same thing was done for the Virgin Mary, who reigns in many places: and they think the vow not binding unless you name the particular place. ANTONIUS. Ridiculous! as if the saints did not live in heaven. ADOLPHUS. Some vowed they would become Carthusians, and there was one who promised to go to the shrine of St. James of Compostella, with his head and feet bare, wearing nothing but an iron coat of mail, and begging his bread all the way. AN. Did no one think of St. Christopher? AD. I heard one—and I could not help laughing at him—in a loud voice, lest he should not be heard, promising the St. Christopher who stands on the top of the steeple in Paris, and is more like a mountain than a statue, a wax-candle as big as himself. As he kept repeating this at the top of his voice, an acquaintance of his, who happened to be standing next him, touched him with his elbow, saying, 'Have a care what you are promising; for though you should sell all you have, you will never be able to pay your vow.' To which the other, in an under-tone, I suppose, lest Christopher should hear, replied, 'Silence, you fool! Do you think I am in earnest? If I once get to shore, I don't mean to give him a tallow dip.'" Adolphus, on being asked why he made no vow himself, replied, "Because I never make bargains with the saints. For what else is it but a formal contract to say, 'I will give, if you will do;' or, 'I will do if you will. I will give a wax-candle if I reach shore; I will go to Rome if you will save?' AN. But did you ask aid from any saint? AD. Not even that. AN. But why? AD. Because heaven is very wide, and if I were to commend my safety to any saint, for example to St. Peter, who would probably be the first to hear, as he stands next the door, before he could enter God's presence and lay my case before Him, meanwhile I am undone. AN. What, then, did you do? AD. I went straight to the Father himself, saying, 'Our Father who art in heaven.' None of the saints hears more quickly than He does, or more willingly grants our requests."

In the next Colloquy Erasmus draws a lively picture of the dirt, discomfort, and confusion of the German inns, which he contrasts unfavourably with those of France. At the latter you are more comfortable than you could be at home; you are waited on by the hostess or her daughter, who cheer up the tired traveller with jest and conversation; the entertainment is elegant and wonderfully cheap; all your wants are anticipated by merry damsels, who gather round, asking how they can serve you; and on your departure an affectionate leave is taken, as if you were quite a near relative. At the German inns it is very different. On your arrival no one greets you, lest they should seem to be looking for a customer. But after you have called aloud for a long time, at last some one pops his head out of the window, like a tortoise peeping out of his shell, nods assent to your inquiries if there is room, and motions you to the stable, where you can attend to your horse in your own fashion. That done, you go into the common room, where you may, if you please, take off your boots, change your shirt, and dry your damp clothes at the stove; if you want to wash your hands you will find water for the purpose, but it is generally so dirty that, after using it, you must look for more water to wash off its effects. In this common room, which is heated past endurance, there are often crowded together some eighty or ninety persons, of all classes and both sexes, and should any foreigner make his appearance among them distinguished by his better dress or superior manners, they all immediately begin to stare at him as if he were a strange animal newly brought from Africa. Late in the evening, when no more arrivals are expected, an old servant, with a white beard, a shaven head, a stern look, and a dirty dress, comes in and counts the guests. He then lays the cloth, and when all are seated, sets before each a wooden trencher, a spoon of the same material, a glass, and, after some interval, a piece of bread. An hour now sometimes elapses before dinner is served. At length the wine is set down, but it is so sour as to be scarcely drinkable, and if you ask for any better kind, even though you pay for it, you are told that no one ever complained of that wine before, and that, if you don't like it, you can go to another inn. The first course consists of soup, which on fast days is made of vegetables, with bread, and this is followed by more soup and pieces of meat or salt fish boiled to shreds. Then comes some kind of vegetable, and then something more substantial, till at last, when the edge of appetite has been thoroughly blunted, they serve roast meat or boiled fish, which is really fit for eating; but this in small quantities, and they take it away almost immediately. All this time no one must leave the table, however exhausted he may be, and at the end of supper the host brings in a plate scored with chalk, on which each one deposits his reckoning. The guests are then shown to their bedrooms, strictly so called, for they contain no furniture but a bed, and the cleanliness there is on a par with that of the rest of the establishment.

The "Inquisition of Faith" is a conversation between a man who has been excommunicated for heresy and a friend who, after a strict examination, can find no fault with his creed. Nevertheless, it seems to border on Arianism in two passages. One is, "The Son also is God, but of God the Father. But the Father alone is of none, and *obtains the principal place among the divine persons.*" In the other, in answer to the question, "Why is the Father alone called God in the Apostles' Creed?" we read as follows:—" Because he is simply the author of all things that are, and the fountain of all Deity. For nothing can be named whose origin does not flow from the Father; and to Him even the Son and the Holy Spirit owe their Divinity. Accordingly the chief authorship, that is, the principle of origination, resides in the Father alone, because He alone is of none. Nevertheless the Creed may be thus understood, that the name of God is not personal but generical, and is afterwards distributed by the terms Father, Son, and

Holy Spirit, in one God; which word, expressive of nature, comprehends the Father, the Son, and the Holy Spirit, that is, three persons."[7]

"*Colloquium Senile*," or the "Old Men's Colloquy," introduces us to four old men, who had lived together forty-two years before at the University of Paris, and who, as they are going to Antwerp in the same carriage, beguile the way by relating the history of their lives. One of them had lived happily for eight years with his wife, by whom he had two sons and two daughters, and since her death, which was the greatest grief he had ever experienced, had remained single. The second had married no less than eight times, and declares that if his wife were to die to-day he would marry the ninth, his only regret being that he cannot have two or three wives at once. The third, who is called Pampirus, or "Jack-of-all-trades," to please his father and gratify his own love of travelling, had become a merchant, but having squandered all his profit in gambling, was reduced to despair, and saw no alternative before him but either to hang himself or enter a monastery. Having decided on what he calls "the milder sort of death," he became a canon in Ireland, but deeming their rule too gentle for one who deserved hanging, he removed, after two months, to Scotland, where he remained about six months as a Carthusian. Finding, however, in that country many whose brains were not very sound, and knowing that he had himself very little brains to lose, he went to France and entered the

---

[7] *Coll. Fam.* i. p. 233 and 238. Where all seems contradictory, it is difficult to say whether these sentences may be reconcileable with the statement of the Athanasian Creed, that "in this Trinity none is afore or after other: none is greater or less than another."

Benedictine order. Among the Benedictines he found more ceremony than true piety, and so left them after eleven months. He then tried the rule of St. Bernard for ten months, and then that of St. Bridget for two days. In that order there was no novitiate, and he had never yet been so insane as to put his neck into a halter which he could not shake off. "At length," he continues, "as I was walking about, I met some persons who wore a cross upon their breast. With this sign I was at first quite taken, but the various forms in which it was worn made my choice difficult. Some wore it white, some red, some green, some particoloured; some simple, some double, others fourfold; in short, it assumed every variety of figure. To make sure of being right I tried them almost all, but I soon found it a very different thing to carry about the cross on one's cloak or tunic, and to wear it in one's heart." At last, in order to attain true sanctity, he determined to visit Jerusalem, but returned, as may be supposed, worse than he went. He then took service, as a soldier, under Julius II., whom he found waging war against the French; but not liking the military life, he began to consider whether he should not abandon the pursuit of religion and return to his old trade of a merchant. Meantime it occurred to him that both might be united. "What!" exclaims one of his companions, "to be a merchant and a monk at the same time!" "Why not? The mendicant orders are very religious, and yet their occupation is as like trading as it could possibly be. They fly through every country and across every sea, they see and hear everything, and there is not a house, plebeian, noble, or royal, into which they will not make their way. EUSEBIUS. Yes, but they do not buy and sell. PAM. Ay do they; often more successfully than we. EU. Which kind did you choose? PAM. I tried them all. EU. And liked none? PAM. On the contrary, I should have liked them all, if I had been allowed to begin my trading at once. But I considered that I must sweat for ever so long as a chorister before any trading would be entrusted to me. So I began to think of hunting for an abbacy; but in the first place the Delian goddess does not bestow her favours on everybody, and one must often follow the chase for a long time. So having spent eight years in this way, hearing news of my father's death, I returned home, and by my mother's advice married, and resumed my former employment as a merchant." Lastly, Eusebius, the fourth speaker, tells how he had become a priest, and lived a quiet life, content with a single benefice. To a remark on the licentiousness and ignorance of the priesthood generally, he replies, "I do not think of what others do, but of what I ought to do; and if I cannot make others better, I choose for my associates the best men of the class." By this time they have arrived at their destination, and repair to the same inn to continue their gossip; and the piece concludes with a lively passage of repartee between two rival postilions.

"The Poor Rich Men."—Two Franciscan friars are repelled from the door of a priest, who tells them he would not trust St. Peter himself if he came in that dress. They then apply at the inn, but at first with no better success, the innkeeper having a special objection to guests furnished with such excellent teeth, but who bring no money with them to pay for what they eat. They say they will pay him in work, on which he offers to show them the kind of work he expects from them, and points to some pictures on his wall—one, of a fox preaching while a goose's head is visible behind protruding from his cowl; another, of a wolf pronouncing absolution, but with part of a sheep peeping out from under his frock; and, lastly, one of an ape in a Franciscan dress, sitting beside a sick man in whose purse one hand is busy, while with the other he presents the cross. Presently, however, mine host's wife appears and turns the tables on her husband, begging him to receive these good men as an atonement for his own sins. "You will be glad enough," she says, "to have them with you when you are dying; so do not turn them out now." Somewhat surlily the innkeeper gives way. The table is spread; whereupon it turns out that the monks are not so poor as they had seemed, but furnish the best part of the entertainment, having brought with them some excellent meat and wine which had been pressed on them at Basle, whence they had last come. In the course of the conversation which follows, the character of the pastor, on whom the monks had previously called, is discussed, from which it appears that he is an excellent customer at the public-house, but that if he possessed any knowledge of Scripture he kept it all to himself. A long discussion ensues on the value of the monastic dress, in which it is shown that the founders of the different orders had simply adopted the plainest and cheapest dress of the time and country in which they lived. The innkeeper is at length quite won over by the conversation of the good monks, and promises them a welcome whenever they shall repeat their visit.

The "Abbot and the Learned Lady" contains some sharp satire on the Church. A luxurious Abbot, visiting a lady and finding her surrounded with Greek and

Latin books, gravely reproves her, and adds that he would be sorry to see his monks given to books. When asked the reason, he answers, "Because I find them less obedient to orders: they appeal to the Decrees and the Decretals; they quote Peter and Paul. LADY. Do your orders, then, conflict with Peter and Paul? AB. What those Apostles may teach I do not know, but I don't like a monk that answers, nor should I choose any of mine to be wiser than myself. LA. That is a thing you can easily guard against, by taking care to have all the wisdom possible. AB. I have no leisure for it. LA. How so? AB. Because I have not time. LA. Not time to be wise? AB. No. LA. What prevents you? AB. Long prayers, house-keeping, hunting, hours, attendance at court." The lady then argues that she finds her books supply her with the necessary wisdom for the management of her household and the education of her children. "AB. Why, I have sixty monks at home, and you will not find a single book in my chamber. LA. Your monks, then, must be well taken care of! AB. I can tolerate books, but not Latin ones. LA. Why not? AB. Because that language is not proper for ladies. LA. I should be glad to hear your reason. AB. It is not favourable to the preservation of their chastity. LA. Then, is the silly trash with which French books are filled, favourable to chastity? AB. That is not it. LA. Tell me plainly what it is. AB. By not knowing Latin they will be safer from the priests. LA. Why, thanks to you, there is very little danger from that source, for you take good care not to know Latin." Presently the lady appeals to the example of the Virgin Mary, and asks the Abbot what he thinks of her. "AB. Most highly. LA. Was she not versed in books? AB. Yes; but not in such as you read. LA. What did she read then? AB. The canonical hours. LA. Indeed! which version of them, pray? AB. That of the Benedictine order. LA. Well, it may be so. But Paula and Eustochium—were they not well versed in the Scriptures? AB. Yes, but that is now rare. LA. True, and in former days an unlearned abbot was a rare phenomenon, whereas now nothing is commoner. In former days princes and emperors were distinguished for their learning no less than their exalted rank. Nor is it so rare now as you suppose. In Spain and Italy there are not a few women belonging to the noblest families who are a match for any man. In England there are the Mores; in Germany, the Pirckheimers and the Blaurers. And if you don't take care, it will soon come to this, that we shall preside in the schools of divinity, preach in the churches and take possession of your mitres. AB. Heaven prevent it! LA. Nay, it is for you to prevent it. But if you go on as you are doing, it is more likely that the geese will begin to preach than that such dumb shepherds as you will be any longer endured. You see the world's stage already turned upside down; you must either give up your character, or else each one must act his own part. AB. By what chance have I met with so accomplished a lady? If you ever come to see us, I will give you a handsome welcome. LA. How? AB. We will dance, drink, hunt, play, and laugh. LA. Truly, I have plenty to laugh at just now."

One of the most entertaining of the Colloquies is the *Peregrinatio Religionis Ergo*, or, "Pilgrimage," the substance of which has been given elsewhere.[a]

[a] Vol. i. pp. 232—235.

The Ἰχθυοφαγία is a conversation between a butcher and a fishmonger, which turns chiefly on the value of ceremonial observances, which the tendency of the times too frequently placed above the weightier matters of the law. Thus, if a priest permits his hair to grow, or puts on a secular dress, he is thrown into prison and severely punished; but though he is a drunkard, a debauchee, a gambler, or an adulterer, he is notwithstanding a pillar of the church. Any one who saw a Carthusian violating the rules of his order, either in his dress or by eating flesh, would be thrown into a frenzy of alarm, lest the earth should gape and swallow both; yet he would express no horror if he saw him drunk, or pouring out calumnies on the character of others, or imposing by manifest deceptions on some poor neighbour. These remarks suggest several anecdotes, some of which are best under the decent veil of a dead language, while others are altogether incredible. Here is one told by the butcher:—"There were lately two ladies here, very sensible women too, one of whom miscarried, and the other fainted, from seeing the prior of a convent of nuns walking about in public, without the black gown over his linen frock. Yet the same ladies had often seen birds of like feather, feasting, singing, and dancing, to speak of nothing worse, without feeling the slightest disgust." This story is capped by the fishmonger, who relates that he had an acquaintance—a learned man and a bachelor of divinity—who was dying of consumption, and who had been long advised by his physicians to have recourse to a diet of eggs and milk, but in vain, even though his bishop exhorted him to comply. At last, when it became apparent that he would die sooner than follow a prescription which would compel him to break the fasts of the church, it was determined to practise a deception upon him, and accordingly a drink was prepared for him, composed of eggs and goat's milk. This he eagerly swallowed, and after some days began to get better, until a servant-maid revealed the trick, when he immediately began to vomit up again what he had eaten. Yet this same man, who was so superstitious in the matter of milk, had no scruple about repudiating a debt, and when his note of hand was somewhat simply presented to him, secretly sliced off his signature with his nail. Being put on his oath, he took it as promptly as if perjury was a positive enjoyment to him, and he would like to commit one once every day at the least! Another story has obviously Erasmus himself for its hero. He was on a visit, by the invitation of his friends, at Eleutheropolis (Friburg), a city which does not altogether correspond with its name. It was Lent, and one or two days were given up to friendly meetings. Meantime, to avoid giving offence, he lived on fish, although he had a dispensation from the Pope to eat what he pleased. Feeling himself threatened with an attack of the cruel disease from which he suffered, he prepared to leave, it being absolutely necessary that he should do so unless he preferred to be laid up where he was. Some people, however, suspecting that he was hastening his departure because he could not endure fish, prevailed with Glaucoplutus, a very learned man and of high authority in the State, to invite him to breakfast. Tired of the crowd which he could not avoid in a public inn, he consented, but on the condition that nothing should be provided but a couple of eggs, and as soon as he had finished, he was to mount his horse. This was promised, but on his arrival he found a roast chicken. Indignant at this breach of promise, he declined to touch anything but the eggs, and bringing the meal to a close, he got on his horse and departed, accompanied by some learned friends. Somehow or other, the savour of that chicken got wind, and reports went flying about as atrocious as if a dozen people had been poisoned. Nor was it one city only which re-echoed with that story: almost on the same day the rumour had flown to other cities three days' journey distant. And, as usual, report had added something to the truth, alleging that the hero of the tale would have been summoned before the magistrates had he not made a hasty flight. This was entirely false, but it was true, nevertheless, that his entertainer was obliged to make an explanation to the authorities. Yet in this same city, during the whole of Lent, but especially on holidays, the people go mad with drink, shout, dance, and fight; they play at dice next door to the church, and make such a noise that it is impossible to hear the sermon, and nobody takes offence.

In the "Charon" Erasmus laments the war between the Emperor and Francis I., and introduces the grim ferry-man of hell come to the upper world to purchase a new vessel in which to carry the shades he expects from that source, as well as from the plague which was then spreading its ravages in every country. Charon also hopes much from the religious dissensions, which have now risen to such a height that no man can trust his brother, no husband can trust his wife. The chief friends of Charon on earth are declared to be "certain animals, who wear black and white gowns over grey frocks, and who, frequenting the houses of the great, instil the love of war into every ear, and exhort thereto princes and people, exclaiming in their sermons that war is just, sacred, and holy. And the more to show the dauntless courage of those men, they shout the same things on both sides. In France they preach that God is on the side of the French, and that no one who has God for a protector can be conquered. In England and Spain they cry that this war is not waged by the Emperor, but by the Almighty; let them only acquit themselves like men and victory is certain; and whoever may fall, he will not perish, but fly straight up to heaven, arms and all." "But what," asks Charon, "moves them to encourage war, or what advantage do they reap from it?" To which the answer is, that they get more profit from the dying than from the living. Being asked how it was that he had come to the upper world to look for a ship, as if there was no timber below, Charon replies that all their wood had been used in burning the shades of heretics.

In the Ἱππεὺς Ἄνιππος, in which there can be no doubt that Erasmus satirizes Eppendorf and his pretended nobility, Harpalus consults Nestorius what steps he should take in order to pass himself off as a knight. He is accordingly recommended in the first place to remove to a distance from his country, then to insinuate himself into the company of young men of really noble birth, whence a suspicion will first arise that he is of equal rank with his associates, and to take care to have nothing plebeian in his dress. He must wear a seal-ring on his finger—a gilt one with an artificial gem will not cost much—he must provide himself with a coat-of-arms and a motto, and having been born in an obscure village, he may take his title from a mountain that stood near it, and call himself the "knight of the golden rock." He may then proceed to write a number of letters to himself, purporting to come from people of great distinction, in which he must be frequently addressed as "most illustrious knight," and these he must take care to drop in convenient places, so as to ensure their getting into other people's hands, or he may sew them into his clothes, and those to whom they are given out to be mended will be sure to talk about it. In the next place, he must gather round him a number of companions, who would always be ready to show him respect and to sound his praises, or he may bribe some of the starving printers with whom the land is overrun, to print his name in their books in large characters, and call him the first man in the country. Nor need he trouble himself about paying those whom he employs; on the contrary, he will find it an advantage to be in debt to as many persons as possible: for "a creditor shows you as much respect as if he had received some great kindness from you, and is in constant fear lest he may furnish you with an excuse for not paying him at all. No one ever found his servants more obedient than a debtor his creditors, who are more grateful for any repayment than if you made them a present." He must maintain a set of active servants, who will remember the purpose for which man is provided with fingers, and who are to be well dressed, in their master's livery, so that if they steal anything, no one will presume to accuse them. Above all, he must ever observe this knightly maxim, that no law forbids that a knight should relieve the plebeian traveller of his money; for what could be more unworthy than that an ignoble merchant should be rolling in wealth, while an honourable knight has nothing to spend on gambling and debauchery? It will be advisable for him to spend most of his time in public places, for should any one drop his purse, or the key of his wine-cellar,—who would dare to suspect so well-dressed and so magnificent a person as the knight of the golden rock? Another way of raising the wind is to invent pretexts for quarrelling with people who have plenty of money, especially monks and priests, who are just now so generally disliked. One has ridiculed your arms, another has spoken insultingly of you, a third has written something which can be so twisted as to read like a calumny. Declare war upon them, threaten them with ruin; they will be sure to come in terror to make terms, when, if you demand three thousand gold pieces, they will be ashamed to offer you less than two hundred. But the best way of all, perhaps, is to entrap some rich heiress into marriage; and this may be easily accomplished by pretending an invitation to enter the Emperor's service, officers of rank having a special attraction for the fair. If, however, the city in which he resides should become too hot for him, and if people should begin to ask such questions as these: What is he about? why is he stopping here so many years? why does he not go home? why is he neglecting his estates? where did he get his arms? where does he get the money for such extravagance?—it is then time for him to flit; his flight, however, should be that of the lion, not of the hare; he may pretend that he has been summoned to the Emperor's court on important business, and will presently return at the head of an army. Those who have anything to lose will never dare to open their mouth against him in his absence.—The portrait was drawn in strong colours. At all events, no one could doubt for whom it was intended.

In the "Seraphic Obsequies," Erasmus ridicules a superstition sanctioned, it would appear, by such a famous man as Rodolphus Agricola, as well as, more recently, by Christopher Longolius the Ciceronian,—that of assuming a monastic habit on the approach of death, with the view of passing into the other world clothed in a vicarious sanctity. Theotimus, returning from the funeral of Eusebius, a learned and distinguished man, describes it to his friend Philecous. Having been warned by his physicians that in all human probability he had not more than three days to live, Eusebius had his head shaved, and putting on the cowl and frock, the girdle and sandals of St. Francis, solemnly vowed, in the presence of witnesses, that he would serve Christ according to the rules of that order if God would grant him his life. He died, however, on the day named by the physicians, and then there came flocking round the corpse several of the Franciscan order, to celebrate his funeral. "You would have wept if you had seen how affectionately the Seraphic brothers washed the body, fitted upon it those holy vestments, leaving the feet, which they rapturously kissed, uncovered, composed the hands in the form of the cross, and even made the face to shine with oil, according to the Gospel precept. " PH. Wonderful humility for men of Seraphic virtue to act the part of undertakers and body-dressers! TH. After that they laid him out on a bier, and following Paul's precept, 'Bear ye one another's burdens,' they carried their brother on their shoulders along the highway to the monastery. Then they buried him with the usual service. While the venerable procession was moving down the street, I saw several shedding involuntary tears when they beheld the same man whom they had before seen clothed in purple and fine linen, now arrayed in the Franciscan dress, girt with a hempen rope, and in all respects laid out so religiously. For the dead man's head was bent over one shoulder, and the hands, as I have said, placed crosswise; while everything else showed a singular respect for religion. The Seraphic brotherhood too, walking with bent heads, with eyes fixed on the ground, and singing so lugubriously that I think the ghosts of the dead could scarcely out-do them, drew tears and sobs from many. PH. But had he the five wounds of St. Francis? TH. That I shall not venture to affirm positively. There were to be seen on his hands and feet certain livid marks, and his dress had a slit in the left side; but I did not venture to examine minutely, because they say that in such matters curiosity has been the ruin of many. PH. But did you see none laughing? TH. I did; but I suspect they were heretics, of whom the world is full just now." Philecous presently proceeds to inquire what advantage the dead man was supposed to derive from this practice, and is assured in reply that whoever takes monastic vows is forthwith enriched with the merits of the entire order, being grafted on the body of that holy fraternity. "PH. What angel has revealed this to them? TH. No angel, my friend, but Christ himself, who, with His own lips, revealed this and many other things to the blessed Francis. PH. I pray and beseech you, by the love you bear me, make me a participator in these communications. TH. They are most profound mysteries, and it is unlawful to impart them to the profane. PH. How profane, friend? There is no order which has more of my good-will than the Seraphic. TH. But you sometimes twit them and abuse them.

PH. That, Theotimus, is precisely a proof of my love. For none do greater injury to that order than those who live basely under its shelter, and whoever takes most interest in the welfare of the order must be most indignant with its corruptors. TH. But I am afraid St. Francis will be angry with me if I tell any of his secrets. PH. What evil do you fear from the most harmless of men? TH. What? Lest he may strike me blind or take away my reason, as he is said to have treated many who refused to believe in the marks of his five wounds. PH. Are the saints then worse in heaven than they were on earth? I am told that St. Francis was of so gentle a nature that, when the boys, as he was going along the road, put cheese, milk, pebbles and stones into his hood which was hanging down behind, he took no offence, but went on his way cheerful and rejoicing; and has he now become angry and revengeful? Another day, having been called by a companion a thief, a murderer, a drunkard, and all the names that could be applied to the greatest villain in the world, he returned thanks, and acknowledged that the other had spoken the truth. As his companion wondered how he could say so, he answered, All these crimes, and worse than these I would have committed, had not the divine favour preserved me. How is it that he has now become so revengeful? TH. It is so. The saints who reign in heaven do not permit themselves to be insulted." Theotimus now proceeds, in answer to further inquiries, to enumerate the revelations imparted to St. Francis. They were seven in number and were as follows:—that the more numerous the Seraphic brotherhood should become, the more abundantly would they be supplied with this kind of pabulum; that on the day sacred to

St. Francis all the souls, not only of the brethren, but of all who wished well to the order, should be released from purgatory; that the sandalled and rope-girdled folk should never fail till the day of judgment; that no one leading an impious life should be able to continue long a member of the order; that none who wished ill to the order should reach half the age pre-ordained by God, but should all perish early by a most miserable death; that the friends of the order, on the other hand, however impiously they might live, should nevertheless obtain the mercy of God, and close a wicked life with a happy end; and lastly, that no one should have a bad end who died in the Seraphic dress. "PH. But what do you call a bad end? TH. It is a bad end if the soul on leaving the body goes straight to hell, from whence there is no redemption. PH. Is not the dress then a safeguard against purgatory? TH. No; except for those who die on the festival of St. Francis. But do you think it a small matter to be safe from hell? PH. I think it a very great matter. But what becomes of those who have the holy dress put on them after death? For they do not die in it. TH. If they intended it while they were yet living, the will is accepted for the deed. PH. When I was residing at Antwerp, I was present, along with other relatives, at the death-bed of a certain lady, and there was a Franciscan friar there, a very holy man, who, observing that she was now at the last gasp, took one of her arms and put it inside his gown, so as to cover part of her shoulder as well. Thereupon the question was raised whether the whole woman was safe from the jaws of hell or only the part covered. TH. She was altogether safe; on the same principle that in baptism only a part of the body is sprinkled with water, and yet the whole man is made a Christian. PH. It is strange that the evil spirits have such a horror of that dress! TH. They fear it more than the Lord's cross. When Eusebius was carried out I saw, and so did others, swarms of black devils leaping at the body; yet none of them dared to touch it." The conversation concludes with some further satire on the Franciscans, and Philecous resolves to die in that holy habit. "For the future," he says, "I shall lead an easier life; I shall not torment myself with the fear of hell, nor waste my time in confession, nor submit to the tortures of penance."

The "Familiar Colloquies," as the successive editions issued from Froben's press, were looked for with eager interest both by friends and enemies, and must have had their full share in the accomplishment of the great religious revolution which was then in progress. The established fame of the author, the intrinsic merits of the work itself, its adaptation to the times, the pungent epigrams which glittered on every page, and, perhaps, not least, the suspicions of heresy which began to be whispered round, all contributed to give it an immense circulation. A bookseller in Paris, it is said, took advantage of the report that the University was about to condemn the work to print no less than twenty-four thousand copies,[9]—a proof that even in that age such interference with the liberty of the press sometimes defeated its own object. But Erasmus was less pleased with another of his editors, a Dominican friar, who was impudent enough to publish an edition with several passages which bore hard upon the monks "corrected," that is, as he says, corrupted, and with a preface, purporting to be by the author himself, in which he was

[9] *Er. Op.* iii. 1168, D.

represented as expressing his anxiety, now that he was so far advanced in years, to correct his writings.[10] Of this forgery he complains bitterly in some of his letters. The dialogue was a form of composition which was admirably adapted to the purposes of Erasmus, since, to any accusation of heresy, he had always the ready answer that it was most unjust to charge him with the sentiments put in the mouth of his fictitious characters. It was his object, he said, to teach Latin, not theology, and it was surely no sin to show how an heretical proposition might be stated in good Latin.[11] This defence, however, did not prevent the work being condemned by the Sorbonne; and eventually it had the honour of being placed by the Inquisition in the first class of prohibited books.[12]

The same plea could not be urged for another remarkable composition of a very different kind, which is especially interesting as throwing light on his relations to the doctrine of the Trinity and to the orthodox system generally. I mean the introduction to his edition of St. Hilary, a work which, owing to the great corruption of the manuscripts, cost him enormous labour, and for which the Benedictine editors of that father give him due credit, at the same time that they regret his "declamatory preface,"[13] which had been

---

[10] *Coronis Apologetica.—Coll. Fam.* ii. 258, 259. According to Burigni (*Vie d'Erasme*, i. 522), the authors of the *Bibl. des Jacobins* (t. 2, p. 53) deny that there is any truth in this story, no such edition as that described by Erasmus being known to them; but as Erasmus quotes from the supposititious preface it is difficult to see how there can be a doubt on the subject.

[11] *Ib.* p. 262, 263.

[12] BURIGNI, i. 516.

[13] "Tredecim post annos (*i.e.* after the Paris edition of 1510) Erasmus ad libros potissimum de Trinitate castigandos animum appulit: tractatus alios ut plurimum aut neglexit

before condemned by the Inquisition and by the Sorbonne. That this should have been its fate is certainly not strange, for Erasmus more than hints a doubt as to the soundness of Hilary on the Deity of the Holy Spirit and some other points of doctrine. Complaining bitterly of the way in which he had been interpolated, especially in those passages where he deviates from the orthodox standard, he quotes a sentence in which Hilary clearly implies that the Father and Son are the only proper objects of worship, to the exclusion of the Holy Spirit, and expresses his surprise that such a sentiment should have escaped corruption. If, he says, the object of these forgeries is to produce the impression that there are no errors in the works of the Fathers, it is labour thrown away, for there is no one so learned or so careful but he sometimes makes a mistake. "By all means, put the best construction you can on what you find written; but for every one to make what alterations he will at his own discretion is rashness, not to say impiety. If, however," he sarcastically adds — he is, doubtless, thinking of his own treatment by the enemies of culture — "the object is to defend the writer, how much better it would be to exercise this charity on the works of the moderns, who have not the sanction of antiquity to secure them from criticism, and whom death has not removed beyond the reach of envy. Instead of this, we are superstitiously indulgent towards the Fathers, while in the writers of our own age we misrepresent even their just and reason-

---

prorsus, aut propter veterum codicum penuriam emendare non valuit; laudem tamen suo ex labore relaturus, si se a declamatoria præfatione abstinuisset, quæ et Sacræ Inquisitioni Romanæ et Parisiensi Theologiæ Facultati censuris digna merito visa est."—*Præf. Gen.* i. 6.

able remarks, and put the worst construction upon all they say, as if by such a method of interpretation we might not find even in the Epistles of Paul some propositions that might be represented as erroneous, heretical, scandalous, or irreverent."

Having noticed that Hilary, in his treatise on the Trinity, deplores the necessity he was under of speaking of things beyond the reach of the human understanding, he remarks that we, in these days, have no such scruples, but move questions and enunciate propositions about matters of which a man may be either ignorant or doubtful without imperilling his salvation.

"Is it not possible," he asks, "to have fellowship with the Father and the Son and the Holy Spirit, without being able to explain philosophically the distinction between the Father and the Son, or between the Holy Spirit and both the other persons; or the difference between the generation of the Son and the procession of the Spirit? If I believe the tradition of the Church, that there are three of one substance, what need of laborious disputation? If I do not believe, no earthly reasoning will convince me." Again: "Thou shalt not be condemned for not knowing whether the Spirit which proceedeth from the Father and the Son consists in one principle or in two; but thou shalt not escape destruction unless thou shalt make it thy endeavour to possess the fruits of the Spirit, which are love, joy, peace, patience, kindness, goodness, long-suffering, meekness, faith, modesty, continence, chastity. . . . The sum of our religion is peace and concord; which cannot easily be maintained unless we define but very few points, and in the greater number leave every one free to form his own judgment." The following passage contains a lesson which is as much needed by Protestant as by Romanist orthodoxy:—

"In old times faith consisted in the life rather than in the profession of a multitude of articles. By-and-bye it became necessary to impose articles of faith, but these were at first few in number and of apostolic simplicity. Subsequently, in consequence of the dishonesty of the heretics, the sacred volume was subjected to a more severe investigation, while their obstinacy compelled the definition of some points by the Synods of the Church. At length faith ceased to be a matter of the heart, and was wholly transferred to written documents; and there were nearly as many forms of belief as there were men. Articles increased, but sincerity decreased. Contention waxed warm, charity waxed cold. The doctrine of Christ, which at first repudiated all strife of words, began to look to the schools of the philosophers for protection: this was the first step in the decline of the Church. Wealth increased, and power too. The interference of the authority of the emperors, moreover, was not very conducive to sincerity of faith. At last, religion degenerated into mere sophistical argumentation, and the Church was inundated with myriads of articles. Hence the progress was easy to terror and threats. And though the Christian life is almost unknown among us, and though faith is on our lips rather than in our heart, though the solid understanding of the Holy Scriptures is wanting to us, yet by the mere force of terror we endeavour to make men believe what they do not believe, to love what they do not love, and to understand what they do not understand."

In turning over the works of Hilary on the Arian heresy, and the reply of Auxentius, Erasmus says it often occurred to him that some might be surprised that, whereas so many precautions are taken to ensure our believing that the Son is very God, of one substance with the Father, hardly any mention is made of the Holy Spirit, although the whole controversy regarding the name of God, the *homoousion*, the equality with the Father, pertains no less to the Spirit than to the Son. The alternative reasons which he gives for this fact are suggestive: "Either because it was more difficult to believe that the Son was God on account of his human nature, or because the early Christians, in their deep reverence for the Divine nature, scrupled to make any proposition concerning it which is not clearly taught in the Bible." He sums up his own conclusion as to the scriptural teaching upon the Three Persons in the following short and emphatic sentence: "The Father is very frequently called God, the Son sometimes, the Holy Spirit never."

Here, indeed, he adds, as usual, a saving clause, or what is meant as such, but it may be questioned whether he does not make matters worse. "And this I say," he continues, "not to throw doubt on what the authority of the orthodox Fathers has taught us from Holy Scripture, but to show how scrupulous the ancients were about pronouncing on questions of divinity, for which they had a much greater reverence than we, who have advanced to such a pitch of audacity that we do not hesitate to dictate to the Son how he ought to honour his own mother. We presume to call the Holy Spirit very God, proceeding from the Father and the Son, which the Fathers do not seem to have ventured upon for a considerable time; yet we do not hesitate by our crimes to drive him from the temple of our heart, as though we believed the Holy Spirit to be no more than an empty name. So, many of the Fathers, who worshipped the Son with the greatest piety, yet scrupled to use the word *homoousion*, because it is nowhere to be found in Holy Scripture."

Does not the following passage, too, betray more sympathy with the Arians than is consistent with an orthodox horror of their creed?—"How furiously Hilary attacks the Arians, calling them impious, blasphemous, devils, pests, enemies of Christ, as if the name of heretic was nothing! And yet it is probable that among the members of the Arian party, there were men who believed that what they taught concerning Christ was in accordance with truth and piety. The doctrine could claim the support of many great authorities; several passages of Holy Scripture were in its favour; nor were there wanting arguments which had the appearance of truth. To this was added the authority of the Emperor, and besides, a vast number of subscribers, who might have justly claimed our adherence, if majorities were always right. Finally, the question was upon a subject which far transcends the limits of the human understanding. I should have deemed any one who thought with Arius a proper subject for advice and instruction, but I would not immediately have called him Satan and Antichrist.] For if such epithets are to be flung at every one who commits an error, what shall we do, to say nothing of so many famous ecclesiastical doctors, to Hilary himself, who, in so many passages, seems to think that Christ had a body which was not susceptible of pain; and that hunger, thirst, weariness, and other affections of that kind were not natural in him but assumed?"

The composition containing these passages was addressed to Carondiletus, the Archbishop of Palermo, to whom the Hilary was dedicated. If episcopal flesh and blood were the same then as they are now—and it is probable they were not very different—the Archbishop's nerves must have been severely tried.

The Hilary was published at Basle in February, 1523.[14] It supplied the occasion for the letter to Marcus Laurinus, quoted in the preceding chapter, who on receiving a copy wrote back that it had quite restored his spirits, he having been informed either that Erasmus was dead or had become a Lutheran;—probably both rumours had reached him. After all, the Preface would seem to have escaped censure in the meantime. However questionable in other respects, it might be taken as an indication that the author had not yet left the Roman Church.

In June, 1523, Erasmus published an enlarged edition of his "Method of True Theology," with a new dedication to the Elector Albert, in which he draws a laboured comparison—more laboured indeed than delicate—between the pains of authors and those of mothers, remarking that some of the former are like bears which bring forth mere lumps of flesh, and then are compelled to lick their cubs into shape. Among these he counts himself. Authors, he adds, are more miserably off even than actors, whose worst fate is to be hissed off the stage, " while in our case the play is performed at the risk of our

---

[14] *Ep.* dcxiii. The dedication is dated January 5, 1522; the date on the title-page is 1523. The former I conjecture to be a mistake, and the latter agrees best with the fact referred to in the text, that a copy sent to M. Laurinus called forth the letter of Erasmus, which is certainly correctly dated Feb. 1, 1523.

lives, and that too at our own expense." His little work, published many years ago, he continues, has been so often revised, and has had so much labour expended on it, that it may now take its rank among books; but should it displease any, this may be imputed to the unhappy state of the times, in which passions are so roused that it is impossible to write anything, however impious, which will not find some to applaud it, or however excellent which will be secure against detraction. "It is part of my unhappy fate that my old age has fallen on these evil times. We must implore the Lord Jesus that He, who alone has the power to do so by his spirit, will turn the hearts of the Christian people to the love of peace and concord. For as long as we permit our own spirit to have free course and to create these disturbances, the more we try to extricate ourselves from our difficulties, the more we shall be entangled in them. How others may like these times I don't know, but I assuredly like them not at all. Party spirit is so hot that fair criticism is impossible. Quarrels and rioting prevail everywhere. Quite gone is the liberty which learning once enjoyed and the pleasure that attended it; and while the good old authors are neglected nothing gives satisfaction unless it savours of revolution. Meantime how Christian peace has suffered! Scarce anywhere will you find the sincere and unaffected friendship of former days not corrupted with some poison. Conspirators you may find, but for friends you will search in vain. And yet what is our religion if peace be gone? The world would be no darker if you were to extinguish the sun. For my part I would rather be a grocer in the possession of Christian tranquillity, and rejoicing in evangelical simple-mindedness, than the greatest and most renowned theologian in the world, and be involved in these dissensions. I, at any rate, for my own poor part, am devoting all my strength to eliminating this poison from the inmost fibres of my heart, recovering the simplicity and peace of the Gospel spirit, and composing myself to that habit of mind in which I may appear with all confidence before the judgment-seat of Christ, to which perhaps to-morrow or any day I may be summoned.

". . . . Let every one judge the writings of others as he would wish his own to be judged. But let those things which must be defined and which all must be compelled to believe, be reduced to a very few, which may easily be done without tarnishing our Christian profession. As to other matters, let it be forbidden that they should be inquired into, or let every one be left to his own judgment. The result of this will be, not only that fewer discussions will hereafter arise, but that the Christian religion will be more easily diffused among all the nations of the world. Then, too, those evils may be corrected under which the world has been long groaning. For if the unjust judge in the Gospel of Luke did not entirely refuse to listen to the appeal of the afflicted widow, how much less ought we to neglect the cry of those for whom the Lord Jesus Christ shed his blood? For it was not for the great only that he died; but the humble and the lowly are his peculiar care. These were the first he gathered round him; by their means the kingdom of heaven began and made progress. These things may be done even without tumult, if kings and princes, in the meantime foregoing the satisfaction of their human passions, will devote themselves with all their heart to the public advantage and the glory of

Jesus Christ, the Prince of princes, and if all participation in this work be forbidden to those whom the world has already endured too long, who care for nothing but their own glory, their own belly, and their own power, and who think that their kingdom cannot stand if the people are permitted to have either brains or judgment. Wherefore we must besiege with our common prayers almighty and all-merciful Jesus, to put this mind into the leading men on both sides, among whom you, as you hold the highest rank, can give the largest amount of aid to the restoration of the peace of the Church, as I am confident you will, and I doubt not you are already about it. Farewell." [15]

On the 14th of September of this year (1523) died Adrian VI., to be succeeded by Giulio de' Medici, under the name of Clement VII. In a letter to the Bishop of Basle Erasmus has left the following just estimate of the character of the new Pope:—

ERASMUS *to* CHRISTOPHER, *Bishop of Basle.*[16]

"*Basle*, 1523.

"I AM waiting for some indication of the spirit of the new Pope. If it shall appear that he is really concerned for the honour of Christ, I mean to give him all the support that can be given by such an insignificant person as myself. I have determined to stop here till March; for so am I bidden by necessity, but meantime I shall not be idle. For, besides other things, I have emended the works of St. Hilary with immense labour, and if Christ will give me strength for it, I will finish my treatise on the art of preaching, which has been long

[15] *Ep.* dclv. [16] *Ep.* dclxi.

promised, and which my excellent friend John, Bishop of Rochester, begs of me in repeated letters. . . . .

"I am well acquainted with the character of the new Pope, with whom I have been on terms of intimacy, and I do not doubt that he will introduce many reforms in ecclesiastical morals: that is to say, he will check the boundless licence that at present prevails in granting dispensations, set limits to pluralism, prescribe a decent dress to the clergy, put down open wickedness, and insist on the frequent celebration of mass. These things are no doubt important as regards the outward form of religion, but I am not sure that they contain the substance of true piety. He will have all obedient to his word by the authority of the Emperor, whose wishes he will consult in all things. The Cardinals, even those who in their hearts wish him ill, will dissemble and submit until he shall establish the now somewhat shaken power of the Roman See. Then his successor, who must follow in no long time, will manage matters as he pleases. I have no desire that the primacy of the Roman See should be abolished, but I could wish that its discipline were such that it might favour every effort that makes for the religion of the Gospel, as for several ages past it has openly taught by its example things plainly averse to the doctrines of Christ."

Here is another letter to the same prelate in a somewhat different style:—

ERASMUS *to* CHRISTOPHER, *Bishop of Basle*.[17]

"ILLUSTRIOUS PRELATE,—Eight days ago I had determined to visit you, in company with Louis Berus, who

[17] *Ep.* delxliii.

has the greatest respect for your highness; but he
thought it would be unkind to ask you in your old age
to leave the warmth of your stove, and I could not
venture to risk exposing myself to it again, having so
often found that it brought on an immediate attack.
But if the milder weather will permit you to leave your
room, I should be glad to see and speak with you. I
have been for some time afflicted with the stone, a
disease with which I was too familiar of old, but which
now recurs more frequently or else with greater danger.
Women become barren with age; it makes me more
fruitful; for I am always either conceiving, or in
labour, or bringing forth. But 'tis a serpent brood,
and I fear may one day kill its parent. Certainly
I have more than once been delivered with serious
danger; and should I ever be brought to bed under
the frowns of Juno and Lucina, all will be over with
Erasmus. They say this disease is related to the gout,
with which I am sorry to hear your highness is
somtimes afflicted. Both of them are recurrent, but that
from which I suffer is attended with the more immediate
danger."

ERASMUS *to* SYLVESTER PRIERAS.[18]

"*Basle*, 1523.

"WHAT your highness means by a letter *smelling of smoke*
I do not very well understand. I am certainly greatly
indebted to you for writing so plainly, and so politely,
what it concerns me to know; and for pointing out how
I may escape the danger with which you threaten me,

[18] *Ep.* dclxiv.

namely, by explaining some passages in my writings; I should have been still more indebted if you had condescended to point out what passages you refer to. It would not be strange that some error should be found in my works, when neither St. Jerome nor St. Augustine could escape, especially considering the great variety of opinions that prevails at present; certainly I have never intentionally admitted into my works anything that conflicted with orthodox doctrine. At Louvain, where I lived so many years, no theologian, whether friend or enemy, ever pointed out anything of the kind, though I frequently begged them to tell me freely if there was. If Stunica is behaving like a madman at Rome—though I am not ignorant at whose instigation he is acting—consider what a precedent he is establishing. Suppose that there are some things in my works which ought not to be tolerated, what a precedent it is that any one should be permitted to publish such scurrilous and impudent attacks on the good name of a man who has certainly never yet been condemned by any one. There is a Carmelite at Louvain, a man perfectly mad and of little learning, and a member of the preaching order, his exact counterpart: these two make me the object of their constant attacks, and will have it that I am a Lutheran, whether I like it or not, though I was the first of all to protest against violent measures. You may think I am boasting, but it is the truth; if I chose to declare, in a single letter, that I had the least sympathy with Luther, you would see all Germany thrown into a fever of joy. I should also have the protection of many of the sovereign princes. But, though provoked by so many reproaches on one side, and solicited by so many flatterers on the other, I have never divested myself of my reverence for the Roman Church. Aleander is doing everything against Luther, but, if you knew all, Erasmus has done more to break the strength and spirit of that faction than all Aleander's engines; in so many private as well as published letters has he set his face against the Lutherans, though I must own many of the reforms urged by that man are necessary; but I do not like dissension on any terms. . . .

"Luther's faction is not yet extinguished, as you in Rome imagine; I would it were! for it is ruining all our studies. There are thousands on thousands who, from detestation of the Roman See, greatly favour Luther; and all they want is a leader. Neither man nor angel shall make me a revolutionist, and yet they are trying all they can to accomplish it. The Emperor is very gracious to me, and I enjoy a salary from him, as his counsellor; of this I am certain. Some of the princes and kings, too, are most friendly; also some of the cardinals and bishops. I beg that I may be allowed to be orthodox in spite of Stunica and such sycophants.

"I could wish to be at Rome, even though I lost half my income; and I mean to go, if health permit. Of the Pope's good will to me, I nothing doubt. He is not one to lend his ear to such calumnies." . . . .

Erasmus speaks confidently to Prieras of the payment of his pension from the Emperor, implying that he would lose it if he accepted the invitation of his friends in Rome to go and live there. In point of fact, however, it was not paid, and he soon found it would not be, except on the condition of his returning to

Brabant. This he was afraid to do, so great was the power of Egmund, who hated him even more than Luther. He and his coadjutor Hulst, he says, "first throw men into prison, and then look out for charges to bring against them." Neither could he accept the liberal offers of the King of France, which, it seems, were still pressed upon him, for fear of offending the Emperor, who was then at war with Francis.[19]

On the 13th of February, 1524, he writes a letter to Clement VII., in which he congratulates him on his elevation to the Papal throne, assures him of his own loyalty to the Roman See, and begs him not to listen to the calumnies of Stunica, who, contrary to the edicts of Leo and Adrian, was publishing infamous libels upon him. The works which this calumniator was thus abusing, he says, were published before Luther's name was ever heard of; but if he had foreseen that such troublesome times were at hand, he would either have been silent, or would have written differently; and as it was, in the later editions of his works he had omitted many passages, in order to give no handle for such attacks, and was prepared to make more changes if the necessity for them should be pointed out. With this letter he sends a present of his Paraphrase of the Acts of the Apostles, and he concludes by saying that nothing shall prevent him going to Rome save death, or the disease, still more cruel than death, from which he suffered, if he can only be assured of protection against his enemies.[20] To this letter the Pope returned a flattering answer, which he accompanied with a present of two hundred florins.[21]

[19] *Er. Op.* iii. 782, A. E.   [20] *Ep.* dclxx.   [21] *Er. Op.* iii. 778, B.

A letter to Carondiletus (March 30, 1524), shows that Erasmus has been pressing for his pension, and that his hints about splendid offers from the King of France had been treated as imaginary. This he assures the archbishop is not the case. The reason the King had so often renewed his invitation was that he had determined to found in Paris a college of three languages, like that at Louvain, and he wished Erasmus to be at its head. He wisely excused himself, remembering the odium he had incurred in connection with Busleiden's college. His servant, however, who had just returned from France, had assured him that a treasurership with a thousand pounds was awaiting him, if he would accept it.[22]

"I have not yet," he continues, "been very burdensome to my sovereign's treasury; for the pension from it has not been once paid. I am living here at great expense, chiefly in consequence of my frequent illnesses, though in other respects I cannot pretend to be very economical. And I have now contracted no little debt, so that if my health would allow me to leave, probably my creditors would not. Wherefore, if it be possible, I pray that at least one year's pension may be paid my servant, the bearer of this, to relieve my present wants. I send the Emperor's letter, which conveys his wishes to this effect, though his I shall always be, with a pension or without it, nor shall I often trouble you in future about so small a matter. This year at frequent intervals, but especially in the months of July and December, I

---

[22] *Ep.* dclxxv. Elsewhere, he calls this treasurership worth at least 500 crowns, and at the same time exclaims against the poverty of the court of Brussels:—"O aulam nostram semper famelicam!"—*Ep.* dclxxxv.

have been so tortured by my enemy, the stone, that I despaired of life, and indeed prayed for death, for no death could be more cruel. And yet these Lutheran tragedies give me more pain than the stone itself. I will venture to say this, too, to one whom I esteem my friend, that the present state of the times has had some influence in preventing my return. You know what a battle I had for the cause of letters with certain theologians before the appearance of Luther; and now the sword has been put into the hands of two of the most bitter enemies of culture, Hulst and Egmund. Egmund's character is known to everybody, and how hostile he is to me he has declared in many ways, and does so still. . . . .

"Though this circumstance had not much weight with me in preventing my return, still, to confess the truth, it has made me less eager to go back to Brabant, especially as in the Emperor's absence there is not much protection to be expected from the Court. Cardinal Campeggio is now at Nuremberg to compose the Lutheran dissension, and has already written me three letters, most affectionately inviting me to give my services, but when I shall undertake the journey I cannot say; all I know is that, instead of being permitted to enjoy the repose so much needed by my years, I am given up to the furies, and torn in pieces between the two contending parties. If I can excuse myself to the Cardinal, till after the German stoves have burned out, I will fly to him, provided I can pay the debts with which, contrary to my custom, I am burdened. Christ, almighty and all-merciful, long preserve your highness."

Such writings as those which I have noticed at the beginning of this chapter by no means tended to reconcile Erasmus with the monkish party, and in fact it would be difficult to conceive anything better calculated to undermine their power, to laugh down their superstitions, and to bring their whole system into contempt, than those Colloquies designed for the instruction of the ingenuous youth. On the other hand, as the Lutheran reformation developed itself, he saw every day more and more reason to distrust it. He had from the first anticipated that the result would be unfavourable to the progress of literature and to practical piety—the two things to which he looked for the deliverance of the world from the yoke of the monks; and however necessary the separation from Rome may have been in the interests of spiritual freedom, it was not given to him to view the future with the eye of Providence, and as regards immediate results he was certainly right. He now saw a new set of fanatics arising on the reformed side, as ignorant, as presumptuous, as hostile to all liberal culture, as the fanatics of the Church; and he dreaded lest the world, instead of being freed from the yoke of superstition, should merely experience a change of masters. He saw men with the Gospel constantly on their lips, but whose lives did not always reflect Gospel purity. As an example of the extent to which they carried their hostility to letters, he notices that at Strasburg they were actually teaching in public that it was needless to learn any language except Hebrew; and although Luther wrote sharply against those who maintained this absurdity, the fact that such an opinion could be broached shows to what the evangelical principles were tending. "This new gospel," wrote Erasmus, and his letters of this period are full of similar complaints, "is producing a new set of men, so impudent, hypocritical, and abusive, such liars and sycophants, who agree neither with one another nor with anybody else, so universally offensive and seditious, such madmen and ranters, and in short so utterly distasteful to me, that if I knew of any city in which I should be free from them, I would remove there at once." [83]

Among those whom he would have included in this description was the reformer Farel, of whom he had formed the worst possible opinion, calling him the greatest boaster and most impudent liar he had ever met. Even the Lutherans themselves, he declares, "cannot endure this man's ungovernable violence, for which he has been often blamed both by Œcolampadius and by Pelican, but without avail, so deep rooted is the disease." [84] William Farel was a young Frenchman of good birth, a native of Dauphiné, who, having gone up to Paris to pursue his studies, became a disciple of Lefevre of Etaples, and having experienced conversion while attending his lectures, from a very bigoted Papist became an equally bigoted evangelical. He has, however, gained for himself a high name in the history of the Reformation, to which no doubt he did good service both in France and Switzerland. Driven from France by persecution, he had taken refuge in Basle, where he was kindly received, along with other French refugees, by Œcolampadius. While here he lost no opportunity of speaking evil of Erasmus —he would rather, he was heard to declare, suffer martyrdom every day than cease to do so—for whom he had conceived a warm dislike, partly on account of his insinuations against some of the evangelicals as men of bad life; but especially because of his advice to

[83] *Er. Op.* iii. 835, A.   [84] *Er. Op.* iii. 823, A.

Pope Adrian as to the best means of extinguishing the Lutheran conflagration, an expression which Farel of course interpreted as if it meant extinguishing the Gospel. On this account he called him a Balaam, implying that he had been bribed to curse the people of the Lord. He was also reported to have said jeeringly that Froben's wife knew more theology than Erasmus. The latter met Farel once, and interrupting an altercation in which he was engaged, took the opportunity of asking him why he had called him a Balaam, a name by which he felt particularly wounded, knowing how impossible it is to refute a sneer, and sensible no doubt that any insinuations of corruption that might be made against him, however false in themselves, would be sufficiently plausible to impose on those who did not know him. On this point, however, he seems to have got no satisfaction. He only learned that the joke did not originate with Farel; he had heard it first from a merchant named Blet and was so pleased with it that he went about repeating it everywhere. On the same occasion, Erasmus, with the view, it may be supposed, of justifying his position, engaged Farel in a controversy on one of the points in dispute between the Romanists and the reformers. He asked him why he objected to the invocation of the saints and whether it was not because it was not expressly enjoined in Scripture. To this Farel assented. He then desired him to prove clearly by the Holy Scriptures that the Holy Spirit should be invoked. "If he is God," said Farel, "he must be invoked." "But prove it," urged Erasmus, "by the Scriptures." At the same time he remarked that there was no difference of opinion between them on this point, his object being merely to show that the absence of Scriptural evidence was not necessarily conclusive against the invocation of the saints. Thus pressed, Farel quoted the text from John's First Epistle: "And these three are one;" to which his antagonist very truly replied that that passage did not refer to sameness of nature, but to consent of testimony, as is evident from the following verse concerning the Spirit, and the water and the blood, where no other construction is possible. Besides, the passage about the Father, the Word, and the Spirit, was not contained in the oldest manuscripts, nor cited by the greatest opponents of the Arians, as Athanasius, Cyril and Hilary. Shortly after this the conversation terminated, not certainly to the advantage of Farel, who, however, wrote to his friends boastful accounts of his victory over Erasmus.[25]

Before leaving Basle, Farel wrote a scurrilous pamphlet against Erasmus, to which indeed he did not put his name, but it was universally ascribed to him, and it was said that he had written another in French, which was not yet published, and which the magistrates were prepared to seize if it should be printed. If Erasmus used his influence to prevent Farel being permitted to return to Basle,[26] it might look as though even he did not quite understand, or at least was not prepared to practise in all cases, the principles of religious liberty; but no doubt he regarded Farel, not merely as a teacher of erroneous doctrine, but far more as a disturber of the public peace.

For a long time Erasmus had resisted the entreaties of his friends to write against Luther, but the pressure put upon him was so strong that he at last felt compelled

[25] *Ep.* dcvii.   [26] D'Aubigné, book xii. chap. xi.

to yield. That he did so with extreme reluctance was perfectly natural. He knew well that he would do no good by it, that he would only exasperate the reform party, who already sufficiently distrusted him; and whether he could satisfy even the less violent of the adherents of the Papacy, must have seemed to him very doubtful. On what ground, indeed, could he attack Luther? Whoever imagined that it was possible for him to undertake the defence of any of the grosser superstitions of Rome, or to uphold the authority of the Pope in any such sense as would please the Roman party, must have strangely mistaken his spirit. He had always admitted, and even in writing to dignitaries of the Church, courageously maintained that in much of what he said Luther was in the right, and had found fault with his manner rather than his matter. He was therefore precluded by a regard for his own consistency from making any general attack on the principles of the reformers, especially so far as they relied on Holy Scripture, and set themselves against monkish superstition; or, if he had attempted this, it must have been with so many concessions and reservations as would have entirely destroyed the force of his reasoning. There were, however, some points of the evangelical faith as held by the leading reformers, which had never commended themselves to his mind. One of these was their view of free-will. On this subject Luther, in his zeal to ascribe everything as concerns human salvation to Divine grace, had expressed himself with an extravagance which, whether or not it was justified by the language of St. Augustine,[17] at all events went beyond the teachings of

---

[17] Luther himself could scarcely have used stronger language than this sentence which Erasmus quotes, without exact reference, from St.

the great majority of the Fathers and the schoolmen, and was opposed to what was understood to be the orthodox faith in the sixteenth century. He utterly denied the existence of any such thing as free-will in man, and maintained that all human actions are the result of an inflexible necessity. Now, the Catholic Church, on the contrary, had always asserted free-will, not indeed pretending that fallen man, without the assistance of grace, can do any works effectual to salvation, but insisting that after the reparation of his nature by grace he then has it in his power, though still liable to sin, to choose whether he will avoid it.[18] Whether, anterior to grace, man could do any work morally good, or whether in that condition all his acts were of the nature of sin and hateful to God, was a point on which doctors differed, the Scotists maintaining the former opinion, and the Thomists the latter.[19] Here then was a question with a clear practical issue. Is the human will entirely passive in the work of salvation, or

---

Augustine:—"Deum et bona et mala operari in nobis, et sua bona opera remunerare in nobis, et sua mala opera punire in nobis." Yet he counts Augustine among those who did not wholly deny free-will.

[18] The Master of the Sentences, the great authority of those days, writes as follows:—"Liberum verum arbitrium est facultas rationis et voluntatis, qua bonum eligitur gratia assistente, vel malum eadem dissistente. . . . . Sed quod bonum est nisi gratia adjuta non eligit, malum vero per se eligit."—Lomb. Sen. lib. ii. Dist. xxiv. 5, *De Libero Arbitrio*. And again, *De quatuor Statibus Liberi Arbitrii in Homine:*—"Post reparationem vero ante confirmationem premitur a concupiscentia, sed non vincitur; et habet quidem infirmitatem in malo, sed gratiam in bono, ut possit peccare propter libertatem et infirmitatem, et possit non peccare ad mortem propter libertatem et gratiam adjuvantem: nondum tamen habet posse omnino non peccare, vel non posse peccare, propter infirmitatem nondum perfecte absorptam, et propter gratiam nondum plene consummatam." —*Ib.* Dist. xxv. 7. Compare Erasmus *De Libero Arbitrio*.

[19] *Er. Op.* ix. 1223, A. B.

can it, by spontaneous efforts, in any degree influence the result? Apart from any respect for the authority of the Fathers of the Church, his common-sense and practical tendencies would naturally have led Erasmus to adopt the affirmative side of the question. This therefore was the point which he selected for his attack upon Luther.

The subject was, perhaps, first suggested by a letter of Tonstall's, who had written to him from London, telling him that the whole Church expected this service from him, and assuring him that however much he might be evil spoken of by the Lutherans, he could not suffer more at their hands than the Deity himself, whom Luther made the author of all wickedness by denying free-will in man, and maintaining that all things happen according to the fixed laws of necessity. Tonstall also mentioned that Luther had just published a book on abolishing the mass, which seemed to him the next step to abolishing Christ, and entreated him by everything sacred at once to grapple with this hydra. This letter is dated July 7, 1523,[30] and it was probably soon after, at any rate before the end of the year, that Erasmus sent to Henry VIII. the first draft of his "Treatise on Free-Will," in answer to Luther, promising that if his Majesty should be pleased with the specimen, he would finish it as soon as his health would permit.[31]

A considerable time, however, was suffered to elapse before the work was put into the printer's hands. Meantime, the report that such a thing was in preparation had reached Luther's ears, who thereupon wrote to Erasmus a letter of warning and protest, not by any means in the most conciliatory style. He does not, he

[30] *Ep.* dclvi.   [31] *Ep.* dclx.

says, find fault with him for having shown an unfriendly spirit towards him in order to secure himself with the Papists: "seeing the Lord has not yet given you the fortitude or even the sense to join us in encountering those monsters." He had, he continues, never wished him to join his party, but he was afraid he might attack his doctrines, and then he would be compelled to withstand him to the face. He then expresses his hearty sympathy with him on the animosity excited against him, but maintains at the same time that those who attacked him were moved by a just zeal, being unable to endure, as he expresses it, "that sarcastic and dissembling spirit which you want to pass off as prudence and modesty." Luther writes quite in the style of an autocrat of his "clemency and mercy towards sinners," and takes great credit for having hitherto kept his pen under restraint; "for," he adds, "however far you are from thinking with us, and however much you condemn, whether wickedly or hypocritically, most of the points of the true faith, still I neither can nor will charge you with obstinacy." He concludes by assuring him that the cause of the Reformation is now far beyond his utmost power to do it hurt, and begs him, if he can do nothing more, to remain merely a spectator of the contest, and above all to abstain from publishing anything against himself.[38]

It is curious that Erasmus should speak of this letter as written *satis humaniter;* and he regrets that for fear of the sycophants he was unable to answer with equal

[38] *Ep.* dccxxvi. A fuller translation of this letter will be found in Jortin, who does not omit to notice that it begins "in the apostolical manner; Grace and peace to you from the Lord Jesus."—*Life of Er.* i. 316, *sqq.*

politeness.[33] His reply was dignified, yet somewhat warm. He refuses to admit that Luther had the purity of the Gospel more at heart than himself, for there was nothing he was not ready to endure for its sake, and claims to be a better friend to the Gospel than many who call themselves evangelicals. But he could not be blind to the disastrous consequences which had already taken place in the ruin of literature, and he dreaded lest all should end in trouble and bloodshed. He had not yet written against Luther, though he might have done so with great applause, because he anticipated from such a course no benefit to the cause of true religion; and as to Luther writing against him, in a worldly point of view nothing more fortunate could befall him. He proceeds to defend his moderation, which Luther had called in question, especially with regard to his answer to Hutten, and concludes with a prayer that Luther's mind may be directed to those counsels which are truly worthy of the Gospel.

This letter is dated May 8, 1524, but the treatise on Free-Will[34] did not appear till September. Erasmus had assured Henry VIII. that there was not a printer in Basle who would venture to print anything containing a single word against Luther; but it was published by Froben notwithstanding.

In this excellent little work Erasmus undertakes to defend the Catholic doctrine in its mildest form, and pleads eloquently for human responsibility, contending that, from the Apostles down, free-will had never been wholly denied, except by the Manichæans and Wickliff.

---

[33] *Er. Op.* iii. 803, B. *Roterod. Primum legito, deinde*
[34] *De Libero Arbitrio* ΔΙΑΤΡΙΒΗ, *judicato. Basiliæ, apud Joannem sive Collatio Desiderii Erasmi Frobennium, anno* 1524. *Sept.*

This point, however, he will not press, because he is aware that numbers are no argument, and that majorities are often wrong. Besides, his antagonist allows no appeal to the Fathers of the Church. He relies, therefore, chiefly upon Scripture, and upon its precepts, promises, and threats, which, he urges, would be quite unintelligible if it were true that all things happen through necessity. The opinion of the reformers seems to attribute cruelty and injustice to God. For, however difficult it may be to explain the inequalities of the present world, it is infinitely more difficult to explain why God should crown his own good deeds in some men with immortal glory, and in others punish with everlasting suffering the evil deeds which, on their hypothesis, equally originate in himself. To explain such paradoxes as these, they are obliged to resort to other still greater paradoxes. Thus, they exaggerate immensely the effects of original sin, by which they will have it that man's best gifts were so corrupted that it is impossible for him to love God, or even when justified by faith to do anything which is not a sin. No doubt their object is to magnify God's mercy; but if they enlarge it in one direction, they contract it in another. For, in the first place, they make God cruel in representing him as filled with wrath against the entire human race for one man's sin; and, secondly, in affirming that even those who are justified can do nothing but sin, they make God very parsimonious of his grace in that he gives no more ample justification. Throughout this treatise Erasmus speaks of Luther with marked respect, but indulges in some sharp and not undeserved hits at his followers. Thus, in reference to their pretence of special illumination, he remarks that, when the

Apostles made a similar claim, they worked miracles in support of it, but these men have never been able so much as to heal a lame horse. If, he adds, you require of them a life worthy of the Spirit, their answer is that they are saved by faith, not by works. Luther himself he excepts from the force of this sarcasm, and the gravest charge he brings against him is a fondness for hyperbole. Luther, he maintains, attempts to drive out one extravagance by another. If the Romanists made a sale of the merits of the Saints, Luther denies that they had any merits, and contends that all their deeds were sins deserving of eternal damnation. In the same way, some of the Catholic party made a profitable trade of confession and penances, and the doctrine of purgatory, with which they have wonderfully entangled the consciences of the people. The opposite party desire to correct this error by alleging that confession is a figment of Satan, and that there is no such thing as purgatory. The one party affirms that the rules of the most petty monasteries are binding under pain of the eternal fire ; the other alleges that all the constitutions of Popes, Councils, and Bishops are heretical and anti-Christian. The one maintains that the vows of monks and priests are perpetually binding ; the other that they are absolutely impious, and ought not to be kept even when they have been assumed. Such hyperboles, however, though they may be admissible in rhetoric, are scarcely to be tolerated in the exposition of Christian doctrine. The words in which he sums up his own views on the subject of discussion are sufficiently moderate and orthodox. "I approve," he says, "of those who ascribe something to Free-Will, but rely most upon Grace."

The work would appear to have satisfied the friends of Erasmus, who were convinced that he had done justice to himself as well as gained a victory over the enemies of the Church. It was praised by the King and Queen of England; and Henry pointed out to Vives a passage with which he was immensely delighted, in which a warning was uttered against prying too minutely into the mysteries of the Divine nature.[35] The Pope expressed his satisfaction, and promised to keep the author in mind; and one of the bitterest enemies of Erasmus, Albert, Prince of Carpi, wrote to him that he had not only refuted but annihilated Luther, and put him to shame, and that the only objection that could be made to his book was the excessive mildness shown to a raging heretic.[36] Even among the reformers the work produced a good impression, and, it is said, induced many of them to modify their views on the subject of predestination. Of this number, it is thought, was Melancthon himself.[37]

In a letter to Wolsey, accompanying the copies sent to himself and the King of England, Erasmus takes credit for his courage in publishing such a work in the present state of Germany, and claims to have done it in obedience to his own and the King's commands. He had determined, he adds, that the work should have no dedication, lest it should be said that he had written it for hire, to please his powerful patrons. Otherwise, it would have been inscribed either to Wolsey or to the Pope.[38]

Whether the Cardinal took the hint obviously contained in this letter, and sent him a handsome compen-

---

[35] *Er. Op.* iii. 899, E.
[36] MÜLLER, p. 322.
[37] *Er. Op.* iii. 854, A. JORTIN, i. 362.
[38] *Ep.* dcxcii.

sation for the risk to which he was exposing himself in defence of the true Church, does not appear; but Wolsey was never one of his most generous patrons.

At the same time he wrote to Aleander, now Archbishop of Brindisi, complaining of many ill-natured things which were said of him at Rome, and for some of which he thought Aleander himself was responsible. He did not, he said, consider it any disgrace that Aleander should be preferred to himself in everything, even in theology, any more than that he was richer and handsomer. "For me, it is glory enough even to be compared with you."[30]

Among those who had most strongly urged upon him the duty of taking up his pen against Luther, was Luther's great enemy, George, Duke of Saxony, who had assured him three years before that there was no other way in which he could free himself from suspicion of collusion with the reformers.

Writing to him, Erasmus now says he has not hitherto obeyed his highness's commands, for two principal reasons, "first, because I not only felt myself unfitted by my age and qualifications for this most perilous work, but also because I have naturally the greatest horror of such gladiatorial contests. Secondly, because I considered that Luther, whatever may be the worth of his doctrine, is a kind of necessary evil, in the present corrupt state of the Church, and I hoped that the effect of that bitter and violent remedy would be a return of good health to the body of the Christian people. Now, however, finding that many interpret my moderation as collusion with Luther, with whom I had never any secret agreement, and perceiving that

[30] *Ep.* dcxciii.

under the pretext of the Gospel there is growing up a new generation, rude, impudent, and intractable, whom Luther himself cannot endure, however much they may despise Luther, whom they treat with the same contumely that they do the Bishops and Princes, notwithstanding my advanced years I have descended into the arena. I send your highness the treatise on Free-Will, on which I long ago saw your very learned epistle. I had a further incentive in the letters of his most serene Majesty, the King of England, and of Clement VII., but by far the strongest motive was supplied by the rascality of certain ranters, who, if they are not stopped, are like to ruin both the Gospel and good letters. I wished the tyranny of the Pharisees to be abolished, not merely changed, but if we must be slaves, I would rather have the Popes and Bishops, such as they are, than those mean tyrants, who are more intolerable than them all." [40]

Two or three days after writing to Wolsey, he wrote to Henry himself, saying, "I expect stoning, and already some furious pamphlets have been flung at my head. But I shall console myself with the example of your Majesty, whose exalted station is no security against their insane violence." [41]

Copies of the tract on Free-Will were also sent to Warham, Tonstall, and Fisher. Here are the most characteristic passages of his letter to the last-named prelate.

ERASMUS *to* JOHN, *Bishop of Rochester.*[42]

"*Basle, September* 4, 1524.

"REVEREND BISHOP,—It was with great grief that I read this expression in your letter, 'I wish your book may

[40] *Ep.* dcxcv.   [41] *Ep.* dccii.   [42] *Ep.* dcxcviii.

find me alive.' My sorrow has been increased by the news brought by my servant, that you are suffering from ill-health. You give yourself no indulgence. I suspect that your ill-health arises in great measure from the situation of your palace: for I will now act the physician if you will allow me. The neighbourhood of the sea, and the shore every now and then laid bare when the tide recedes, gives a sharpness to the atmosphere. Then, your library has glass in all the walls, and this admits through the cracks a subtle and rarified air, to use the medical phrase, which is charged with pestilence to thin and weak people. Nor do I forget how constantly you are in your library, which in fact is your paradise; if I were to stay in such a place for three hours I should be unwell. A room with a wooden floor, and with the walls constructed of beams of wood, would suit you better; for bricks and lime give out a kind of noxious vapour. I know that death is not formidable to those who lead a pious life, but it concerns the whole Church that in such a dearth of good men, the life of such a Bishop should be spared. . . .

"You congratulate me on my triumphs. How I triumph, I know not; I certainly sustain a three-fold contest: with those Roman Pagans who are jealous of me; with certain theologians and monks, who are turning every stone to destroy me; and with some rabid Lutherans who roar at me, because I alone, they say, retard their triumph. I do so, because I do not choose, at the risk of my life, to profess the whole doctrine of Luther, in which there is much that I do not understand, much that I am in doubt about, much that, even if it were safe, on conscientious grounds I would not venture to profess. I could wish that the result of this disturbance, which Luther has stirred up, might be a return of health to the Church. And yet when I see the bad lives of some who never have the word 'Gospel' out of their mouths, my mind presages an unhappy and a bloody end. The Lutheran faction is increasing every day, and now extends to Savoy, Lorraine, Spain, and even Milan. Burgundy, next door to us, is thrown into confusion by one Farel, a Frenchman, who being driven from France, has come here; he is a ranter, and keeps neither tongue nor pen under any sort of restraint. . . ."

The publication of the tract against Luther gave Erasmus the opportunity of writing a letter to Melancthon, in which he states more fully than anywhere else his reasons for writing against Luther, and in which he by no means spares those whom he calls the pseudo-evangelicals. It is to the credit of his honesty that he speaks of them to the full as bitterly when writing to Wittenberg itself as if he were addressing one of the dignitaries of the Roman Church. "I know not," he says, "what sort of Church yours is, but I am sure there are in it men of such character that I fear they will turn the world upside down, and drive the authorities to use force, and put the good and the bad alike under restraint. They have 'the Gospel,' 'the word of God,' 'faith,' 'Christ,' and 'the Spirit' continually upon their lips, but if you look at their lives they speak quite a different sort of language. It is for this that we are dethroning our masters, the Popes and Bishops, that we may submit to more merciless tyrants, to such madmen as Otto and Farel." He even accuses Capito of dissimulation, and discovers in Œcolampadius a want of perfect sincerity. "How seditiously Zwingle is acting, to say nothing of the rest! They do not assent to you, nor agree with one another, and yet they require us to rebel against all the orthodox Fathers and Councils, in reliance on their authority! You say that they are in error who reject images as an impiety, but what disturbances Zwingle has stirred up about images! You teach that dress is perfectly indifferent; several here are teaching that the cowl must be altogether given up. You maintain that Bishops and Episcopal constitutions may be submitted to, save where they lead to impiety; they say they are all impious and anti-Christian." After complaining of the attacks made upon himself by some of the more violent of the reform party, he asks, "How can I believe that these men are led by the Spirit of Christ, whose lives are so much at variance with the teaching of Christ? Once the Gospel turned ferocity into meekness, rapacity into kindness, turbulence into peace, cursing into blessing; these men are made mad, they rob and steal, they stir up tumults everywhere, they curse even those who do them good. I see new hypocrites and new tyrants, but not the least spark of the Gospel spirit." He then explains why he had written the tract on Free-Will. The monks had persuaded every one that he was in close confederacy with Luther, and his friends, seeing the danger he would be in if so damaging a charge were to go unchallenged, had on the contrary given currency to the report that he would write against Luther. This expectation he had himself encouraged, and now, had he not published his treatise, he would have put it in the power of his enemies to charge him with cowardice; and rabid evangelicals would have fancied that the suppressed work was far more violent than the actual one, while the sovereigns who expected from him this service to the cause of the Church would have had their worst suspicions confirmed. Moreover, Luther's letter, now published, in which he promised not to write against Erasmus, on condition that he also would be silent, made silence no longer possible. At the same time, all that he had written was quite in accordance with his real sentiments, which, however, he was ready to abandon as soon as he was convinced that they were erroneous.

The reply of Melancthon to this letter was as gentle as his own spirit. "It is not without reason, my dear Erasmus, that you complain of the manners of those who profess the Gospel at this time. . . . . Luther, however, bears no resemblance to those men, and often deplores that private passions lurk under the cloak of religion; but as he holds that these scandals are caused by the devil for the destruction of the Gospel, he thinks that he ought not on their account to retract, or abandon the public cause." He finds fault with Erasmus, however, for judging of the cause itself by the vices of some of its unworthy defenders, and points out that, although he dissents from Luther on the question of free-will, he agrees with him on the far more important question of the value of ceremonies. Very justly, also, he takes him to task for classing such a man as Œcolampadius and some others like him with the low scoundrels who disgrace the cause of the Gospel. He ends by assuring him that the treatise on Free-Will has been received in a most friendly spirit. "Your moderation has given us much satisfaction, although you have certainly sprinkled your pages with plenty of black salt."[43]

The answer of Luther was delayed somewhat more

[43] *Ep.* dcciv.

than a year. He had promised, through Melancthon, that he would reply with the same moderation with which Erasmus had written, but the latter begged that he would write in his usual style, as otherwise collusion would be suspected. Luther perhaps wished to be moderate, and distrusted himself; at any rate, he does not appear to have entered on his task with eagerness. "I can't tell you," he wrote to Spalatin, "how I loathe the 'Treatise on Free-Will;' I have not yet read more than a few pages of it. It is unpleasant to me to have to reply to so unlearned a book by so learned a man." Besides, he had other work on hand. "I shall not answer Erasmus," he told Amsdorf, "until I have finished off Carlstadt, who has excited a strange disturbance in Upper Germany."[44] In December of the following year, 1525, the answer at length appeared under a title which sufficiently indicates its purport, and which may be rendered, "Man's Will not Free."[45] The book proved that Erasmus had neither misunderstood nor misrepresented the doctrine of Luther. He here asserts, in the most unqualified manner, the absolute dependence of man for good or for evil upon the Divine will. That God's foreknowledge is not contingent but absolute—that was the single thunderbolt with which he undertook to scatter to the winds all the arguments of his antagonist. Nor does he, for one moment, shrink from the apparent practical consequences of his doctrine. Erasmus had asked, If men be satisfied that all their actions are necessary, who will take the trouble to amend his life? Luther's answer was distinct and emphatic:—

[44] MELCHIOR ADAM, *Vit. Luth.* In the letter to Spalatin for "Molestum est tam erudito libro respondere tam eraditi viri," we ought, no doubt, as Jortin conjectures (vol. i. p. 359, note), to read "Molestum est tam *inerudito*," &c.

[45] *De Servo Arbitrio.*

"*No one* will amend his life; the elect will have theirs amended for them; the non-elect must perish in their misery." If the doctrine that all human actions, evil as well as good, proceed from God, was a hard saying, Luther avoided the seeming impiety by the following argument:—As God, he contends, moves and works in all beings, it necessarily follows that he moves and works even in Satan and the wicked. But as he does so without changing their nature, of course the bad are driven to do evil, by the same divine impulse by which the virtuous are prompted to do well. A man driving a lame horse proceeds exactly in the same manner as he who drives a sound one, and yet the horse goes badly; and so God, although incapable of doing evil, yet does evil deeds through wicked men whom he uses as his instruments. The illustration, if not quite reverent, is at least ingenious, but it need scarcely be said it does not reach the bottom of the problem of evil. It must be regretted that the great reformer did not, in this treatise, preserve the moderate, courteous tone of which his antagonist had set him the example, and which it seems he himself wished to maintain. But moderation was a virtue with which Luther's nature had no affinity, and which perhaps would not have been of advantage to his cause. And although he did not upon this occasion permit himself to fall into mere railing, he did not hesitate to charge his opponent with ignorance, and even to apply to parts of his work such words as impious and sacrilegious. No doubt he was more deeply in earnest than his antagonist, and it is impossible not to admire the noble rebuke with which he met the complaint of Erasmus that the discussion of such questions as that of free-will was likely to bring confusion and discord upon the world. The latter had treated the

question very much as a matter of speculative interest, as a subject on which learned men must agree to differ, and in regard to which the evidence on either side was pretty equally balanced. He had, in fact, taken up in respect to this question very much the same position as is generally assumed towards what they may consider dangerous opinions by modern clergymen, who are wont to urge that if a man is unhappy enough to hold views of which they disapprove, he is bound in common decency to keep them to himself. He had gone so far as to say that even if Luther's doctrine were true, it was nevertheless so dangerous that it ought to be concealed, certainly not discussed in the vulgar tongue and in presence of the multitude. And to this Luther indignantly replied:—
"I tell you, and I pray you lay it well to heart, that to me this matter is serious, necessary, and eternal; of such momentous interest that it must be asserted and defended at the risk of life itself—ay, though the result should be not only to plunge the world in conflict, but to bring chaos back again and annihilate the universe!"

Erasmus, however, had much to urge in self-justification. Luther's treatise called forth a lengthened rejoinder, which was chiefly taken up with the defence of this very position. There he completely clears himself of the reproach of indifference to the truth. The great central doctrines of the Church he declares he is ready to defend, if need be, with his life. But there are many minor points—for example, Whether God creates all things through necessity, Why the derivation of the Son from the Father is called generation, and that of the Holy Spirit procession, and so on—which he thinks theologians may very usefully debate among themselves, but which ought not to be broached before the multitude. And of the number of those questions are such points relating to free will as the Church has left undecided. In this treatise, which was published in two books in the years 1526, 1527, and which he called *Hyperaspistes*,[a] Erasmus takes Luther severely to task for his treatment of him. His expressions of respect he regards as hypocrisy, nor does he thank him for ascribing to him the greatest eloquence, when he at the same time accuses him of impiety. The object of this intermingling of praise with abuse, he thinks, was to increase the odium which already attached to his name, and convey the impression that, while secretly sympathising with the reformers, he concealed his real sentiments through fear or worldliness; and so he compares Luther's treatise to a cup whose honied edge deceives the eye and tempts the lip, while its contents are charged with deadly poison. That this accusation, so far as it implied deliberate malice, was unfounded, may readily be admitted; but it cannot be denied that Luther wrote with too much of that affectation of being animated by the deepest love in the infliction of the severest wounds, with too much of that assumption of superiority, if not in human at least in heavenly graces, which have usually been characteristic of those who in more recent times represent his opinions. The following sentence, for example, has the true evangelical ring:—" Who knows, most worthy Erasmus, but God may condescend to visit you, through me, his miserable and frail vessel, that in a happy hour I may come to you with this book of mine, and gain my dearest brother."

After the publication of the *Hyperaspistes*, "my dearest brother" became "that enraged viper, Erasmus of Rotterdam, the vainest creature in the world."

[a] *Desiderii Erasmi Hyperaspistes Diatribæ adversus Servum Arbitrium Martini Lutheri.*—*Er. Op.* x. 1249.

CHAPTER XVI.

Erasmus attacked on both Sides—Bedda—Louis de Berquin—Persecuted by the Sorbonne—Warned by Erasmus—Thrown into Prison — His Sentence — And Execution — Correspondence between Erasmus and Bedda — Reply to Sutor—Erasmus addresses the Sorbonne—Answers Bedda—Appeals to Francis I.—The "Familiar Colloquies" condemned—Erasmus's Declarations—Bedda makes the amende honorable—The Prince of Carpi—His attack on Erasmus—Reply — The Prince's Death — The Spanish Monks — Erasmus accused of Heresy — His Defence — Letter to Fonseca—Erasmus's farewell to his Persecutors.

HAVING thus called down on his head the wrath of the Lutherans, Erasmus now found himself fairly between two fires. To borrow his own expression, he was pelted on both sides. He was assailed with threats, with calumnies, with furious pamphlets and vile caricatures. Even his person, he fancied, would scarcely have been safe, had it not been for the protection of the Bishop and the magistrates of Basle. The Papists ascribed to him all the evils of the time. In the latter part of the year 1524 the great peasant insurrection broke out, swept like a torrent through Germany, and for a time threatened universal revolution. The monasteries were plundered, the images torn from the churches, the castles of the nobles set on fire, community of goods and equality of rank proclaimed: deeds of great cruelty were perpetrated and torrents of blood shed. All these things, which Erasmus regarded as the natural fruit of Luther's revolt against the Papacy, were laid at his own door by the monks. It was he, they cried, who laid the egg which Luther had hatched, and it was in vain that he replied that he had laid a hen's egg, while Luther had brought out a very different sort of bird. On the other hand, the Lutherans complained that it was altogether owing to his cowardice that their cause was not long since triumphant. Thus it was that while in Brabant and Italy he passed for a Lutheran, in Germany and Switzerland he was *Anti-Lutheranissimus*.[1]

He was still in the thick of his controversy with Luther and the evangelicals when he was called on to bear the brunt of an attack from the opposite side much more formidable than any which had yet been made upon him. Hitherto neither the Pope nor any recognized authority,—in fact, no one but a few spiteful monks, provoked by his gibes at their hypocrisy and superstition,—had accused him of heresy or condemned anything he had written. Now, however, in the year 1526, the University of Paris was roused to pass a severe censure on the "Paraphrases," many propositions in which were declared to be heretical and impious, and especially to condemn and prohibit the "Familiar Colloquies." We must now briefly follow the steps which led to this result.

The principal actor in this "tragedy," as Erasmus calls all these disturbances, was Noel Bedier, or Bedda, the syndic of the Sorbonne, an ignorant and narrow-minded fanatic, wedded to scholasticism, a bitter enemy of all generous culture, a bigoted Catholic and a most determined heresy-hunter, of whom Erasmus, who knew

[1] *Ep.* dccxix. dccxlii, and *passim.*

him well, said that in Bedda alone there are three thousand monks.[1] This man, in concert with his colleague Duchesne, had, as early as 1521, procured a decree from the University of Paris that Luther's books should be burned. They had next turned their attention to the signs of reform which were visible in France itself, and which, considering the high places in which they appeared, the Court itself, under the influence of Margaret of Valois, the King's sister, being infected with the new principles, might well have seemed to prognosticate the greatest danger to the Church. Conspicuous among the objects of their persecution was a gentleman of Artois, Louis de Berquin, a councillor and high in the King's favour, in whose fortunes Erasmus must have taken a special interest, seeing that his chief crime consisted in translating into French some of his own works, and that the heresies of which he was accused were unquestionably learned, not from the monk of Wittenberg, but from the scholar of Rotterdam. Berquin, according to the latter, who has left us a picture of his character, was an unmarried man, but of so pure a life that there was never so much as a whisper against his chastity, remarkable for his singular kindness to the poor, and most observant of the rites and ceremonies of the Church, of her fasts, holy days and masses, and whatever else was believed in those days to be a part of true piety. He had no sympathy with the doctrines of Luther, and his real offence was that he had spoken too freely of "certain sour theologians and monks whose ferocity was equalled

---

[1] *Er. Op.* iii. 1066, B. Erasmus had known Bedda during his residence in Paris, when a young man, and speaks of him in some of his letters as "Natalis Theologus."—*Ep.* xxxvii., lliii.

only by their stupidity." In a book which he had published there occurred such sentiments as these, that in sermons the Virgin Mother ought not to be invoked instead of the Holy Spirit, nor was it right to call her the "fountain of all grace," and that at even-song she should not be called, contrary to the custom of the Scriptures, "our hope and life," seeing that these epithets rather belong to the Son; and on such frivolous charges as these,[3] he was thrown into prison and was in danger of life for heresy. Being set at liberty by the interference of the King, who was indignant at this treatment of an officer of his court—this happened on the 8th of August, 1523—he was tried by the King's council and acquitted. The accusers alleged that the judgment was inspired by fear of the King's displeasure, but Berquin not unnaturally regarded himself as lawfully victor in the conflict, and immediately wrote a tract to celebrate his triumph. It was at this juncture that he first became known to Erasmus, with whom he entered into correspondence, and who at once conceived a high opinion of his character. He, however, gave him the sensible advice not to stir up a nest of hornets by publishing his panegyric on himself, but to pursue his studies in peace. "And pray do not," he added, "mix me up with your affairs; for that would be of no advantage to either of us."[4] His advice was thrown away. Meantime several tracts appeared, including translations into French of some of the works of Erasmus, which were suspected or known to be Berquin's. The "Praise of Marriage," the "Complaint

[3] "Ob hujusmodi nænias."—*Er. Op.* iii. 1208, A.
[4] "Deinde, ne me involveret suæ causæ, quod utrique nostrûm foret incommodum."—*Ib.* 1208, B.

of Peace," and two short pieces on the Lord's Prayer
and the Creed, were the works which Berquin thus
made accessible to every monk, however ignorant, to
every clown who could read his native tongue, but with
them the author tells us his translator had mixed some
remarks of his own.[5] That this proceeding of Berquin's
should have roused the monks to still greater fury,
considering how severely they and their superstitious
practices were handled in these works, need not surprise
us; but Erasmus, anxious to save his character for
orthodoxy, gives an explanation of the matter which
puts it in quite another light. The monks, he says, had
been accustomed to proclaim, in their sermons, their
conversations and over their cups, wherever they went
by land or by water, at every cobbler's stall, in every
weaver's shop, and in the confessional itself, that
Erasmus was a far more pestilent heretic than Luther,
and they had succeeded in convincing many fools,
many old men, and many women, of the truth of what
they affirmed. But now that the works on which they
pretended to base these charges were translated into the
vulgar tongue, they were afraid that these calumnies
would be exposed, and themselves convicted of malice
and falsehood.[6] According to this view the monks
were enraged, not because the works of Erasmus were
pestilent and heretical, but because they were not so;
but if this was not an after-thought, he ought, surely, to
have been grateful to Berquin for the service he was
rendering him. Instead of that, he proceeded to
remonstrate with him still more strongly than before,

---

[5] "Prorepserunt interim libelli clam excusi, quibus ex meis versis interjecerat sua quædam." *Ib.* 1208, C. No doubt the translation was sufficiently free to justify this remark.

[6] *Er. Op.* iii. 1014, C, D.

assuring him that by these translations he would do no good to the cause of religion, and again begging him, if he was determined to engage in conflict with the monks, not to involve his friend, who had already so much odium to bear on his own account; but to these expostulations Berquin only replied that the surest way to relieve him of that odium was to popularise his works and thus prove the supreme wickedness and folly of the monks. For some time Berquin was now permitted to go on his way in peace, his enemies not daring to renew their attack on a man who stood so high in the royal favour; but after the disastrous battle of Pavia, where the French King was made the Emperor's prisoner and carried into captivity to Spain, they recovered their courage, found new articles against him, and once more threw him into prison. His books were condemned to be burned, he himself was required to retract his errors or else he must go to the stake. Berquin nobly refused to yield on a single point, and would have been put to death immediately, had not the parliament, at the instigation, it was supposed, of the King's mother, interfered by declaring that they desired to go over the whole case once more from the beginning. Meantime Francis, who had now returned from Spain, was informed of the state of affairs, and without a moment's delay sent word to the parliament to take care what they were about, as he would certainly require Berquin's life at their hands. Thereupon he was removed from prison to a comfortable apartment, in which, however, he was still kept for some time in custody. At last he was for the second time restored to liberty, on the plea that he might have greater facilities for preparing his defence.

Berquin might now have escaped his doom had he acted with moderation and prudence; but instead of this he became more confident than ever, boasted loudly of his victory, and actually turned the tables on the Sorbonne by accusing them of impiety. It was in vain that Erasmus warned him that such an offence could never be forgiven, in vain that he begged him to leave the country under pretence of an embassage, which he might easily procure through the influence of his friends. He assured him that if he had a better cause than Christ himself the monks would never rest till they destroyed him, and advised him not to place too much confidence in the King's favour, which was necessarily only temporary and liable to be influenced by the whispers of calumny. These warnings seemed to have no effect on Berquin except to make him more bold. He broke out with unbridled licence against the monks and theologians, and especially the Syndic Bedda, and his influence was sufficient to procure from the King a letter requiring the Faculty to condemn twelve articles in the works of the latter charged with impiety and blasphemy, or else to prove them by warrant of Holy Scripture. The Sorbonne, however, was not thus to be cheated of its prey. Hounded on by Bedda they pursued the unfortunate man to his death. Berquin seems to have imagined that Erasmus might now have interfered with effect to render his victory secure, and he used every persuasion to induce him to do so, but on his pointing out how impossible this was, and once more urging him to fly from the country, he began to write to him more coldly and less frequently than before. At last the catastrophe which Erasmus had foreseen arrived. Berquin's case was delegated to twelve judges, and as the day of trial approached, if trial indeed it could be called, he was thrown into prison—an evil omen of what was to follow. His sentence was to abjure the condemned articles in his works, to have his tongue bored through with a red-hot iron, and afterwards to be imprisoned for life. On hearing this unexpectedly atrocious sentence, he appealed to the King and the Pope, whereupon the judges informed him that if he would not submit they would soon put it out of his power to appeal; and the next day they condemned him to the flames. Berquin submitted to his fate with heroic fortitude, neither in his countenance nor his gesture betraying the least apprehension, while his whole bearing indicated a conscience at peace with itself. Before his death he addressed the people, but the six hundred soldiers who were assembled to prevent any outbreak made such a clatter with their arms that it was impossible to hear him. The multitude, it seems, had been carefully instructed as to the deadly nature of his crime, for when the fire was kindled no one ventured to call out the name of Jesus, which was customary even in cases of murder and sacrilege. A Franciscan friar who was close by was asked whether he had acknowledged his error before his death, and affirmed that he had, adding that he had no doubt his soul had passed into rest; but Erasmus, who records these particulars, gave no credit to the Franciscan, especially as it was customary to spread such reports for the honour of the true faith, and to deceive the multitude.

It is difficult to see how Erasmus could have done anything to avert the fate of this learned and brave, but somewhat imprudent, nobleman. The King of France was certainly more powerful than even the illustrious monarch of letters, and he, after twice rescuing his favourite from the rage of the monks, was at length compelled to give way. He could at best only have made himself responsible for the heresies charged upon his friend, and this would have exasperated rather than mollified the wrath of Bedda and his compeers. It is clear that Berquin courted his doom, and what, asks Erasmus, can you do for a man who is resolved to bring destruction on himself? Still one could wish that he had expressed his disapprobation of the horrible wickedness of his sentence a little more warmly, and that he had more plainly acknowledged that if Berquin's fate was deserved, he himself had no right to live. "I offer no opinion on the justice of his sentence," he cautiously observes, and no doubt he spoke within the letter of the truth, "because the grounds of it are quite unknown to me. If he did not deserve his punishment I am sorry for his fate; but if he deserved it I am doubly sorry, for it is better to die innocent than guilty."[7]

It was on the 22nd of April, in the year 1529, that Berquin was executed, so that I have somewhat anticipated by recording it here, but it seemed natural to follow his story without interruption to its melancholy end.

In the meantime, the attempt made by the unfortunate nobleman to popularise in France some of the most daring of the writings of Erasmus, must have greatly stimulated the fury of the monks against the alleged author of all the heresies of the day. What a triumph, too, it would be for the enemies of light if the great and influential University of Paris could be induced to condemn and humiliate the proud scholar whom Kings honoured and even Popes had acknowledged. Francis I.

[7] *Ep.* mlx.

had been known to say that those divines who were bold enough to attack any one, had yet never had the courage to lay hands on Erasmus,[a] and was it worthy of those who feared neither Pope nor King to decline such a challenge? Bedda had long had his eyes fixed in the direction of Basle. He was neither a scholar nor much given to study, for which, indeed, his life of bustling intrigue must have left him little time, but like the rest he probably knew when he was hurt, and there was no reason why he should not scent a heresy as well as another. With the punctilious exactness in little things which marks a small mind, or which was perhaps acquired under monastic training, Bedda has noted the precise moment at which he began to read the "Paraphrase of St. Luke." It was on Sunday, the 10th of January, 1523, at four o'clock in the afternoon. He noted several errors in it, but either his work must have progressed very slowly, or he may have thought the time was not yet come for an open attack,—in fact he was shortly afterwards, as we have seen, wholly occupied with the persecution of Berquin,—for it was not for more than two years that Erasmus obtained a copy of the notes. They were not then forwarded by Bedda himself, but were procured with some difficulty through a friend, Francis Deloinus, the late President of the Parliament of Paris. Erasmus thereupon wrote to Bedda thanking him for his diligence, and begging that he would do the same thing for the rest of his "Paraphrases," and especially for his "Annotations on the New Testament," of which he was just then preparing the fourth edition. Several learned men, Atensis, Latomus, Fisher, Bishop of Rochester, had been

[a] *Er. Op.* iii. 1713, F.

entreated to point out the faults of this work, but had given it nothing but praise. Still, if Bedda would take the trouble of indicating any passages which could justly give offence to learned and good men, he would put him under a lasting obligation.

In the course of this letter, perhaps as a gentle hint to the Syndic in what spirit he should enter on the task proposed, if, indeed, he ventured to engage in it, Erasmus refers to a book against him which had just appeared in Paris, probably not without the connivance of Bedda himself, by one Lecouturier, a Carthusian friar, formerly a doctor of the Sorbonne, whose Latin name, Sutor, inevitably suggests the proverb, "*Ne sutor ultra crepidam.*" The book, he says, is filled with abuse, and is a monument of incredible presumption and ignorance. "What will be said by men of sober judgment, and there are more than can be counted everywhere who have no dislike for Erasmus, when they see such books issuing from the Sorbonne? I am aware, indeed, that all the really learned men of your order must disapprove of it; but, meantime, sound theologians are brought into contempt by the folly of a few."[9]

Bedda answered Erasmus in a hypocritical letter, dated May 21, 1525, in execrable Latin, in which he my-dearest-brothered him with all the unctuous affection of evangelical piety, and besought him to accept the advice of "the poor Bedda" in the spirit in which he gave it, assuring him that he desired only his soul's salvation. His advice was this. In the first place, it was perilously suspicious that he should thus go on, without intermission, writing new books which were not necessary to the Church; for the future, then, let him

[9] *Ep.* dccxli.

abstain from any further publications, and, content with the fame he has already acquired, prepare himself for the judgments of God, which cannot now be far off. Secondly, let him follow the example of his patron Saint Augustine, by carefully reviewing his works, and striking out from them whatever may conflict with good morals or sound faith. There are many things in his writings, Bedda continues, which have given great scandal to Christian people, especially on the celibacy of the clergy, the vows of the monks, fasts, feasts, evangelical councils, translating the Scriptures into the vulgar tongue, human laws and canonical hours, divorce, the creeds of the Church, and many similar questions. Finally, he informs him that his " Praise of Marriage " and some other works, translated into French, as was suspected by Louis de Berquin, had been presented to the Sorbonne to determine whether they were fit for publication, and that when the commissioners, according to custom, read aloud before the Faculty the passages they considered unsound, all were mute with astonishment, showing how much they disapproved of his doctrines. If, however, he would follow the advice of Bedda, it would yet be well with him.[10]

This epistle called forth from Erasmus a long rejoinder, written in studiously civil language, but full of that ironical humour of which he was such a master. Although, he said, he was in receipt of letters which made unfavourable mention of Bedda, yet he had never ceased to regard him both as a sound theologian and a good man. Bedda, on the other hand, by addressing him as brother-priest, seemed to withhold from him the title of brother-theologian, which he thought a little

[10] *Ep.* cccxxxii. App.

hard, seeing that neither Leo nor Clement, nor even Adrian, who was himself unquestionably a great theologian, had refused him that title. If, indeed, the name theologian implied great learning, he had certainly no pretensions to it; but, on the same principles, the name priest would imply great piety, and to that he had even less pretension, although more anxious to be pious than learned. Bedda seemed to think that he was one of those who have a passion for worldly fame. There may, he admits, be some vestiges of that infirmity in his character, and he confesses that he did derive a certain amount of pleasure from the praises which used to be heaped upon him, when he was called the Prince of Letters, the Star of Germany, and so on; but as he bore his honours meekly, so he is not greatly lessened in his own eyes now that he is once more plain Erasmus. To the recommendation of his correspondent that he should read Gerson and other such writers, in order that he might appear vile in his own eyes, he answered that he had read some of Gerson's works when he was a young man, and had liked them very well, but the more he read of the scholastic writers the more highly did he think of himself, and he found no book so well adapted to humble his pride as the writings of the Evangelists and the Apostles. Bedda is mistaken in supposing that he has not time to devote himself to the things that make for true piety because he writes so much; this might, indeed, be difficult for Bedda, who is not accustomed to it; but to him it is an easy matter after his long practice, and for some years past he has been preparing seriously and with all his heart for that day which his advanced years and failing health assure him cannot be far distant.

He then enters into a long defence of his labours on the New Testament, showing how willing he had ever been to accept advice.

As to Berquin, he knew him only by his letters; but from these he judged him to be a modest and sensible man. He had, however, constantly advised him to keep clear of strife and contention.

He then proceeds to denounce the theologians, or rather those who disgraced theology, in language which Bedda might, no doubt with great justice, have applied to himself. It is most true that the name of theologian is everywhere becoming disreputable; "and I am afraid, most excellent Bedda," he continues, "that if you are not careful, you and your friends may soon sink as low as the theologians of Germany, whose authority in these times is such that, if they find fault with anything, their condemnation is itself a sufficient recommendation." Look at Standish. Look at Egmund. Look at Sutor. "What would not the man do who corrupted my 'Colloquies,' and added a preface of his own with my name attached? And these things are done in the University of Paris, where it is not lawful to print the Paraphrases of Erasmus. . . . Sutor's book is printed with your approval, unless the title-page lies. . . . Do you suppose that such books do not concern the honour of the University? . . . Nor am I ignorant what virulent abuse some of your fraternity have been launching against me this long time; I need not mention their names, which must be well known to you, as, indeed, they are known to far too many. . . . For there are not a few, particularly among those of advanced years, whom nothing can please which savours in the least of polite literature, or which differs from what they learned in their childhood, and who do not consider that the world is turning round, and that we must accommodate ourselves to its revolutions. There are some men, sour by nature and without any great ability, on account of their poverty possessing no good books nor time to study them, and having learned nothing but what is taught in the schools, and taught very badly, as you know is generally the case, who pass at once from the hair-splitting discussions of the University to the head of a school of boys, among whom they grow old and over whom they domineer, ordering what they please by their mere nod, and terrifying with threats those who will not obey. As no one resists them, they think whatever accords with their own wishes must be right, and these manners they carry with them into public life, being complete strangers to all civility and almost wholly devoid of even common sense, imagining that they are always among children, and regarding all mankind in the light of their pupils. When such men assume the office of critic, and find their prejudices touched, what will they ever approve of, especially considering there are so many excuses for fault-finding?—this is derogatory to the honour of the saints, that is disrespectful to our masters, this is contrary to a laudable custom, that savours of the heresy of the Waldensians, the other approximates the error of the poor men of Leyden."

Returning to Sutor, Erasmus asks Bedda why he has not given him some of the advice which he so freely lavishes on himself. "I thank you," he says, "for what you do for me, but I am surprised that you feel no concern for him. I write books which you say do no good to the Church, and without such books as Sutor writes, would the house of God fall? You are afraid that

I may not have time to attend to heavenly things, but those who write thus are lifted up to the third heaven."

As to leaving off writing, he would be following his own wishes if he were to do so, his years and failing health now requiring that he should rest from his labours, but Bedda was the only person who had ever given him such advice. On the other hand, he was entreated by many learned and eminent men to persevere in this course. It was only lately he had received a letter from the King of England, earnestly entreating him to write something on the Psalms, and another from the Queen requesting a work on marriage. More than once he had been called on by Pope Clement, and frequently by Cardinal Campeggio, to continue his services to literature. The Bishop of Rochester was entreating him for a work on the art of preaching, and the late Pope Adrian, while still a Cardinal, had begged him to do for the Old Testament what he had already done for the New. Highly as he esteemed Bedda, he was sure he would not expect him to place his judgment before that of so many learned and distinguished people. He then thanks Bedda for pointing out the passages in his works in which he thinks he has expressed dangerous opinions, but adds that he has not yet been informed where the offence lies. "Certainly when I read them over again I find nothing to regret, even though death should be staring me in the face, so may God love me." After pointing out the injustice of judging him from translations of his works, when the originals are accessible, and further defending the works translated, he concludes by assuring Bedda that he cannot offend him by any freedom he may use in giving his advice.[11]

[11] *Ep.* dccxlvi.

This letter is dated the 15th of June, 1525. Later in the year, Erasmus wrote his "Reply to the Ravings of Sutor."[12] By his account Sutor's book was a strange mixture of ignorance, folly, and presumption; it was written in something even worse than monkish Latin, and contained offences against grammar which not only the flogging Orbilius of Horace, but the meekest dominie that ever plied the ferule would have visited with stripes. Its sole motive was vanity. While Sutor was a Doctor of the Sorbonne he had no time to read the Scriptures, nor even Peter Lombard; but having more leisure as a Carthusian, he read the two Testaments and some of the Fathers, not, however, straight through, but here and there according as a passage might be cited by Erasmus, or by Lee, or Stunica. On this principle he constructed his calumnious volume, stringing together materials which were supplied by others, and hoping that as Lee and others before unknown to fame had become suddenly notorious, he too might gain celebrity on the like easy terms. His attack embraced three points. The first was the Version of the New Testament. Sutor assumed that Jerome translated the Old and New Testaments by special inspiration of the Holy Spirit, such as the evangelists and prophets enjoyed; that the edition now used by the Latin Church is Jerome's, and that to doubt whether there is any error in it, or anything that needs change, is heresy or blasphemy. The Church, he seemed to think, would fall and everything go to ruin if a single word was altered in the Vulgate, or a doubt thrown on its infallible correctness; quite ignoring the fact that the

---

[12] *Apologia adversus Debacchationes Sutoris* — Er. *Op.* ix. 739. The letter to Selva, President of the Parliament of Paris, which accompanied the work, is dated August 25, 1525.—*Ep.* dccliv.

Version of Erasmus had been so many years before the public, and had received the sanction of the highest authorities. The second point was languages and literature, which Sutor referred to diabolical origin. A knowledge of languages, he maintained, was utterly unnecessary to the understanding of the Holy Scriptures, and to desire to know Greek or Hebrew for this purpose was insane and heretical. The third was the question of translating the Scriptures into the vulgar tongue. Here, again, this fanatical monk saw the seeds of ruin to the true faith. On all these points Erasmus answered him at great length. He afterwards regretted that he had taken the trouble of replying to so contemptible a production, but said he was urged to it by his friends. It is unfortunate that he so far lost his temper, or forgot his manners, as to speak of Sutor's "rotten brains."

The reply was dedicated to the President of the Parliament of Paris, to whom he appealed for protection in the absence of Francis I. This, however, did not prevent Sutor returning to the charge in another pamphlet even more scurrilous than the first. Of this, also, Erasmus vouchsafed a brief notice,[13] in which he said that he never regretted anything so much as having replied to Sutor's former book, and had no intention of answering this one, of which he had read only a few pages.

He continued for some time to correspond with the Syndic, always preserving the same courteous tone, and professing his willingness to be corrected, until at length there reached him certain criticisms for which Bedda

---

[13] *Desiderii Erasmi Appendix respondens ad quædam Antapologiæ Petri Sutoris.—Er. Op.* ix. 807.

and Duchesne made themselves responsible, and which undertook to prove that the doctrine of Erasmus, where it treated of the Scriptures or of theology, was in many respects erroneous, schismatic, and contrary to good morals.[14] These, as was apparent from their date, had been in circulation for a considerable time without his knowledge, and bearing the names of two such prominent men, there was great reason to fear lest they might be understood to convey the judgment of the University; so that it now became clear that Bedda's object was not to convince him of his errors in a charitable spirit, but to stir up feeling against him by calumnies and falsehoods, and thus if possible secure a public censure. At once, therefore, on the 6th of February, 1526, he addressed himself to the Faculty of Theology, complaining of the treatment he had received, and at the same time sending his "Guesses in Answer to Bedda's Notes,"[15] so called because it was often extremely difficult to see exactly in what the alleged error consisted. Duchesne had in the meantime "gone to his own place," so that it is only with his surviving adversary that he has now to deal. Of him he here observes that "he is, in my opinion, a good man, but even good men have their failings; they are apt to over-estimate their own pursuits, and to undervalue those of others; they are too ready to yield to suggestions from without, too willing to listen to false reports. In short, even good men are human.

[14] "Quæstionis propositio. Jesus Maria B. Si phalerata Erasmi doctrina comprobatur sana, catholica, atque religiosa, si religiosis viris licita, salutifera, ac amplectenda sit absque ullo discrimine, et si nullum lucidæ hæresis hujusce tempestatis virus sub mellis ornatu lateat." Responsio N. Beddæ, Gymnas'i Montis-acuti Primarii. April 7, 1524.—*Er. Op.* ix. 451.

[15] *Desiderii Erasmi Divinationes ad notata per Beddam.*—*Er. Op.* ix. 453.

At all events, he honestly professes a deadly hatred of languages and polite literature, and that may perhaps be the reason that he is a somewhat hard censor of my works. Of myself I will say nothing, except that when I wrote those works I was perfectly sincere, and desirous of promoting Christian piety. Therefore, if there is any error in them, it has proceeded either from ignorance or want of care."[16]

The errors charged upon Erasmus were found chiefly in his "Paraphrases," to which, however, were added some from his other works, and especially from his tract addressed to the Bishop of Basle on the prohibition of flesh-meat, and consisted of such propositions, inuendoes, and implications as, however true and useful they might be in themselves, could not fail to offend the monkish piety of the sixteenth century. Such were his statements that "all the epistles which are ascribed to Paul cannot be said to be incontrovertibly his," that "there are some passages in the Gospels which in his opinion are inexplicable," that "the Scriptures ought to be read by clowns and mechanics, and even by the Turks," that "the Scriptures should be translated into all tongues;" his doubt whether the creed called the Apostles' really came from the Apostles; his assertion that Christ alone was free from all stain of sin,—a proposition which denied the immaculate conception of the Virgin so stoutly maintained by the Scotists. Bedda found errors even in such apparently innocent and incontrovertible propositions as that "the Gospel condemns all oaths, execrations, and whatsoever binds the promiser by fear," or that "the Law merely forbids us to kill, while Jesus commanded that we should not even be angry with our

[16] *Er. Op.* ix. 451.

brother." He was offended because Erasmus had spoken of "the foreign ring" of Paul's style; and even the opinions which he quoted from others were ascribed to him as errors. Thus he had not said on his own authority that the Dionysius who described the ancient rites of the Church was later than Dionysius the Areopagite, but merely that this was the opinion of the learned. If he had said that "scruples about meats may make a man superstitious but by no means pious," it was St. Paul, and not Erasmus, who was responsible for the sentiment. If he had said, as in following Paul he could not help saying, that "the benefits of Christ are bestowed on faith alone, not on merits," this was far from implying that he agreed with Luther that there could be no such thing as merit. If he had said that "belief is the only path to immortality," this no more excluded the good works which faith produces or carries with it than the proposition that "the young lady went in alone" would imply that her dress and ornaments remained outside. It was easy for Erasmus, with his great learning, to show that in none of these propositions had he really violated the orthodox faith, as represented by the Fathers and Councils of the Church; with his rhetorical power and skill in logical fence it was easy for him to escape from the interpretation put upon his words by his critic, or even to explain away their actual meaning, but it is not at all surprising if he entirely failed to convince the bigots of the Sorbonne that he was sound in the faith, and that his teachings were not contrary to the interests of the Catholic Church.

It need scarcely be said that Bedda made no attempt to reply to the defence of Erasmus. That was not his method of controversy by any means. He dealt chiefly in assertions, in misrepresentations, in suppression of the truth, and in direct falsehoods. He was so far successful that after the most persevering efforts he at last obtained the permission of the Faculty to print a little work purporting to expose the errors of Faber Stapulensis and Erasmus.[17] The second and smaller part of the work, which was devoted to the latter, consisted of a repetition of the former charges, with some omitted and the addition of others, and as each page was headed with the "Errors of Erasmus," while the same words in enormous capitals were prefixed to every chapter, it was ingeniously calculated to make an impression on the many who read nothing more than the index, the preface, and the headings. For the rest, Bedda wrote in the most dogmatic and oracular style, as who should say, "What I have written I have written; I am a God, and can neither err nor be deceived." He seemed to think that the object of his hostility had nothing to do but to recant, even though he did not understand the charges against him. Leaving Faber to take care of himself, Erasmus now wrote a most elaborate reply to the criticisms of Bedda,[18] declaring that he had counted in his little book no less

---

[17] In 1519, Bedda had published a work against Faber, entitled, *De Unica Magdalena, contra Jacobum Fabrum, et Jodocum Clichtoveum*. The work referred to in the text was entitled, *Contra Commentarios ejusdem Fabri in Evangelia et Epistolas, Lib. II., et contra Erasmi Paraphrases, Liber I.*, and was printed at Paris in 1526.—See Bayle, art. Beda (Noel).

[18] *Desiderii Erasmi Supputatio Errorum in Censuris Beddæ:* printed, according to Bayle (art. Beda), in 1527.

There is also a third work, entitled, *Desiderii Erasmi in Natalis Beddæ Censuras erroneas Elenchus.* These, together with the *Divinationes*, will be found in *Er. Op.* ix.

than one hundred and eighty-one lies, three hundred and ten calumnies, and forty-seven blasphemies. In this work he handles his adversary in his happiest style of ironical sarcasm, ridicules his Latin, and deliciously exposes his ignorance, folly, and malice. Bedda, he says, begins his sentences like Cicero, and there are only a few additional peculiarities wanting to make him a perfect Tully, but unfortunately Cicero imagined there was some difference between the indicative and subjunctive moods—a circumstance of which Bedda does not seem to be aware. He fears that in engaging in controversy with the Syndic he may be unwittingly attacking many others, who hide themselves under his antagonist's gown; and his apprehension reminds him of a mock-fight which he once witnessed at Sienna, where a bull was let loose to be run down and destroyed by certain huge machines, consisting of a wooden framework with leather stretched over it, which outwardly resembled a tortoise, a ram, or some other animal, but within which there were concealed a number of men, who, by means of ropes, made the creature's mouth open, turned its head to this side and to that, and so terrified the unfortunate bull almost to death by making as though he were about to be devoured. With such a machine he fears that he, who is no bull, but a timid deer, may have to do; and if so he begs that those who are thus concealed will not suppose themselves attacked, his desire being that only one person, or if possible not even one, may be brought to grief by this combat. The consent of the Faculty, he is persuaded, was given through complacency, Bedda having asked for it in vain for more than two years, and at last obtained it when many of the members were out of town, and from the terms in which it is conveyed it is clear that it does not imply approval. Even if it did, there are means by which a small but violent minority often gets the better of the more sensible majority, and it may be that the Faculty, occupied with graver matters, has not given to this case the attention it deserves. But be that as it may, Bedda has been guilty of so many palpable falsehoods that if the supreme Pontiff himself should sanction them, it would be necessary to appeal from the Pope asleep to the Pope awake; for black would not be white even though the Pope of Rome were to say so.

Bedda had, of course, revived the old charge of collusion between Erasmus and Luther, to which the former replies that he agrees with Luther as the nightingale does with the cuckoo. It was said that Luther had borrowed from his works, but how could that be, seeing that Luther would not admit that he knew anything whatever of theology? So that it was very foolish to say, as some did, either Luther *erasmises*, or Erasmus *lutherises*. In one respect, it might be admitted that Bedda had not lied, for it was true that in some passages of his works, Erasmus had taxed those theologians who, despising all literary culture, having no knowledge of the Fathers or even of the Scriptures themselves, spent their years in the discussion of thorny and unprofitable questions. If there were none such in the world when he wrote, his admonition was superfluous, but nevertheless well-meant; but if there were, alas! too many everywhere, his advice had not been in vain, nor had he injured but benefited the theologians thereby. " For we now see in our universities quite another kind of divines, who understand both the old learning and the new, and whose judgment is accordingly more trustworthy and of greater weight, who dispute more soberly, preach more piously, and write with greater erudition." But Bedda had a high opinion of the scholastic theology as a protection against heresy; "what then had become of that safeguard these many years, while Luther, like a wild-boar, was devastating the Lord's vineyard? Where was then the zeal with which the unhappy Bedda is now eaten up? How is it that a man provided with so many remedies, permits the Jews to persist in their blindness, the Bohemians and Greeks in schism, the Turks and such like half-Christians to perish without help? At any rate he ought to have engaged hand to hand with Luther. There would have been a well-matched pair of gladiators! But, doubtless, there was more fame at less cost to be had by quarrelling with Erasmus, who by his writings had urged many to the pursuit of piety, had always hated faction, and had never led any one astray." Bedda had charged Faber and Erasmus with introducing a new mode of handling theological topics and recommending heathen literature as though of itself it would conduce to salvation, whereas that was an assertion he had never ventured to make even of the Aristotelian philosophy, much less of polite letters, and in his translations and paraphrases he had ever aimed to be simple and unaffected, and not superstitiously observant of Latin elegance, preferring to be esteemed a Christian rather than a Ciceronian. Again he had undertaken the panegyric of the Sorbonne, which Erasmus had never attacked. "Of that college," he says," I have always entertained the highest opinion, nor do I doubt that many of its members are such as

Bedda describes, but I do not think they would be less numerous if Bedda himself were absent." He had put himself forward as the champion of the Christian religion. "In truth," says Erasmus, "it is through such defenders that the Church has fallen into her present unhappy state, the little spark having grown into this tremendous blaze." After a new and more detailed examination of the criticisms of Bedda he advises him to cast himself at the feet of Almighty God, and ask pardon for his calumnies, then to acknowledge his errors and retract his censures. Finally he recommends him to go back to his Greek and Latin grammar, his ignorance of which had caused him to utter such gross calumnies against his neighbour, and prevented him from understanding the Latin not less than the Greek Fathers. "Let him not be ashamed to learn, though late, what it is needful for him to know. But if, without noticing all my answers to him, he shall continue to disseminate similar criticisms, I declare that I will waste no more time, of which I have already lost too much, on these unlearned and insane controversies. Let him not expect that the Church will ever sink to such a depth of folly as to give her sanction to censures which have neither reason nor modesty. Should that ever come to pass I shall then be glad to leave such a Church. But as it is certain that this will never be, so is it my fixed resolve never to leave the society of the truly religious."

He did not strictly adhere to the resolution expressed above, for we have yet another rejoinder to some further remarks of Bedda,[19] from which it would appear that the Syndic, as might be supposed, was by no means pleased

---

[19] *Desiderii Erasmi Responsio ad Notulas Beddaicas.—Er. Op.* ix. 701.

with the way he was handled, held himself up as a
deeply injured person who had been animated by the
very best intentions, and reproached Erasmus with his
inconsistency in having before addressed him as an
excellent man and most accomplished divine, while he
now applied to him such different epithets. His
refutation of Bedda, he tells us, cost him a month's
labour, most of which, however, was employed in
reading his calumnies, and examining the passages
which he had attacked. On the 16th of June, 1526, he
wrote a letter to King Francis I.,[20] in which after
congratulating him on his happy return to his kingdom,
and on the peace which the world might expect from
his reconciliation with the Emperor, he calls attention
to the doings of Bedda and Sutor, who by their
mendacity and violence are bringing disgrace on the
University of Paris, and begs his Majesty either to put
some restraint on their fury, or to secure for him the
right of printing and publishing his defence in Paris.
"For it would be most unjust," he reasonably says,
"that they should be permitted to disseminate their
poison, and that we should not be permitted to apply
the antidote." This appeal was successful; or rather
had been anticipated by Francis, who had already
issued an edict prohibiting the sale of Bedda's work,
which Bedda himself was compelled to publish to the
booksellers "with his own sacred lips;" but the law
was evaded and the work clandestinely circulated
notwithstanding.[21]

[20] *Ep.* dcccxxvi.

[21] "Id edictum, ne gravaretur Facultas, ipse Bedda sacro suo ore bibliopolis edere coactus est, quanquam nihilo secius clam distrahebatur, delusa regis auctoritate, quæ mirum quantum laudatur, cum reponit statuam adorandam."—*Er. Op.* ix. 705, E. The King's edict, according to M. Chevillier (*Orig.*

Not even the King's authority would have availed to prevent the condemnation of the arch-heretic. Already, indeed, the "Familiar Colloquies" had been censured. On the 15th of May, 1526, the Faculty met in the Church of St. Maturin, to consider finally what should be done with the book bearing that title, and after a long debate, which was adjourned till the next day, when the Faculty met again in the College of the Sorbonne, and the grounds of complaint were again gone into in the presence of all the Masters, it was concluded that by the author of that book the fasts and abstinences of the Church were undervalued, vows to the Virgin Mary and other saints ridiculed, virginity, in comparison with marriage, held of little or no account, and entrance on the religious life indiscriminately discouraged. Accordingly, after mature deliberation, it was unanimously decreed that the reading of this book should be prohibited to all, and especially to young men, inasmuch as by reading such a work the youth, under the pretence of acquiring an elegant style, would be corrupted rather than instructed. In support of this decision there follow some "erroneous, scandalous, and impious propositions, contained in the book called 'Familiar Colloquies,' by Desiderius Erasmus of Rotterdam, in the year of our Lord 1526, in which work the author, as though he were a heathen, ridicules, satirizes, and sneers at the Christian religion and its holy ceremonies and observances, tears them to shreds and decrees their abolition."[22]

Again, towards the end of July, the Dean and Faculty of the Theological School of Paris met to

de l'imprimerie de Paris, quoted by Bayle *ubi supra*), was dated from Amboise, the 9th of April, 1526, and thus preceded the letter of Erasmus, supposing both dates to be correct.

[22] *Er. Op.* ix. 928, 929.

consider "a question proposed to them by many grave men, what was to be thought of certain propositions extracted from the Paraphrases of Desiderius Erasmus on the New Testament, and some others taken from a book of his in defence of the said propositions called his *Elenchus*, as well as a few others found in his other works."[23] The propositions were embraced under thirty-two heads, and were for the most part identical with those already charged with heresy by Bedda; and thus was the persecuted scholar, who unwillingly left his more congenial studies to engage in these wearisome controversies, compelled for the third or fourth time to travel over the same ground, meeting point by point these annoying and incorrigible adversaries.

The judgment of the University of Paris could not be treated with contempt, and in the "Declarations"[24] which he published in reply, Erasmus, without yielding one inch of his ground, preserves throughout that tone of respect which he considered due to so powerful and influential a body. He had hoped, he said, there had been an end of wrangling, were it only from the weariness of his assailants, but now that the censures of the Theological Faculty of Paris have unexpectedly appeared, he felt uncertain what to do, thinking it safe neither to be silent, nor to reply, lest, on the one hand, his silence might be construed into contempt for so famous a university, or possibly into an acknowledgment of the justice of the charges against him, while, on the other hand, his venturing to answer so great an authority might be set down to obstinacy. He chose, however,

---

[23] *Er. Op.* ix. 813, 814.
[24] *Desiderii Erasmi Declarationes ad Censuras Lutetiæ vulgatas sub nomine Facultatis Theologiæ Parisiensis.—Er. Op.* ix. 813.

what appeared to him the least of the two evils, to be considered presuming rather than the author of impious dogmas, but promised that he would answer with the greatest deference, and wherever he had fallen into an error from carelessness or ignorance he would acknowledge and correct it. If, on the other hand, he had been misrepresented, he would not throw the blame on the Faculty itself, but on the commissioners and others who had been entrusted with the task of reporting on his works. Erasmus very justly complains that he was judged by far stricter rules than the ancient Fathers, Basil, Chrysostom, Ambrose, Jerome, or Augustine, in whose works might be found thousands of propositions meriting graver censure than any in his own. Moreover, in his dialogues, it was very unfair to object to him what was said by one speaker merely in order that it might be refuted by another. Finally, he expresses his approval of the pious watchfulness of the theologians, who are not satisfied with plucking up the tares of false doctrines, but study also not to offend the scruples of weak brethren. But he thinks this object might have been better accomplished if they had exercised more care in making their extracts from his works, and had not attributed to him opinions which he did not hold.

In the declarations which follow this introduction, and which are a careful examination of the charges brought against him by the Sorbonne as well as the restatement of his own position, he was generally able to say that he had merely stated his own private opinion, which as a loyal son of the Church he was, of course, perfectly at liberty to do, so long as he did not know it to be heretical, and had not, in fact, made any dogmatic assertions whatever. In many cases he was able to prove, as he had done before, in replying to Bedda, that he had really said no more than the sacred writer whom he was paraphrasing. Sometimes, no doubt, he repeated the alleged heresy, or even made it worse. In other cases his meaning had been mistaken ; for example, on the question of divorce, though charged with heresy for affirming that a wife guilty of adultery ceased to be a wife, he declared that he had referred only to her civil and social rights, but had not intended to contradict the doctrine of the Church, that by Divine law the marriage bond is indissoluble. On many other points on which he was charged with heresy, his learning enabled him to show that he had the authority of the orthodox Fathers on his side, and it may also be remarked that there were at that time many open questions, decided it may be by public opinion, but which the Church had not yet finally settled, and on which therefore differences of opinion were in the meantime permissible.

That Erasmus's declarations were not satisfactory to the Sorbonne may be considered certain. Whether they would be deemed in all respects a valid defence before a modern ecclesiastical tribunal—say the Judicial Committee of the Privy Council, or, a closer parallel, the General Assembly of the Kirk of Scotland—seems also very doubtful. It may be that he had not in any direct way contravened orthodox dogma as laid down in the decrees of the councils of the Church, and his heresies, if so they may be called, were of that intangible kind which it is always extremely difficult to bring within the letter of a written law; at the same time there can be no doubt that in the whole spirit of his teaching he was entirely opposed to Rome and to Rome's policy, and that the monks were guided by a perfectly true instinct in regarding him as their deadliest foe. They acted as the priests of all ages have acted in the same circumstances, and especially were they bound by every consideration of interest and safety to destroy the credit of, and if possible to extirpate, that most scathing exposure of their vices and superstitions, the "Familiar Colloquies." It was, indeed, too late for them to succeed. As always happens, where such a contest is waged on anything like equal terms, the attempt to repress freedom of speech defeated itself. In a reading age nothing helps the sale of a book like an ecclesiastical censure. And so it was, as we have already seen, in the present case. The enterprising bookseller, who, on hearing that the "Colloquies" were likely to be forbidden by the University, had twenty-four thousand copies printed, showed some knowledge of human nature, while Bedda, by his interference with the liberty of the press, succeeded only in gaining thousands of readers for a work which he deemed more dangerous than all the writings of Luther.[85]

The declarations in answer to the censures of the Sorbonne belong to the year 1529. In fact, it would appear that the censures themselves, though passed, as we have seen, in the summer of 1526, were not published for about two years afterwards, the approval of the other faculties being waited for,[86] and when at length they reached Erasmus he was too much occupied with other important works to give them his immediate attention. Burigni thinks there is room to doubt whether the decree forbidding the use of the "Colloquies" was ever literally executed. At any rate it is satisfactory to know that Bedda was not always triumphant. Some

[85] See above, p. 179. [86] BURIGNI, i. pp. 513, 514.

years afterwards, several persons having been burned alive at Paris, on a charge of having disseminated seditious books, among others Bedda was accused, and was compelled to make what was called the *amende honorable*, by confessing publicly after the crier, in the presence of a great concourse of people, before the church of Notre Dame, that he had spoken against the truth and against the King; after which he was thrown into prison, to be confined during the King's pleasure. He died on the 8th of February, 1537.[17]

If Bedda was the most pertinacious and the most successful of his antagonists at this time, he was not the only one who was labouring to undermine his influence, and bring upon him the condemnation of the Church. Another enemy, of higher consideration in the world, but fortunately with less power to do mischief, appeared at Rome in the person of Albertus Pius, Prince of Carpi, a man of considerable influence at the Pontifical court, who went about declaring that Erasmus was neither a philosopher nor a theologian, and was often heard to repeat that he was the prime author of all the disorder which then prevailed in the world. It does not appear that these representations made any impression on the mind of Pope Clement: but Erasmus, on hearing the report, wrote the Prince a letter of remonstrance—its date is the 10th of October, 1525—in which he assured him that his first charge did not greatly trouble him, as it was merely what he had always said of himself, but as to the other assertion, nothing could possibly be more utterly groundless. On the first appearance of Luther, when all the world was applauding him, he had been foremost in

---

[17] "Bedda tuus fecit amendam, ut vocant, honorabilem," &c.—*Er. Op.* iii. 1505, D. See also Bayle.

advising his friends not to mix themselves up with a movement which he foresaw would have a bloody end. He had constantly declared that he had himself nothing to do with Luther, and in fact Luther's opinion of him was precisely the same as that of the Prince of Carpi, namely that he was no theologian. If he was asked why he had not resisted the evil at its origin, he answered that it was because, like many others, he thought Luther was a good man, divinely sent to correct the depraved morals of mankind; besides, when there were so many universities, and the movement met with the approval not only of the vulgar but of some of the leading Bishops and Cardinals, what rashness it would have been in him, a mere private individual, to set himself against the judgment of the whole world. The real cause, he added, of all our trouble is the openly wicked life of certain priests, the pride of certain divines, the tyranny no longer endurable of certain monks. He begged therefore that the Prince would cease to entertain so injurious an opinion regarding him, and would not say things which were calculated to do him so much injury.[28]

This letter, far from producing the intended effect, only called forth a volume from the Prince, in which he repeated and aggravated his charges.[29] It reached Erasmus about two years afterwards, at a time when Italy was all in confusion, in consequence of the invasion of the Germans, and when therefore it would have been

[28] *Er. Op.* ix. 1093.

[29] *Alberti Pii, Principis Carpensis, Responsio longa ad Erasmum Rot. Roma Basileam, anno* 1526. "Quod Erasmus bonis litteris suscitatis, Novo imprimis Testamento Græco cum versione, et annotationibus, anno 1516 edito, reformationi ansam dederit, cum exhortatione, quin in Lutherum scribat, cui ad reformandum occasionem dedisset.'
—Von der Hardt, l. c. p. 114.

hopeless to attempt sending a reply. Soon after came the news of the capture of Rome by the Imperial troops and therewith doubtful reports about the Prince, some to the effect that he was sharing the Pope's captivity, while others intimated that he had provided for his safety by a seasonable flight. It was not till towards the close of the year 1528 that Erasmus at length learned that he was at Paris, and that his book, which had hitherto existed only in manuscript, was about to be given to the public. He therefore immediately wrote to the Prince once more, begging him to reconsider his determination, or at least to modify his expressions in the printed copies,[30] but either his remonstrances arrived too late, or would in any case have proved unavailing. The book came to his hands, in type, in the beginning of the following February, and finding that he had then just ten days before the Frankfort fair, though overwhelmed with other work, in order, he said, that he might not seem to despise his antagonist, he produced his reply, trusting to the Prince's courtesy to excuse the haste with which he was obliged to write.[31]

In the meantime, however, nearly a year previously, he had taken the precaution of writing to the Pope himself, to assure him how false were the charges against him, and to exhort him to keep a strong hand over the monks, who hated learning even more than they hated Luther.[32] Nor would he believe that the Prince of Carpi, in his attacks upon him, was acting an

---

[30] *Ep.* dccccxcv.

[31] *Ad Exhortationem clarissimi doctissimique Comitis, Alberti Pii, Carporum Principis, Desiderii Erasmi Roterodami Responsio. Da-* *tum Basiliæ idibus Februarii, anno* MDXXIX.—*Er. Op.* ix. 1095-1122.

[32] *Ep.* dccccvi. The date is April 3, 1528.

altogether independent part. He thought, perhaps justly, that he could detect a more powerful hand pulling the cords from behind the scenes. This he hints in his letter to the Pope. He afterwards wrote more plainly, "I can easily believe that when Pius wrote against me at Rome he was set on by others; nor am I ignorant who they are. One is a gentleman of Jewish extraction, a class of men with whom I have never agreed." The allusion, of course, was to Aleander; and Erasmus was informed, by persons who were present at the time, that when the Pope had determined to give him a rich living in the Church, he and Pius together had prevailed on him to alter his resolution.

The Prince's attack upon Erasmus was full of compliments to his learning and genius, and in reply Erasmus treats his opponent with remarkable courtesy, but gives him many home thrusts, which wounded not the less because they were planted with all the grace of a master of fence. He convicts him of not having read the works which he attacked, of repeating old charges without taking the slightest notice of the answers which had been already made to them, and of utterly failing to support the points which he had undertaken to establish. These were, that Erasmus was the occasion, cause, author and leader of the Lutheran movement, and that his writings undermined the authority of the sacraments, put marriage above continence, assailed the teachings of the Fathers and the dignity of the Pope, and derided the monastic profession and the prayers of the Church. All these charges he totally denied. If he had ever raised a doubt it was on points which either required further investigation, or which the Church had not yet defined. He had never said a word against the authority of the sacraments; on the contrary, had increased their authority as far as he could. If it was to attack the priesthood, to remind them occasionally of their duty, he admitted the charge, but it was one which applied no less to Jerome, Cyprian, Chrysostom, and Bernard. He had always reverenced the ceremonies of the Church; he had sometimes found fault with an extreme, superstitious, or unreasonable observance of them. He found fault with those, of whom the world is full, who, to the neglect of true religion, put their whole trust in ceremonies, which may indeed be sacred, but which are designed to help us forward to better things. "Show me," he said, "a single monk whom I have attacked as a monk. There are none for whom I have a greater veneration, none with whom I would sooner spend my life than with those who are truly dead to the world, and live according to the Gospel rule, were it not that my bodily infirmity made me useless for any kind of society."

One of the principal subjects of accusation against him was the *Moria*, a book which Albert *had* read, and which he maintained had been the ruin of many. "I never heard," replied Erasmus, "that so much as a fly was lost through my *Moria*, except that it brought upon me some odium, but only with the theologians and pseudo-monks; and yet no book was ever received with greater applause; I do not say by young men, but by the leading men and primates of the Church." As to the charges, founded on this work, of turning sacred things into ridicule, a retort lay open to him of which he did not fail to avail himself. "I think, Prince Albert, that you are a man of Christian piety, for which reason I will speak my sentiments the more freely. You will much more readily find scoffers at sacred things in Italy, among men of your own rank, ay, and in your much lauded Rome, than with us. *I could not endure to sit down at table with such men.* Once more I beg that you will not be offended by my freedom."

Another point into which he enters at some length is the confessional. The Prince had charged him with having collected, in a book which he had written on the subject, the advantages and disadvantages of confession, and then left it to the reader to determine whether it should be abolished or not. This Erasmus maintained was an entire misrepresentation of his meaning. He had not said that confession was the cause, but only the occasion, of many evils, and he had never left it to the judgment of the reader to decide on its abolition, but had merely proposed the question for consideration in the proper quarter; he was speaking of course of the authority of the Pope and the consent of the Christian people, that is, the authority of the whole Church. And surely confession might be abolished by the same authority by which it was established. Nor had he dogmatically affirmed that it was an institution of the Church; he had merely argued on that supposition. He believed confession to be a most salutary practice, and one that ought to be observed with the same reverence as if it had been instituted by Christ, and he would be glad if it could be proved that it was so instituted. This had been often attempted both in ancient and in modern times, but with less success than might be desired. Even Latomus, who wrote expressly on the subject, and from the Roman point of view, had left it an open question whether it was taught by Christ, or inferred from

Scripture, or instituted by a general decree of the Church. To what purpose, then, would he have pronounced an opinion unless he had been able to support it with sound arguments? We need not follow him into the discussion of other points. This may serve as an example of his method of repelling the attacks made on the soundness of his faith. Admitting that the Church could ever acknowledge herself so far in the wrong as to retrace her steps in a matter of such moment, his reasoning was sufficiently logical; but was it consistent with the claims of Rome to admit that one of her most cherished institutions and most valuable instruments of power was the occasion of so many evils that it must be abolished?

In regard to the often repeated and not altogether unfounded charge of being the virtual author of the Reformation, he was now able to point to his writings against Luther, and still more effectively to Luther's attack on himself, which he often declared was the most bitter he had ever sustained. These indeed the Prince had not seen when he wrote his work, with the exception of the treatise on Free-Will, but that at least he admitted that he had read, and yet he spoke of the silence of Erasmus, as if he had done nothing whatever. He had, he admitted, delayed to take up his pen, but why should he, a mere private individual, and no expert in theology—so at least his enemies said—have come forth like a second David to challenge the Lutheran Goliath to single combat, and so draw down upon his head the fury of almost the entire world? He could name, he said, many at Rome who scarcely ascribed to him the sense of a man; but now, when the object is to injure his reputation, from a mere fly he is suddenly transformed into an elephant.

"Was there none but Erasmus," he continues, "to come forward in such a mighty up-turning of the world to bear the brunt of the battle? How much more effectually might you have done so, Albert, who to the gifts of fortune, the influence of your high rank and a character unspotted by envy, add a profound knowledge of philosophy and theology, great eloquence and great moderation. In this way you would certainly have become more favourably known to the world than by repeating the complaints of others concerning Erasmus." Even when thus put on his defence he is far from taking refuge in abuse of Luther, or admitting that the whole duty of man consists in hating him. Indeed he still speaks of him as having been raised up by Providence to punish the sins of the world. "All," he observes, "are not truly religious who go to Rome, nor all Christians who call Luther a pestilent beast."

Pius, expelled from his principality and now living at Paris, where he was hand and glove with Bedda, made immediate preparations to renew his attack on a formidable scale, thus giving occasion to the obvious pun of his antagonist, that though he had ceased to be Prince of Carpi he could not refrain from carping. He gathered round him a number of assistants, some to make the extracts on which his charges were founded, some to polish the style, some to supply the Scriptural testimonies, some to provide matter and arguments, some to point out the doctrines alleged to be impugned. This, of course, is the humorous account of Erasmus himself, but among those who aided in the work he was able to name at least two, the learned Spaniard, Sepulveda, and Peter Cornutus, a Franciscan friar. The result was a work in twenty-four books, in which all the old charges and some new ones were marshalled in due order, collected especially from the "Annotations on the New Testament," the Paraphrases, the *Moria*, the "Colloquies," the Scholia on St. Jerome, and the Preface to Hilary. Before the publication, or even the completion of the work, of which, however, he had assumed the responsibility, the Prince died, and was carried to the grave in the dress of the Franciscan order, which, according to a superstition then very prevalent, he had assumed three days before his decease. The reader will not doubt that he is the Eusebius of the "Seraphic Obsequies."[33]

Erasmus would willingly have avoided the odium of fighting with the dead, but what can you do, he asked, when the dead attack you? He wrote another long defence of himself,[34] in which he went through the charges one by one, not without invoking a curse on the head of his accusers for the trouble they had given him by omitting the proper references to his works, so that he sometimes could not even find the passages objected to. It must be admitted that he is not so courteous to the Prince dead as he was to him when living; but Albert had shown himself an inveterate foe, and one not to be soothed by kind words. He remembered, too, that under his name he was replying to others who were still able to do him mischief. The success of the defence itself will be differently estimated according to the sympathies of the reader. It was easy for Erasmus to say that he had always attacked manners, not men, not the monastic orders, but their vices and super-

---

[33] See above, p. 175.
[34] *Desiderii Erasmi Roterodami Apologia brevis ad viginti quatuor libros Alberti Pii quondam Carporum Comitis.*—*Er. Op.* ix. 1123.

stitions. It will always be easy for a cautious writer to repel a charge of heresy. He has merely quoted the opinion of others, but pronounced none of his own; or, the extracts from his works have been garbled; or, his meaning has been misunderstood, or maliciously perverted; or, stronger things may be found in the Fathers, or in the Scriptures themselves. Such was the line of defence which he took up, but it may be doubted whether any arguments could heal the wounds inflicted by the *Moria*, or remove the impression produced by such a sentence as, "We venture to call the Holy Spirit God," from the preface to St. Hilary. Erasmus, however, did not expect to conciliate the monks, nor was he afraid of them. It was enough for him if he could justify himself in the eyes of the moderate adherents of the Papacy and the ruling authorities; and even in this very apology he breaks out with his wonted bitterness against the corruptions of the Church. Thus in reference to some remarks supposed to be derogatory to the Papacy, but which really referred only to the character of some of the Popes, Albert had wished that God might have mercy on him. "Nay, rather," retorts he, "may God have mercy on the Popes, who are sometimes such a scandal to the Church of Christ!" And again, in answer to the question, what is a useless or unnecessary vow, he replies, "To go to Jerusalem is not necessary to any one who has not vowed to do so, as he may trace the footsteps of Christ better in the Gospels. It is also useless if he leaves at home a wife and children, who require his presence, and perhaps not useless only, but also pernicious."

Nowhere, perhaps, was he attacked more furiously than in Spain. The Dominicans and Franciscans there, moved, as he believed, by Edward Lee, who was then on an embassy to the Imperial Court, and had disseminated among them his criticisms on the Annotations, were exceedingly mad against him and clamoured for his destruction. They exerted their influence to have his books prohibited; they appealed to the Emperor and the Bishops; they whispered calumnies against him in private, and took care that no priest who was suspected of admiring him should be admitted to any place of trust. At Salamanca they went the length of raising a popular tumult, which was with difficulty suppressed by the authorities, and one of their leaders, a Dominican, named Peter a Victoria, absolutely set the Emperor and his officers at defiance, exclaiming that "we ought to obey God rather than men."

Erasmus, hearing of these disturbances, and knowing well the power of the monks, was somewhat anxious as to the result. He wrote to Alfonso Fonseca, the Archbishop of Toledo, from whom he received a most friendly reply, assuring him of his own personal interest in his safety, and exhorting him to moderation and courage.[35] From a private friend also he learned that so far the machinations of his enemies had had no other effect than to give still greater celebrity to a name already known everywhere, and held in the highest honour by all the friends of learning. Public curiosity was excited regarding him, and even those who could not read Latin were eager to know something of his writings. Accordingly his *Enchiridion* had been translated into Spanish, and, though several thousand copies were issued, so great was the demand that the printers were scarcely able to supply it. Not only men, but weak

[35] *Ep.* dccclviii., dated April 24, 1527.

women too, were eager to have his works, and even nuns contrived to have copies of them smuggled into their cloisters. At length, in order to prevent any further disturbance, the monks were directed, if they had any charges worthy of consideration, to lay them before the proper authorities, and not turn the country upside down by these seditious clamours. "If Erasmus *is* a heretic," said Fonseca, "by all means let him be burned." They accordingly collected together a vast mass of articles of the most incongruous character, and without any form or order, which, however, were returned to them to be reduced into proper shape. Finally they presented to the Arch-Inquisitor, the Archbishop of Seville, a number of articles purporting to show that Erasmus had written, among other points of faith, against the Holy Trinity, the Inquisition, the Sacraments, the authority of Holy Scripture, against Christianity and the orthodox Fathers, the honour of the Blessed Virgin, the fasts of the Church, Indulgences, Celibacy, the rights of property, the freedom of the will, and hell-punishments. "Surely," said he, "they have gone far enough in descending from the Supreme Trinity to the infernal regions?" The Court of Inquisition, consisting of the Archbishops and of the leading divines of the three universities, was opened with all due solemnity, by the chanting of the *De Sancto Spiritu*. The President, the Archbishop of Seville, earnestly exhorted to moderation and calmness, but the defenders having begun their remarks with some modest praise of the accused, the monks immediately broke out into tumult, and made it impossible for the case to proceed. A pestilence which just then began to show itself furnished a plausible excuse for the dissolution of the court, and the Archbishop, who seems to have been friendly to Erasmus, did not again summon it.

These events took place in the course of the year 1527, and on the 15th of October of that year Erasmus sent his answer to the monks to the Archbishop of Seville.[36] It is of the same character as his other apologies, and appears to have given satisfaction to his friends in Spain. "I should be guilty of falsehood," he writes to Fonseca, "were I to pretend that I feel no annoyance while I am thus bitten, pelted, and barked at on every side; still, with the assistance of Christ, who by the breath of his grace will temper these storms, I have never so far given way to this weakness of the flesh as to think of leaving my post, nor have I permitted myself to yield to despondency. Indeed, I think I have gained some strength from the insults to which I am subjected. . . . I am exceedingly glad that you are pleased with my 'Apology.' I thought you must approve of my moderation, considering the stupid folly of the monks and what it deserves. Such articles to lay before such men—who ever saw the like?"[37] Meantime, the monks, foiled in their attempt to procure the condemnation of Erasmus, took their revenge in all sorts of scurrilous pamphlets, in one of which the author, a Franciscan of that strictest class called Observants, undertook the defence of all the monastic rules against his attacks. One of the charges brought by this silly writer was that he, the constant preacher of peace and forbearance, was the cause of the war between the Emperor and Francis I., and that he was responsible for the sack of Rome the preceding year. The unlucky

[36] *Ep.* dcccclii. *Desiderii Erasmi Apologia adversus articulos aliquot per monachos quosdam in Hispaniis exhibitos.*—*Er. Op.* ix. 1015.
[37] *Ep.* mxxxiii.

fellow supplied excellent materials for his antagonist's wit by his modest claim to be well versed in logic, physics, and metaphysics, and still more by his frank confession that he had written while suffering under an attack of fever, which made it impossible for him to look at a book. Erasmus vouchsafed a brief reply, in which he did not fail to take advantage of the opportunities thus afforded him.[38]

Thus, in his quiet retreat at Basle, by the banks of the green Rhine, did the great champion of letters stoutly carry on his warfare with the legions of darkness, who were now rushing upon him on all sides, bent upon his ruin. They had persecuted Wimphilingus; they had brought down the grey hairs of Reuchlin with sorrow to the grave; they had destroyed Berquin in the face of one of the most powerful monarchs in Europe; and who was this decrepit old man that he should escape? He saw in these almost simultaneous movements a vast conspiracy, in which Lee and Aleander were the principal actors, and whose object was to confound Erasmus with Luther, learning with heresy, and thus destroy both together. He might well feel that he had now done his duty as a soldier of the truth, and he accordingly took leave of his persecutors in a short farewell, in which the absolute contempt he expresses for them shows that he considered himself safe from their attacks, while, at the same time, its naïve simplicity proves that, though the admired of all the world, he does not forget that he is still a plain monk speaking to the brethren who hated him, but for whom he desired nothing worse than a changed spirit. It is entitled,—

---

[38] *Desiderii Erasmi Responsio adversus febricitantis cujusdam libellum.*— Er. Op. x. 1674.

The EPISTLE of DESIDERIUS ERASMUS to CERTAIN MOST IMPUDENT JACKDAWS.[30]

"I SEE what you are about, Brethren and Fathers," it begins; "you have bribed a number of young men, whose ignorance is matched only by their effrontery, to make a combined attack upon Erasmus and put an end to him. They are equally devoid of shame and feeling, having nothing to lose, and so continually are they changing their shape that it is impossible to take hold of them—they are now here, now there, and a single buckler hides an army. . . . I now, therefore, by this present writing, Brethren and Fathers, give you notice —bribe, invent, deceive, despise the decrees of Emperor and Bishops, publish your anonymous scribblings as you will, for the future I will not condescend to read or to refute your trash. God will find out all impious hypocrites, and to his just judgments I deliver them. What a decrepit old man they think me! Why, Budæus is but two years younger, Bedda, perhaps, four or five, Latomus three. Up to the present moment I am constantly overwhelmed with work, and to this, for the most part, is owing my ill-health and any signs there may be on me of old age. Old man as I am, it would take four pair of strong young shoulders to bear the burden that I carry unaided. My eyes are not dim, thanks be to God, though many wonder that I was not blind long ago. I have never yet used spectacles either by day or by candle-light. I have never touched a stick. I walk firm and erect; my hands tremble less than those of any youth; I am less troubled with the stone

---

[30] *Desiderii Erasmi Epistola ad quosdam impudentissimos Graculos.*— *Er. Op.* x. 1745.

every day; and if I moderate my work, with the help of God, I may yet live fourteen years with all my senses entire. Length of life, however, is in God's hand. They who live with me observe no great failure of either mind or memory. Where, then, is that decrepit old man, tottering on the brink of the grave? Oh! the buffoons, whom the world can no longer endure! But what object do they hope to gain by all this ignorant and wordy trash? The learned will not read it, while the pious will detest it. I have never yet been able to find any one to read their nonsense for me. But with such books they intend to finish 'the decrepit old man.' They had better use daggers; for it is all one what weapon they employ if they have the spirit of assassins. And yet this 'decrepit old man' has given you Jerome, Cyprian, Augustine, and is now giving you Chrysostom, from whom, and from Athanasius, he has translated so much. Of the Greek authors he has illustrated so many passages in the New Testament; let them read the index and see how much this decrepit old man has given them which conduces both to learning and to piety. . . . But I must now bring my admonition to a close, for they are only growing worse every day. For the future I shall despise them, and I would I had always done so, for it is no pleasure to try and drown the croaking of frogs. Let them say, with their stout defiance of divine and human laws, 'We ought to obey God rather than men.' That was well said by the Apostles, and even on *their* lips it is not without a certain appropriateness; only it is not the same God in the two cases. The God of the Apostles was the Maker of heaven and earth; their god is their belly. Fare ye well."

CHAPTER XVII.

ERASMUS AT HOME — HIS INCOME — HIS SUFFERINGS — LETTER TO WARHAM — JOKES AT THE REFORMERS — DEATH OF LINACRE — LONGOLIUS — FROBEN — TRACT ON CONFESSION — DEVOTIONAL WORKS — THE "LINGUA" — THE INSTITUTION OF CHRISTIAN MARRIAGE — THE "CHRISTIAN WIDOW" — PLINY — IRENÆUS — ST. CHRYSOSTOM — ST. ATHANASIUS — ST. AMBROSE — THE "DE PRONUNCIATIONE — THE "CICERONIAN" — BEMBO AND SADOLETI — JULIUS CÆSAR SCALIGER'S ORATIONS — QUARREL WITH EPPENDORF — CONDUCT OF ERASMUS — NEW EDITION OF SENECA — ST. AUGUSTINE.

DURING these stormy times he would seem to have kept himself pretty much at home, pursuing his studies in his own room, or perhaps wandering as far as Froben's garden, where on fine days he often spent the afternoon, walking up and down, or writing in the summer-house. Nor, while the peasant war lasted, would it have been very safe to have ventured far beyond the walls of Basle. "Every day," he writes to Polydore Virgil, in the autumn of 1525, "there are bloody conflicts between the nobles and the peasants so near us that we can hear the firing, and almost the groans of the wounded;" and in another letter he estimates the number of slain peasants at far more than a hundred thousand, "and every day," he adds, "priests are imprisoned, tortured, hanged, decapitated, or burned."[1] He was living now, he tells Cardinal Campeggio, in a house of his own,

---

[1] *Er. Op.* iii. 888, F. 900. F.

provided with an open fireplace, on account of his well-known horror of the German stoves.[2] One of his letters gives us a pleasant glimpse of the interior of his bedroom, either wall of which was adorned with a cast of his friend Pirckheimer, and a picture of him by Dürer, so that, as he remarks, his eyes fell upon him whichever way he turned.[3] Being compelled to keep three servants, one of whom was always abroad on some mission, he lived at considerable expense—in one place he estimates his expenditure at six hundred golden florins a year—and meantime his pension as a councillor of the Emperor, notwithstanding repeated orders from Charles himself, continued unpaid. "If it is ever paid now," said Erasmus, "it will come too late, unless indeed there is any use for money in the Elysian fields."[4] The truth may have been, as he suspected, that the Imperial exchequer was too much exhausted to afford this tax upon it, and as he was not residing in the Emperor's dominions, this furnished an excuse for withholding the pension. He could not, however, have been in any want of money. Besides the pensions which he received regularly from his English friends, Warham and Mountjoy, and which he sent to collect every year, there were wealthy and powerful men in almost every country of Europe willing to do him honour. Handsome presents, whether of money or of plate, poured in upon him almost daily.[5] Pope Clement VII., on two different

---

[2] "Quæ res me cogit ut Basiliæ in propriis ædibus habitem, quæ aulam habent cum fumario."—*Er. Op.* 913, A.

[3] *Ib.* 849, A.

[4] "Lenta solutio nescio quid mihi profutura sit, nisi forte in campis Elysiis opus erit pecunia."—*Ib.* iii. 874, F., cf. 901, F.

[5] "Regum, cardinalium, ducum, episcoporum literis honorificentissime scriptis habeo plena scrinia. A multis veniunt et munera nequaquam vulgaria."—*Ib.* 972, A.

occasions, sent him two hundred florins. Sigismund I., King of Poland, to whom, at the earnest request of his young friend the Baron à Lasco, he wrote, praising his wisdom, his clemency, his moderation, his chivalrous qualities, and pointing out to him the means by which he might pacify the world,[6] sent him in return an ample present.[7] The Chancellor of Poland gave him a watch.[8] From Duke George of Saxony, whose suspicions of collusion with Luther were removed by the publication of the *Hyperaspistes*, he received a handsome silver cup,[9] as well as other presents. The Bishop of Lincoln was a liberal patron.[10] Polydore Virgil, though a literary man himself, could afford to give him a sum of money to *procure* a horse; "I wish," said Erasmus, "you could give me anything to *cure* the rider."[11] From the sale of his works, too, he must have drawn a very considerable and steadily-increasing revenue, and Froben was ever most generous. Besides, he had usually one or two young men of the highest position residing with him, who were anxious to benefit by his conversation, or perhaps merely to have the honour of sitting at the same table with the great Erasmus, and who must have contributed handsomely to the expenses of his housekeeping. One of these was the Polish Baron à Lasco, just mentioned, of whom he speaks in the highest terms as a delightful companion, and whom we find him playfully upbraiding for having so corrupted the simplicity of his household with his luxurious living that it would take some time to restore it to its former

---

[6] *Ep.* dccclx.
[7] *Er. Op.* iii. 1097, E.
[8] *Ep.* dccexxxvii.
[9] *Ep.* dcccxci.
[10] *Ep.* dcccxiv.
[11] "Dedisti quo paretur equus, utinam dare possis quo reparetur eques."—*Er. Op.* iii. 934, F.

frugality.[12] We also find mention of his old pupil Thomas Grey, who was with him for a time along with his youngest son.[13]

He still continued to suffer grievously from his old enemy, the stone. Sometimes he speaks as if it had almost proved his death, and he wished for nothing but release from pain; but it is clear that he makes the most of his sufferings, which, however, were no doubt real enough, whenever he wants to use them as a plea for resisting the entreaties of his Italian friends to settle at Rome, or the commands of the Emperor to return to Brabant. On the other hand, he tells his friend Pirckheimer that he suffered less since he had begun to take his wine diluted with a decoction of liquorice. At one time the physicians quite despaired of him; but fortunately the character of his disease underwent a change; instead of stones he now discharged large quantities of chalk,[14] a circumstance which he ascribed to the use of wine and sugar, both of which were adulterated with that substance. After that the pain became more constant, but at the same time somewhat more tolerable.

Happily his sufferings were unable to conquer his good spirits, or repress that vein of pleasantry which was always ready to break out on every opportunity. Warham, ever generous, had not only increased his pension, but also sent him a present of a horse, for which he thanks him in the following characteristic terms, at the same time forwarding to him the second edition of the "Jerome," then just out, and with the ink so wet that the volumes could not be bound:—

---

[12] *Er. Op.* iii. 917, A.   [13] *Ib.* 908, C.
[14] "Calculus meus versus in calcem."—*Ib.* 1139, C. Conf. 946, D, 1814, A, B, C.

"I thank you," he says, "for the increase in my pension. A plague on those wars which take tithes of us so often! but I thought pensions were free of taxes.

"I have received the horse, which is no beauty, but a good creature notwithstanding; for he is free from all the mortal sins, except gluttony and laziness; and he is adorned with all the virtues of a good confessor, being pious, prudent, humble, modest, sober, chaste, and quiet, and neither bites nor kicks. I suspect that by the knavery or mistake of your servants another horse is come in place of the one you ordered. I had instructed my servant not to accept a horse unless a very handsome and good one should be spontaneously offered. And yet I am most grateful to you for your good intentions. I was thinking of selling my horses, as I have now ceased to be a rider."[15]

He must have his jokes too against the reformers. "They have only two objects," he wrote, "a wife and a fortune."[16] Referring to the marriage of Luther, "I hoped," said he, "that his wife would have tamed him, but he has written against no one with greater virulence than against myself." "If," he added, "the popular story is true that Antichrist will be born of a monk and a nun, how many thousand Antichrists must there now be in the world?"[17] When the Basle reformer followed the example of his leader, he thus reported the circumstance:—"Œcolampadius has lately married. His bride is not a bad-looking girl. He wants, I suppose,

---

[15] *Ep.* dcxcvii.
[16] "Duo tantum quærunt, censum et uxorem."—*Er. Op.* iii. 1139, B.
[17] *Ep.* dccci.

to mortify the flesh. Some talk of the Lutheran tragedy; I think 'tis a comedy, for it always ends in a marriage." [18]

If the tortures of his disease had not kept death constantly before his eyes, there was the loss of old and valued friends to remind him that he too must soon cast off the hull of mortality.[19] Linacre died in England in the year 1524, of a disease very similar to his own.[20] Longolius, his countryman, the most Ciceronian of the Cisalpine scholars, died at Padua, in 1524, at the premature age of about thirty.[21] Martin Dorpius, long a convert to the cause of letters, died at Louvain about the same time, and Erasmus mourned his loss in an epitaph in iambic verse.[22] To compensate in some degree, however, for these losses, two of his bitterest enemies were also removed by death; though it may be doubted whether Erasmus took precisely the same view of their fate as Mercurinus Gattinarius, the Chancellor of Charles V., who saw in it an evident judgment of heaven, and wrote to him that he was glad to observe that the same thing had happened in his case which he himself had often experienced; "for," he continues, "I have seen a great many who hated me most bitterly, and wished for my removal from the Court, themselves first removed out of this world. I hear that this fate has now befallen two of your opponents; thus does God favour His own." [23] One of these was Egmund, the Carmelite, who was choked in vomiting; the other was Vincentius, a Dominican friar, who, with three others, had written

---

[18] *Er. Op.* iii. 1071, F.
[19] "Brevi, ni fallor, abjiciatur hoc syphar, et exsiliet nova cicada."—*Ib.* 887, E.
[20] *Ib.* 946, F.
[21] *Ib.* 789, C.
[22] *Ib.* 899, C.
[23] *Ep.* dcccl.

a scurrilous book against Erasmus, of which we hear often in his letters.

But the greatest loss which he sustained during his residence at Basle was that of his friend Froben, the printer, who died in the midst of his labours in the year 1527. "I bore my own brother's death with the greatest calmness," wrote Erasmus, "but I cannot endure the loss of Froben." "He was a true friend, so simple and sincere, that, even if he had wished to conceal anything, it was so repugnant to his nature that he would have found it impossible; so ready to do good to all that he was glad to have conferred a favour even where it was not deserved; and this made him an easy prey to thieves and impostors. . . . . To me his kindness was unbounded. What plots would he not lay, what occasions would he not seek, to force some present upon me! nor did I ever see him better pleased than when he had prevailed upon me, either by artifice or entreaties, to accept one. In this respect I had need of the greatest caution against his attempts to catch me, nor did I ever find more use for my rhetoric than to invent pretexts for declining his munificence, without giving umbrage to my friend; for I could not bear to see him disappointed. If it happened that I had given orders by my servants for a piece of cloth to make a gown, he had already guessed my purpose, and paid the bill before I suspected it; nor could he be prevailed on by any entreaties to take back the money. If, on the other hand, I wished to save him from any loss, I was obliged to deceive him with similar arts. This kind of contest went on between us continually, very different from the vulgar method of dealing, where the sole object of the one party is to extort the most possible, and of the other to give the least possible. I could not prevail upon him to give nothing at all; but I am sure all his family will bear witness that I availed myself of his kindness very moderately. Whatever labours I undertook for him I undertook for love of learning. Considering that he gave up his whole life to the adornment, the illustration, and the advancement of such labours, avoiding no fatigue by day or night, but esteeming it a sufficient gain if a good author came into the hands of the public with due dignity, how could I prey upon a man thus minded? Sometimes, when he showed me and other friends the first pages of some great author, how he danced for joy, how his face beamed with triumph! You would have thought that he was already reaping in the greatest abundance the fruits of his labours, and expected no other reward. I will not here enhance the praise of Froben by throwing blame on others; but it is well known how full of errors and how badly printed are the books which have been sent out by some printers, even from Venice and Rome. But within these few years how many volumes, and in what noble type, have issued from Froben's office! And on this account he has refrained from having anything to do with controversial tracts, from which others have made no small profits, lest he should bring useful learning into disrepute. He printed Jerome twice, and was so bent on reprinting Augustine with equal splendour, notwithstanding the discouragements of several friends, of whom I was one, that he was wont to say to his intimates that he desired no longer life than would suffice to finish Augustine. He saw the completion of the first and second volumes only;—it was a pious wish, and the spirit by which he was animated was deserving of immortality; but it seemed otherwise to Providence, whose unsearchable counsels it were impiety either to examine or to reprehend. He was somewhat advanced in years, but his health was so strong and vigorous that throughout his entire life he was never laid up with illness. Six years ago he fell from the top of the stairs on a tiled floor, and the fall had almost proved fatal to him. He recovered, nevertheless, but the accident, as usual, left its effects behind it, however he might try to conceal them; for he was a man of such a high spirit that he was ashamed to let it be seen that he was in pain. The year before he died he was seized with the most excruciating pain in his right heel. Medical aid was at once called in, which however had no other effect but to exasperate the disease, on the nature of which the doctors disagreed, and while one tried one remedy and one another, some recommended that the foot should be cut off. At last a physician came who succeeded in subduing the pain so far as to render it tolerable, and permit of the patient taking food and sleep. Afterwards he felt so strong that he went twice on horseback to Frankfort, his disease having passed into the toes of his right foot, which he was unable to bend, though otherwise in good health. Being frequently advised by myself as well as by his doctor to go more seldom out of doors, or to go better protected against the cold, he refused to listen, thinking it a disgrace, by making any change in his usual habits, to admit that he was suffering from disease. Two of the fingers of his right hand now became paralysed, showing that death was not far off; but this also he concealed, thinking it unmanly in any respect to give way to disease. At last, as he was one day standing on an elevation for some purpose, the exact nature of which I do not know, he fell down on his face on the pavement, and gave himself a severe wound on the head. He was at once carried to his bed, when he neither raised his eyes, nor gave any evidence of feeling, nor any sign of life at all, except by moving his left hand—for the whole right side was paralysed. Thus for two days he lay as one asleep, but wakened up before his death, when the lid of his left eye was with difficulty slightly opened, his tongue, however, remaining immovable; nor did he live after that for more than six hours. So passed our Froben from the world to a more blessed life, leaving his wife, his children, his friends, the whole city, and all who knew him, bitterly to lament his loss. Let all who love letters array themselves in black, let them weep and exhibit the signs of woe, adorn his tomb with parsley and with flowers, sprinkle water and burn odours, if there be any avail in such ceremonies. This at least gratitude demands, that we all offer our prayers for the happiness of the deceased, and celebrate his memory with praises due; and that we give our support to the office of Froben, which not only will not cease on account of the decease of its master, but will make the most strenuous efforts that what he has begun may ever improve and grow."[84]

Fortunately the pitiful squabbles in which Erasmus was obliged to engage with his monkish persecutors did not prevent him giving most of his time to those more useful labours which he hoped would carry his name down to future ages. The biographer is naturally led to pay the greatest attention to those writings into which the personal element enters most largely, but these the author would have been well content to see consigned

[84] *Ep.* dcccexxii.

to oblivion. We must now rapidly pass in review the other works on which his pen was employed during this portion of his life.

The little work on the confessional, which provoked the animadversions of the Prince of Carpi, belongs to the early part of the year 1524.[25] It enumerates several advantages which, from the Romanist point of view, may fairly be claimed for the institution, but contains also a scathing exposure of the evils to which it gives rise, showing how it may become not only a formidable instrument of sacerdotal power, but also a means of propagating vice. Young and inexperienced priests, it informs us, frequently hear from their penitents of vices of which they would never have dreamed without such suggestion, and are consequently tempted to practise them, while on the other hand unscrupulous confessors often become the abettors of crime. On the whole, the impression is left that the institution does more harm than good. After condemning the handbooks of confession in common use, which enumerate all the crimes that either are or can be committed, the treatise concludes with some excellent practical remarks, pointing out what sins ought to be confessed, and suggesting that the penance should have some special application to the character of the sin.

In the course of the same, or the following year, he published several devotional works which he would have been glad to see translated into the vulgar tongues, instead of those which were likely to do him injury with

---

[25] *Exomologesis, sive Modus confitendi, per Erasmum Roterodamum, opus nunc primum et natum et excusum, cum aliis lectu dignis, quorum catalogum reperies in proxima pagella. Basiliæ, apud Joannem Frob. anno* MDXXIII.

the common herd of ignorant monks. One of these was a treatise on prayer,[26] in the course of which he takes occasion to defend the invocation of saints, on the ground that, if we ask good men on earth to pray for us, there seems to be no reason why we may not seek to benefit by their intercessions after they have departed this life. Others were a Sermon, or Oration, on the boundless mercy of God;[27] a Liturgy in praise of the Virgin of Laurentum,[28] for which he obtained the sanction of the Archbishop of Besançon; and a prayer to the Virgin in adversity.[29] This last has no date, while an exposition of the Lord's Prayer,[30] arranged under seven heads, for the days of the week, belongs to the year 1523. In his comparison of the Virgin and the Martyr,[31] written for a convent at Cologne, in acknowledgment of some delicacies sent him by the inmates, he had an opportunity of making some amends for his frequent commendations of the married state and his biting attacks on monasticism, of which to some extent he availed himself. "Married women," he remarks, "have no time for singing hymns, and sometimes lose all taste for it. They have to please their husbands, scold their servants, and whip their children. Our virgins, free from all the cares of this world, have

[26] *Modus Orandi Deum, per Desiderium Erasmum Roterodamum.*—Er. Op. v. 1099, where there is no date, but it is mentioned Ep. dcccxxxiii., which belongs to the year 1526.

[27] *De Immensa Dei Misericordia, Des. Erasmi Rot. Concio.* The dedication of this work to Christopher, Bishop of Basle, is dated July 29, 1524.

[28] *Liturgia Virginis Lauretana.*—Er. Op. v. 1327.

[29] *Obsecratio ad Virginem Matrem Mariam in rebus adversis.*—Er. Op. v. 1233.

[30] *Precatio Dominica, in septem portiones distributa, per D. Erasmum Roterodamum.* Oct. 24, 1523.

[31] *Virginis et Martyris Comparatio.* July 30, 1524.

nothing else to do but sing sweet hymns to their divine spouse." "To a virgin who loves her spouse, the convent is not a prison, as some falsely say, but a paradise." He, however, makes no retractation of principles previously avowed, but takes occasion to blame Tertullian and Jerome for being almost extravagant in their admiration of virginity; "for its excellence," he maintains, "should not be exalted to the disparagement of chaste marriage."

A commentary on Prudentius's hymn on the nativity,[32] written on Christmas day, 1524, and dedicated to Margaret Roper, Sir Thomas More's daughter, besides being admirably adapted to its purpose, enters into some details which, but for the practice of ecclesiastical writers, it might be thought blasphemous to discuss. Was it in those days the received belief that the Divine Son entered the Virgin's womb through her ear?

There is also a Commentary dedicated to John More, Margaret's only brother, on Ovid's little poem *De Nuce*.[33] In the preface Erasmus speaks of the many letters he had received from More's daughters, so excellently composed, and in such good Latin, that he would not have believed they were their own, did he not know it as a fact which admitted of no doubt.

In August, 1525, he published a work on the use and abuse of the tongue.[34] It is an eloquent treatise, abounding with all sorts of anecdotes illustrative of the

---

[32] *Commentarius in Hymnum Prudentii, De Natali Pueri Jesu.*—Er. Op. v. 1337.

[33] *P. Ovidii Nasonis Elegia de Nuce, cum commentario Desiderii Erasmi Roterodami.*—Er. Op. i. 1187.

[34] *Desiderii Erasmi Roterodami Lingua, sive de Linguæ usu atque abusu, liber utilissimus.* August 6, 1525.

subject, and may consequently be still read both with profit and pleasure. Its description of the tongue itself, as the organ of speech, embraces, I presume, all that was known at the time of its anatomy, and besides testifying to the author's extensive general knowledge, may show how much he had profited by his acquaintance with Linacre, Cop, and other celebrated physicians. On the publication of this work he wrote to his friends, "Erasmus will henceforth be mute, having parted with his tongue;" and the joke must have pleased him, for we find it repeated to several different correspondents.

He had been often entreated by his friends, and especially by the Bishop of Lincoln, to undertake a commentary on the Book of Psalms, and accordingly, he, at different times, made several of the Psalms the subjects of expositions or sermons, some of which were of a general character, while others were applied to the circumstances of the time. As early as 1515, he had written at St. Omer an exposition of the first Psalm, which in the Latin begins *Beatus vir*, and which he appropriately dedicated to his friend Beatus Rhenanus. A sermon on the fourth Psalm was dedicated to the Bishop of Lincoln in the year 1525, and to the same prelate some years afterwards an exposition of the eighty-fifth. The second and third Psalms were also appropriately handled, and in the latter years of his life he returned to the work;[35] but to have paraphrased, or commented on, the entire book, on the scale of those specimens, would itself have been the work of a lifetime. Of some at least of these expositions, as well as of his other devotional works, it may be remarked that they do not often rise much above what we might be inclined

---

[35] *Er. Op.* v. 171. *sqq.*

to consider common-place; but to those who were wearied with the logic-chopping and barren disquisitions of the schoolmen, we may well believe they would come as a stream of the water of life.

His most remarkable work of the year 1526, was the "Institution of Christian Matrimony,"[36] which he wrote at the request of Lord Mountjoy, and dedicated to Queen Catherine of England, by whom probably the work was suggested. So far as I can pretend to judge, it is an admirably full and complete treatment of the subject, in its social, legal, and religious aspects; and contains many good practical remarks on the choice of a mate, on the duties of husbands and wives, and on the education of children. On some parts of his subject he might perhaps have enlarged more if he had had the advantage of practical experience to guide him, but he certainly does not deserve to have his own joke applied to him by any one but himself, that in writing on marriage he was acting as absurdly as the philosopher who, never having been in a battle, undertook to lecture Hannibal on the art of war.[37] He gave great offence by seeming to place the married state above celibacy, and still more by suggesting a doubt whether marriage is a sacrament. On the first point, however, he expresses himself very cautiously, warned by the attacks which his "Praise of Marriage" had called forth, and on the other he confines himself to saying that such was the opinion of the early Fathers, adding that the more plausible opinion of the moderns has now prevailed.

This was shortly followed by "The Christian Widow,"

---

[36] *Christiani Matrimonii Institutio, per Desiderium Erasmum Roterodamum.*—*Er. Op.* v. 615.

[37] *Er. Op.* iii. 953, A.

written in compliment of Maria, sister of Charles V., whose youthful husband, the King of Pannonia and Bohemia, was prematurely snatched from her by the fortunes of war.[38]

Nor, while he was enriching the literature of his day with these original compositions, was the work of restoring the ancients neglected. In the year 1525, in a letter dated February 8, he dedicated to the Bishop of Olmutz an edition of Pliny's "Natural History," in which he claimed to have restored from a very old manuscript several passages which had before seemed hopelessly corrupt. While acknowledging the merit of previous restorers of Pliny's text, among whom were Hermolaus Barbarus and William Budæus, he claims for his own edition that it surpasses all its predecessors both in correctness of text and beauty of type.[39]

In 1526, he translated some treatises of Galen's, the whole of whose works had appeared at Venice, from the press of Aldus, in the original tongue.[40] Linacre was also a translator of Galen, and had done the work so well that Erasmus generously declared his translation to be more elegant than the original.

The same year he published an edition of Irenæus, which he dedicated to Bernard, Bishop of Trent. This is a *princeps editio*, and is said to be very defective and full of faults, owing to the want of good manuscripts.[41]

---

[38] *Vidua Christiana, per Desiderium Erasmum Roterodamum, ad inclytam quondam Pannoniæ Bohemiæque reginam Mariam, Caroli Cæsaris et Ferdinandi regis sororem.*—*Er. Op.* v. 723.

[39] *Ep.* dccxxx.

[40] *Ep.* dcccxxi. Erasmus translated the *Exhortatio ad bonas artes*, the *De optimo dicendi genere*, and the *Quod optimus Medicus idem sit et Philosophus.*—*Er. Op.* i. 1049, *sqq.*

[41] Massuet, in the preface to his own edition, speaks of it thus:— "Quoiqu'on ait beaucoup d'obligation à Erasme, qui d'ailleurs a si

In 1527 he translated into Latin several sermons of Chrysostom from a very old Greek manuscript which had been sent him from Venice, and also some works of St. Athanasius which had recently come to light. The former were dedicated to John III., King of Portugal: the latter to the Bishop of Lincoln.[42] The same year he assisted in an edition of Ambrose in four volumes, which he inscribed to John à Lasco, the Primate of Poland. The preface to this work is a very elegant composition, in which Erasmus graphically describes the contest between Ambrose and the Emperor Theodosius, draws a parallel between that time and his own, and laments that there is now no such peace-maker to heal the divisions of the Church. He dwells particularly on the moderation of Ambrose, observing that he usually writes more in sorrow than in anger; and to this circumstance he attributes it that his works have been so widely acceptable, and so little assailed by envy, and that, whereas the writings of other Fathers have been exposed to every species of hostility, Ambrose is quoted honourably by every one, even by heretics. Jerome alone, he remarks, seems to be sometimes unfair towards him. This was by no means the first edition of Ambrose. There were no fewer than three in the fifteenth century, the earliest of which is ascribed to the year 1485, while the second was printed at Milan in 1490. Both these, however, were very imperfect, and the credit of

bien mérité des lettres, d'avoir le premier publié les livres de S. Irénée, il est fâcheux que, privé des meilleurs manuscrits, il n'ait pas pû mieux faire. Son édition est si pleine de fautes, de lacunes, de périodes inutiles, que souvent on cherche Irénée dans Irénée, sans pouvoir decouvrir ce qu'il pense."—Quoted by Burigni.

[43] The translations from the Fathers will be found in vol. viii. of Le Clerc's *Erasmus*.

the first edition, approaching to a complete collection of his works, is due to John Amerbach. This was published at Basle in 1492, and reprinted in 1506. To this Erasmus added a few tractates, which had not appeared before, and some notes, which, however, were scarcely worthy of his fame. As usual, he complains, and no doubt with reason, of the great labour which had been expended on the restoration of this Father, but, as in other instances, he may be suspected of having relied more upon conjectures than on the authority of manuscripts.[43]

Early in 1528 Erasmus published an essay on the right pronunciation of Latin and Greek,[44] in which he exposes with great learning and ingenuity the incorrectness of the methods usually followed, and advocates principles which, though they have not yet been adopted in practice, would now be generally admitted to be substantially sound. The treatise takes the whimsical form of a conversation between a lion and a bear, and opens with a preliminary discussion of the qualifications requisite in schoolmasters, complaining that they are an underpaid class, and claiming for them a greater amount of respect than they usually receive. It then explains the formation of the letters of the alphabet, traces the causes of mispronunciation, discusses the vowel sounds, distinguishing between accent and quantity, discusses the pronunciation of the consonants, distinguishing F, Ph, and V, and showing that C and G had always uniform sounds both in Greek and Latin,

[43] *Ep.* dccclxxviii.—"Quantum autem sudoris in hoc restituendo, dum collatione veterum codicum emendantur depravata, restituuntur amputata, resecantur assuta, reponuntur Græca, quæ vel aberant prorsus, vel figuris nihil significantibus fuerant addita, tuæ prudentiæ fuerit æstimare."—*Conf.* MIGNE. *Pref.*

[44] *Dialogus de recta Latini Græcique sermonis pronunciatione.*—*Er. Op.* i. 913.

whatever vowel might follow, and is interspersed with several anecdotes and many wise and witty remarks. A story told by Voss respecting the origin of this treatise, on the authority of Rutgerus Rescius, professor of Greek in the College of Busleiden, and who lived for about two years in the same college with Erasmus, is on the face of it incredible. It is that Henry Glareanus, having come from Paris to Louvain, being invited to dinner by Erasmus, and asked what news he brought, knowing his curiosity and credulity, told him a story which he had invented on the way, to the effect that some very learned Greeks had recently arrived in Paris who pronounced their language very differently from the vulgar method; whereupon Erasmus immediately wrote his dialogue on Pronunciation, advocating the new method and passing it off as his own discovery, but afterwards perceiving that he had been imposed on, he did not make any change in his practice. But there is no evidence that he wrote the dialogue till long after he had left Louvain. Moreover, it is fatal to the truth of the story that it implies that the method of pronunciation advocated by Erasmus was erroneous, whereas it is really founded on sound principles, and, in fact, this treatise alone would entitle its author to a high rank among the pioneers of philological science.

Accompanying the dialogue on pronunciation was another work, which, as it concerned the character of Erasmus as a scholar, and involved him in a new controversy, demands some fuller notice. This was his celebrated "Ciceronian,"[45] which he wrote to ridicule the folly and absurdity of those pedants, chiefly Italians, who carried their admiration of Cicero to such an

[45] *Ciceronianus, sive de optimo dicendi genere, Dialogus.*—*Er. Op.* i. 973.

extreme that they made him their exclusive model, and would employ any circumlocution, however cumbrous, rather than use a word or a phrase which they could not support by his authority. The result of this pedantry was that they were obliged either to avoid treating Christian themes, or to apply to them, most inappropriately, names and titles borrowed from the pagan mythology, and accordingly it seems to have been a maxim with the Ciceronians to abstain from reading Christian authors as well as from the study of Greek. Erasmus, of course, had far too much good sense to permit himself to be led away by any such absurdity. He had formed his perhaps not highly polished but very effective and expressive style on no exclusive model, but on his wide acquaintance with all the principal Latin writers of all ages, both Christian and heathen. He knew well that he could not enforce Christian truth or discuss questions of Christian divinity unless he freely used words for which there was no classical authority, and he believed that if Cicero himself were to live again he would not hesitate to employ phrases of which as a heathen he had not felt the want. The Ciceronians, therefore, appeared to him semi-Pagans, and he did not scruple to call them so. They, on their part, could not endure that a barbarian, and especially one who did not fall down before the divinity they worshipped, should have so completely eclipsed Italian fame. Accordingly at Rome they were not satisfied with charging him with heresy; they would allow him no merit as a scholar or a critic. His translations of Hecuba and Iphigenia they said were stolen; his emendations of Jerome were mere guesses; his Seneca was a series of blunders. They called him

Er-rasmus to indicate that he was always in error; they
nicknamed him *Porrophagus*, from his frequent use of
the word "*porro*." Some years previously Erasmus
had written to Aleander to protest against these
calumnies,[46] either suspecting that he was their author,
or persuaded that by addressing himself to so influential
a person he must reach his less-known tormentors. He
now resolved to silence for ever the pretensions of these
pedants if possible, but in any case to hold them up to
the laughter of the world.

The Ciceronian also takes the form of a dialogue
between a member of the sect and two others who
resolve upon his conversion, and by pretending the
greatest sympathy with his weakness draw him on to
reveal all the mysteries of the craft. Nosoponus, the
subject of this experiment, proceeds to state that for
seven entire years he has read nothing but Cicero,
abstaining from all other literature as religiously as a
Carthusian friar from flesh meat. Having thus prepared himself, he next made a list in alphabetical order
of all the words contained in Cicero, another of the
phrases peculiar to that author, and a third indicating
the feet with which he begins and ends his sentences, as
well as the various ways in which the intervening words
are modulated. The first of these vocabularies distin-
guishes the different uses of the same word, nor is it
enough to note one or two examples; account must be
taken of every one, with the number of the page, the
number of the line, and whether in the beginning,
middle or end of the line. The true Ciceronian will not
use any word which is not actually found in Cicero,
even though it should have the sanction of Terence or

---

[46] *Ep.* dcxciii. Conf. *Ep.* dclxxxix.

any other equally approved author, nor will he even use any part of a Ciceronian word, unless Cicero has used that part: thus if he finds *amo, amas, amat,* but not *amamus* or *amatis,* he must confine himself to the former and eschew the latter. In short, he is no Ciceronian in whose writings there is found the lightest word for which the authority of Cicero cannot be quoted. Being thus provided with the necessary apparatus, the Ciceronian is now prepared to exercise his art. The time chosen is the dead of night. The place a study in the middle of his house, with thick walls and double doors and windows, and with every chink so carefully stopped, that even in the day-time it is scarcely possible for a ray of light to enter, or a sound from the outside to be heard. No one must sleep near in case they should talk in their sleep, or by their snores interrupt the flow of thought. Nor is this perfect seclusion sufficient. The worthy votary of the Tullian muse will bring to his task not only a pure heart, but a mind absolutely free from care, and with this view it is better that he should be a bachelor and never accept any public office. In preparation for that night he must dine lightly and abstain altogether from supper; only, lest a complete fast should affect his brain, he may partake of ten currants, which have the advantage of being both meat and drink, and of three coriander seeds coated with sugar. Having selected a favourable night, for it is not every night that will serve his purpose, he may now proceed to compose. He wants to write a letter, perhaps, for some papers which he had lent to a friend, and which he wishes to have returned. He turns over a number of Cicero's letters, consults his vocabularies, selects some very Ciceronian words; then figures of speech, phrases, numbers; then considers what ornaments would be appropriate. In this way it may take a long winter's night to complete a single sentence. Nor is one writing by any means enough. The composition must be recast again and again; again and again compared with the vocabularies, so that not a word may escape; and finally, before it can be considered perfect, it must be laid past for several days, and then re-examined with a cool head, with the possible result of being ultimately condemned. Having thus drawn out the Ciceronian, Bulephorus, the chief speaker on the other side, under pretence of asking for further advice, begins to expose the absurdity of the whole affair. He first obtains the admission that whoever desires to excel in composition ought to choose the best models for his imitation, and M. Tully, he remarks, is selected merely because he possesses more of the graces of eloquence than any other Latin writer. Yet even he is deficient in some very necessary qualifications. For instance, no one doubts that humour is part of the art of rhetoric, but there Cicero entirely failed. Brevity is sometimes required in an orator, and of that Sallust and Brutus are better models than Cicero. For explaining an involved subject Hortensius is preferable. For trustworthiness, which is one of the principal qualities of an orator, we must go rather to Aristides, Phocion, Cato, or Brutus. Moreover, Cicero did not write upon all subjects. Some of his works too are lost, so that it is impossible for any one to be a complete Ciceronian. By-and-bye Nosoponus is prevailed on to admit that he does not speak well who does not speak aptly, and that, in order to speak aptly, our speech must adapt itself to present persons and things. But the present state of the world, Bulephorus continues, does not at all resemble the times of Cicero, seeing that our religion, government, laws, manners, studies, and even the very appearance of men, are all changed. It is an impertinence, then, to ask us to express ourselves in all things as Cicero did. Whoever would impose that rule, "let him first restore the Rome of old, let him restore the Senate and the Senate House, the Conscript Fathers, the equestrian order, the people marshalled in their centuries and tribes; let him restore the colleges of the Augurs and the Auspices, the Pontifex maximus, the flamens and vestals, the ædiles, prætors, tribunes of the people, the consuls, dictators, emperors, the comitia, laws, decrees of the senate, plebiscites, statues, triumphs, ovations, supplications, temples, shrines, sacrifices, the gods and goddesses, the Capitol and the sacred fire; let him restore the provinces, colonies, municipal towns, and allies of the city that ruled the world." No one will be inclined to dispute the justness of this reasoning. Erasmus afterwards gives several examples of the substitution of Ciceronian for Christian phrases, and maintains that the preference for the former is due to the secret paganism which lurks at the heart of those apes of Cicero. He shows that the advantage of being a Ciceronian is not worth the pains, since business is now transacted in the vernacular, and as to public addresses, the vulgar do not appreciate Ciceronian eloquence, while nothing can be less adapted for sermons. To what use, then, will you put this accomplishment? Writing letters to the learned? But there are very few of these, and they care nothing for Ciceronian phrase, provided your language be good, pure, and tasteful. To whom then? To four Italians, who have recently begun to boast themselves Ciceronians, although they do not bear the slightest resemblance to Cicero, and have not a single feature the same.

But enough, perhaps, has been said to indicate the nature of this admirable piece, in which wit, learning, and eloquence all perform their due part. It concludes with a review of the principal writers of Latin from Cicero down, among whom it is shown that not one was a Ciceronian in the Italian sense of the word. In this part of his essay, in which it was necessary to touch on the merits of living writers, although he was liberal of his praise, Erasmus did not escape giving offence. Some were angry because they were omitted altogether; others because they thought they were not sufficiently commended. Quite a ferment was excited among the literary men of France because Budæus seemed to be somewhat disparaged, and it was no doubt with a mischievous intention that Erasmus placed his great rival by the side of Badius the printer, and appeared almost to imply the superiority of the latter. The supposed affront gave occasion to a variety of epigrams, and called forth several letters of remonstrance recommending that Erasmus should write an apology. He could not, however, admit that there was any necessity for doing so, as it was entirely owing to the circumstance of them both living in Paris that Budæus and Badius had been mentioned together, and he had compared them only in one particular, admitted to be of no account, while he had added that Budæus, if no Ciceronian, was to be admired for many other excellent gifts. It would, he thought, show a very poor opinion of one for whom he had in reality the highest esteem, to assume that he could have taken offence where there was so little cause for it. The letter to his French friend, Germanus Brixius, in which he makes these remarks, was, perhaps, received as a sufficient atonement.[47]

The two Italian scholars, Bembo and Sadoleti, well known as the apostolic secretaries of Leo X., who, as the principal representatives of the Ciceronian party, might have considered themselves specially aggrieved by the attack of Erasmus on their favourite pedantry, would not seem to have taken any serious offence, and may, perhaps, have been rather inclined to profit by his good-humoured criticism. Both of them, indeed, are mentioned with just commendation in the "Ciceronian," but Bembo, who carried his classical pedantry to a ridiculous extreme, might well have suspected himself of having suggested the Nosoponus of the piece. We find him, however, afterwards corresponding with Erasmus on friendly terms,[48] while with Sadoleti, who shared his own moderate views of reform, the relations of the latter would seem to have been of a particularly pleasing character. There is a letter which he wrote to him on the occasion of the sack of Rome by the Imperial troops, under the Constable Bourbon—this, however, was before the publication of the "Ciceronian"—to condole with him on the loss of property which he had then sustained, and especially on the destruction of his splendid library; and this was followed by a further correspondence, which extended to considerable length, Sadoleti having hinted to Erasmus how much better it would be for him to abstain in his writings from controverted points, and from running counter to popular prejudice in respect to questions which did not involve

[47] *Ep.* dccclxxxi.
[48] *Ep.* mxlii. mxcix. mccxxxii. mcclix. mcclxxii.

true piety, and Erasmus defending himself with his accustomed vigour and fulness, but with the most perfect good temper.[49] On the other hand, the indignation provoked by the attack on the Ciceronians found a vent in a furious oration by the famous scholar, Julius Cæsar Scaliger, in which Erasmus was loaded with abuse, and Cicero defended in no very Ciceronian style.[50] Erasmus, with the approval of his friends, wisely resolved to take no notice of this philippic. He would not believe that Scaliger was the real author, but strangely ascribed it to Aleander. "I, who have lived in the same house and slept in the same bed, and know the man inside and out, am as sure it is his as I am that I live."[51] Scaliger, taking this to mean that he was incapable of producing such an oration, was only the more enraged, and wrote another invective still more furious than the first; but this was never even seen by its object, who died before it was published. It would appear that he afterwards made some atonement and endeavoured to do more justice to the merits of Erasmus.

---

[49] *Ep.* dccclxxxviii. dcccxciv. mlxxxv., &c.

[50] *J. Cæs. Scaligeri pro M. Tullio Cicerone contra Desid. Erasmum Roterodamum Oratio I.* Tolosæ, 1620. The oration was sent to Paris in 1529, and, after many difficulties, printed in 1531.—See Bayle.

[51] "Cum Aleandro per literas expostularam de libello Julii Cæsaris. Is, quo se liberet stolidissimi facinoris invidia, excusat se literis accurate scriptis, sed utitur lemmatibus multo frigidissimis. Exemplar ad te mitto. Ut video, tibi propemodum persuasit : at ego, qui de domestico convictu ac lectuli quoque contubernio totum intus et in cute novi, tam scio esse ovum illius, quam scio me vivere. Sed huic tempori serviendum."—*Ep.* mccxviii. The date of this letter is May 3, 1532, but it was from a later letter, dated March 18, 1535, that Scaliger learned that the credit of his composition was denied him. His second oration was written in that year, but not printed till the close of 1536.—See Bayle.

The "Ciceronian" was dedicated to John Ulattenus in a preface, dated February 14, 1528, in which Erasmus explains that his object is not to discourage the imitation of Cicero, but to show how we may truly copy him and combine his great eloquence with Christian piety. And still more efficiently to guard against any perversion of his real meaning, he afterwards dedicated to the same friend an edition of Cicero's "Tusculan Questions," with a beautiful preface, doing full justice to the great Roman. When Froben, he said, asked him to assist in this work, he readily acceded to his request, being delighted to have the opportunity of reading Cicero again, not only for the sake of polishing his own style, but because such a study tended so much to the regulation and control of the passions. When reading he often felt indignant with those who say that Cicero has no excellence but pomp of words. "What may be the case with others," he proceeds, "I know not; but for myself, such is the impression made upon me by M. Tully, especially when he treats of the rules of moral conduct, that I can not doubt that the heart from which such sentiments flow must be inspired with some divine fervour. And this opinion of mine pleases me the more as often as I consider how infinite and inestimable is the goodness of God, which some would fain make as narrow, I fear, as their own hearts. Where Cicero's soul may be now, is a question which, it may be, lies beyond the reach of the human understanding. I at least will not dispute with those who entertain the hope that he is now living peacefully in heaven." This opinion he defends on the ground that Cicero had just notions of God and immortality, and lived an upright and even a holy life. Very few Jews, before the publication of the Gospel, had exact notions of the Son and the Spirit; many did not believe in the resurrection of the body, and yet no one doubts their salvation. "When I was a boy," he says, "I did not like Cicero so well as Seneca, and I was twenty years old before I could bear to sit long at him, though I enjoyed the other classical authors. Whether I have made progress with the advance of years I do not know, but I certainly never loved Cicero more than I do now when I am an old man, not only on account of a felicity of expression which is almost divine, but on account of the sanctity of his mind."[58] These sentiments may not have pleased the monks, but they ought to have satisfied the Ciceronians.

Erasmus was busily engaged on the "Ciceronian" and the treatise on Pronunciation, when he was interrupted by an affair which was very nearly involving him in a lawsuit, and which ended not altogether to his advantage. Ever since his quarrel with Hutten, the *soi-disant* knight, Henry Eppendorf had continued sending him threatening letters, with the view, he suspected, of extorting money, or possibly even of terrifying him to death—a thing which might readily enough have occurred, Erasmus thought, in the case of an old man like himself, an invalid and naturally timorous—and at last having found out that he had written to Duke George about him complaining of his conduct, he threatened him with a lawsuit for defamation of character. Arriving in Basle, apparently at the beginning of 1528, he encountered Beatus, into whose bosom he immediately poured out all his wrath, telling him how the Duke, who had hitherto been his best friend, had now be-

[58] *Ep.* ccccxcix. App.

come his most bitter enemy, and how he had in consequence lost a large fortune, meaning perhaps by marriage. Beatus, ever a lover of peace, advised that he should see Erasmus, which Eppendorf did not altogether refuse, but he declared that he would not go to his house. Meantime he went about, loudly complaining everywhere how badly Erasmus had used him. The day after his arrival he called upon the chief magistrate, and intimated that he intended to take legal proceedings, but was told that the Council was then very much occupied and that he would have to wait for some days. The day following an interview took place. Eppendorf produced a letter to Duke George, which, however, as it was written in a strange hand, and without date or signature, Erasmus declined to acknowledge as his own, and an altercation arising on this point, Beatus interposed and begged them to be reconciled, to which Erasmus replied that he had no objection. The discussion, however, was renewed, on Eppendorf again complaining of the injury done to his character; but, after much mutual recrimination, he at length agreed that peace should be made, but on certain conditions to be proposed by himself. Being desired to state them, he replied that he was too much excited to do so just then, but he would send them the next day by Beatus. The terms which he then proposed were that Erasmus should publicly retract his accusations by dedicating some work to him; secondly, that he should write to the Duke to restore him to his good graces, the letter to be first read by Eppendorf; and thirdly, that he should give one hundred ducats for the poor of Friburg, as many for those of Basle, and two hundred, which Eppendorf himself would carry to Strasburg, where he was then residing, and distribute at his own discretion.

Erasmus, feeling sure that Eppendorf would never be able to prove that the letter to the Duke was not a forgery, and confident that he had a counter case equally strong in the threatening letters addressed to himself, and in other acts of hostility, was at first disposed to try the chances of the law. Against this course, however, he was advised by his friends, Beatus, Boniface Amerbach, and Berus, who recommended him to make any terms rather than put it in the power of this talkative and idle profligate to fill the whole country with the report that Erasmus had been arraigned before the court of Basle. They urged, besides, that among his judges there would be many personally hostile to him on account of his opposition to Luther. The force of these considerations could not be denied; but what chiefly determined him was the loss of time, and the mental annoyance, which a lawsuit must inevitably occasion. He was compelled to reflect, moreover, that, after all, his suspicions of Eppendorf rested on a number of minute circumstances, which, however conclusive they might appear to his own mind, might yet fail to carry conviction to others. For these reasons, then, he resolved, if possible, to come to terms, and drew up a counter-proposal in which he agreed to the dedication, adding that he would do even more for the sake of friendship, only, however, if he saw a real change in Eppendorf's conduct. In regard to the second condition, he said he could not tell what cause the Duke might have for displeasure, but if it arose from his own complaint he had no objection to endeavour to soften it by writing such a letter as he might presume to address to a person of such exalted rank. As to the proposed alms, that was a matter he would attend to himself, and the less Eppendorf said about it the better, lest it should be thought that money was the only object he had in view in bringing his charge. Rhenanus and Amerbach being chosen arbitrators, decided that Erasmus should accept the two first conditions proposed by Eppendorf, and should besides pay twenty florins, to be lodged in their hands for the benefit of the poor. The transaction was completed with all due solemnity in the presence of Louis Berus and Henry Glareanus, who acted as witnesses. The arbitrators first shook hands with the two parties, and exacted a promise that they would abide by their decision. The judgment was then read aloud, and each one signified his assent, first verbally, afterwards by subscription. They then broke the same bread in token of friendship, and drank from the same cup—the cup which Duke George had given to Erasmus. The latter next proposed that their friendship should be for ever, to which Eppendorf agreed, and thereupon they again shook hands. The next day Erasmus received them all at supper; everything was done to show that he had forgotten all offences, but no sooner was supper over than Eppendorf began to ask for the letter to Duke George, which he said he must have against the following morning. Although no time had been prescribed when it should be given, still, as he was urgent, rather than run the risk of putting an end to their friendship almost before it had begun, Erasmus complied. Eppendorf then declared that he must have the dedication as well, and, however absurd it might seem to write a preface to a book which was not yet in existence, at the request of the arbitrators this second demand also was acceded to.

A form of dedication was drawn up and handed to Eppendorf, and so the party separated.[53]

Altogether it was a very awkward affair, and, notwithstanding his own defence of his conduct, in the letter to his friend Pirckheimer, from which the above particulars are taken, it must be confessed that Erasmus does not appear to as much advantage on this occasion as his admirers could wish. In the first place, even supposing that Eppendorf was as bad as he believed him to be, it may be thought that there was a certain degree of meanness in his calling in the aid of the powerful Duke of Saxony to relieve himself of a troublesome persecutor.

On the other hand, it should be remembered that Eppendorf had been specially recommended by Duke George to Erasmus, and the latter may accordingly have thought himself called upon to exercise some sort of *surveillance* over the young man's conduct. Still, if he denied his own letter—and it is not easy to escape from the impression that the letter produced was really his, or rather a copy of it—it looks as if he was conscious that he had written it under the influence of personal feeling, and felt that Eppendorf had some real grounds of complaint against him. That Erasmus himself believed the letter to be his may be inferred from the way in which he attempts to justify himself for disowning it. How, he asks, could he be expected to remember after so many years? The Duke's answer to Eppendorf, which he called upon him in vain to produce, would have proved that he had never penned such libels. Besides, supposing it to have been his, he did not say that he had not written it, but only that he

[53] *Ep.* dcccclviii. cccxlvi. App.

did not recognise it; and even if he had said that he had not written it, it would have been the truth, as it was not in his handwriting. Assuredly the memory of Erasmus was not so treacherous that he could not trust it on such an important point after any length of time, and had he really suspected forgery his denial would have been far more explicit and indignant. On the other hand, before a court of law, he would certainly have been justified in throwing the burden of proof upon his adversary, and it may be remarked that in the letter to Pirckheimer he goes into the question with lawyer-like minuteness, even discussing the hypothesis that the letter had appeared to be in his own handwriting, and arguing that even in that case it would have been a folly for him to acknowledge it, such forgeries being far from uncommon. Admitting, however, that he was entitled to call upon his adversary to prove the genuineness of his document before founding any charge upon it, to promise to write a dedication to such a man as Eppendorf, to place a worthless adventurer, as he regarded him, on the same level of honour with the Warhams and the Mountjoys, was a humiliation to which he ought never to have consented. It is strange indeed that his friends should have permitted it, but probably they would never have done so had he not himself first accepted the proposal. No doubt the almost certain alternative of his refusal was the payment of a large sum of money, but any payment would have been better than the degradation of being compelled publicly to acknowledge as an equal a man whom he had previously insulted, and whom he still hated and despised. He was convinced, however, that Eppendorf's main object was the extortion of money, and on that point he resolved to be firm. He would not, he declared, give him anything for the poor of Strasburg, suspecting that Eppendorf himself was the poorest man there. The truth may be, perhaps, that Erasmus was deficient in that fine sense of honour which would have enabled him to see at once the full extent of the humiliation to which he was submitting; while, on the other hand, he very properly had strong objections to being imposed upon. Probably he had never intended to keep his promise of a dedication, and when he made it depend on Eppendorf's sincerity, he left himself a loop-hole by which he might have escaped had not his adversary insisted on its immediate fulfilment. After all, the dedication was comparatively worthless without the book which ought to have accompanied it.

Eppendorf, having thus gained at least one of his objects, made the most of his victory, and boasted everywhere that he had reduced Erasmus to terms to which he himself would not have condescended for a thousand guineas. The evangelicals were in ecstasies. The report flew through Germany that Erasmus had been atrociously used by Henry Eppendorf, and had been reconciled to him on the most disgraceful conditions. It was not long before Eppendorf began to accuse him of a breach of faith for not having sent him the promised book, and on this he wrote him a letter of expostulation, excusing himself on the plea of being overwhelmed with work, besides having so many controversies on hand. No time, he urged, had been prescribed for the fulfilment of his promise, and even if there had been, he was not on that account chargeable with breach of faith. Otherwise every debtor who failed of payment on the appointed day would be open to a similar charge. "How unreasonable this would be," he pointedly adds, "no one knows better than yourself." The letter called forth an angry rejoinder, in which Eppendorf, in the strongest language, repudiated this last insinuation against his character. "I have nothing to do," he added, "with your theological quarrels, which no doubt you bring upon yourself: all I ask of you is that you should keep your word."[34] The adventurer carried his complaint to the court of Saxony, but the Duke refused to see him, saying he would have nothing to do with a man who was ashamed to acknowledge his own father. At the same time he wrote a kind letter to Erasmus, who, of course, had lost no time in informing him of the real state of the case, in which he expressed his regret that at his years and with his great learning he should be persecuted by such a fellow, and advised him to take no more notice of him than if he were a fly buzzing about his head.[35] By persevering applications, however, Eppendorf at length prevailed on the Duke to commit the case to Julius Pflug, from whom he hoped for a favourable verdict, as he knew nothing of his character, and he had induced him to listen to his own version of the story. Pflug wrote in the most friendly style to Erasmus, but desired him to fulfil the terms of the agreement by adding a book to the preface already written. This, however, he declined to do on the ground that Eppendorf had violated the agreement before leaving Basle, and since then had not ceased to speak and write against him in the most hostile manner. He was now at all events sensible that he had made a false step in writing the dedication, and he afterwards declared

[34] *Ep.* mlxxxvii., mlxxxviii.   [35] *Ep.* cccxlviii. App.

that he had resolved to endure anything rather than stain his paper with the name of such a worthless person. And so the matter ended; for there was no power to compel him to go farther in the performance of his promise. He suspected, however, perhaps justly enough, that Eppendorf continued to circulate falsehoods regarding him, and to stir up enemies to attack him.[56]

During this, the last year of his residence at Basle, Erasmus was very much occupied with two other works which we must now notice. One of these was a new edition of Seneca. Several years ago he had published an edition of Seneca, which, however, was altogether unworthy of his fame, and which he was now anxious to repudiate. It was indeed only partially his own work. Having found some manuscripts of Seneca at Cambridge, he brought them with him to Basle, and having hastily run through them, noting on the margin the various readings and such emendations in the very corrupt text as his own judgment suggested, on being obliged to leave town he put the work into the hands of a friend, who promised to finish it for him. On his return home some months afterwards he found the work printed, but so full of errors that he felt quite ashamed of it. For this, however, he blames himself, who had entrusted to another what he ought to have done himself, rather than his friend, who had undertaken a task to which he was unequal. The book was dedicated to the Bishop of Durham, and nearly cost him the friendship of that prelate. He sent the Bishop his copy through a bookseller, who happened to be going to England, but who never delivered it, though he positively affirmed that he had done so. The Bishop, accordingly, when

[56] *Ep.* mcxlvi.

Erasmus wrote to him mentioning the book and the dedication, thought he was laughing at him, and having afterwards discovered how many blunders there were in the edition, he was still more angry, and on his calling upon him on his return to England, gave him a most freezing reception, whereas previously he had been most cordial. Thus stimulated by the prospect of retrieving his character, Erasmus undertook, as he hoped with better auspices, the new edition, on which he spent so much care that he considered himself quite justified in repudiating the former one. "I will not," he says, "attempt to describe the labour it has cost me; for I know no one will believe it, unless he compares the former edition with this one. If any one will take the trouble to do that, he will immediately see that this is quite another Seneca from the former one; not that nothing is left requiring further elucidation, but that by a happy as well as bold criticism, aided by various manuscripts, some of which were of very great antiquity, I have removed innumerable monstrosities." Erasmus alleges two special reasons for the extraordinary corruption of the text of this author, independently of the usual carelessness of transcribers. The first was his affected and obscure phraseology, which made it very easy to misread him. The other was the great esteem in which he was held by the ancient Christians, who almost regarded him as an orthodox writer, partly on account of the excellence of his precepts, and partly for the sake of his pretended correspondence with the Apostle Paul. This respect for him was still farther increased by St. Jerome, who entered him in his catalogue of saints, and the consequence was that Seneca was more widely read than any other heathen writer, and that, abounding as he does with unusual words, with historical allusions, Græcisms, and other difficulties, unlearned and half-learned readers were tempted to alter his text to suit their own ignorance or caprice; and to such an extent was this carried that Erasmus tells us he often found the same place so variously corrupted that not in a single word did the different copies agree with one another, nor yet with the true reading according to the old manuscripts. The sound critical perceptions of Erasmus led him of course to reject as spurious the correspondence of Seneca and St. Paul, as well as the absurd story of his being a Christian in disguise. For supposing the philosopher could have been such a coward as not to give the least hint of his faith even in his latest writings, and so wary as to have escaped the suspicions of Nero, who, when bent on his death and anxious to find charges against him, never reproached him with Christianity, how are we to explain or defend the fact that to the end he goes on speaking of gods and goddesses, and in several places expresses doubts whether man survives the tomb? "Besides, what end does this fiction serve? Is it to recommend his works to Christian men? For my part, I think it would be more to the reader's advantage to read the works of Seneca as of a man ignorant of our religion. For if you read him as a pagan, he wrote like a Christian; but if you read him as a Christian, then he wrote like a pagan." The preface from which these particulars are taken proceeds with some further remarks on the philosophy of Seneca, contains a learned disquisition on his style, and gives an account of his extant works.[57]

[57] *Ep.* mx.

It had never been the custom of Erasmus to dedicate the different editions of his works to different patrons, still less, like some beggarly authors, who, as they expressed it, boasted of procuring several sons-in-law by perhaps their only offspring, to inscribe different copies of the same book with the names of various great men. As we remember, he disappointed the not unnatural suspicion of Warham in this matter, by adding the Iphigenia in Aulis of Euripides to the Hecuba already presented to him, and through the various editions of the "Adages," immensely increased as the later ones were compared with the first little volume, he never changed from his pupil and patron, William Mountjoy. From this practice, however, he departed on the present occasion, and in order to mark the complete want of identity between the two editions of Seneca, the new one was dedicated to his new friend, the Bishop of Cracow and Chancellor of Poland.

The other work to which I have referred was the complete edition of St. Augustine, which it had long been the ambition of Froben to bring out with equal splendour to his "Jerome." Several of the works of the great African Father had been printed separately even before the close of the fifteenth century, and in 1506 John Amerbach had published, for the first time, a collected edition which had given universal satisfaction. Since that time, however, the art of printing had made great progress, and Amerbach's text, however creditable it might be to his industry and zeal, was now found to be full of faults, which it would be desirable to remove in a new edition. Scarcely any other author, Erasmus complained, had suffered so much from the rash and impious trifling of lazy monks as Augustine. His involved style rendered him peculiarly liable to corruption, while both labour and judgment were necessary to separate the ridiculous interlineations of the monks from the genuine text. Erasmus had no intention at his time of life, and in the infirm state of his health, of undertaking a task which required a man in the vigour of youth and strength, but John Froben with some difficulty at length prevailed upon him to undertake the correction of a single sheet of the Epistles, to be shown as a specimen at the next Frankfort fair. He made the promise on condition that no more would be asked; but afterwards, finding that Froben was bent on completing the volume of the Epistles, and that no one else was prepared to act as editor, he allowed regard for his friend as well as the piety of the task to overcome his first resolution. He consented to take charge of the entire volume, but on the understanding that he was not to be asked to do more, and he repeatedly assured Froben that if he was determined to proceed he must find some other editor. No one, however, offered himself, and as Froben declared that he was resolved to print the whole on his own responsibility, partly from respect to his friend, to whom he could refuse nothing, but chiefly because he thought it would be disgraceful if one of the most distinguished fathers of the Church should be permitted again to appear with all the errors of the transcribers made more conspicuous by splendid print and paper, he submitted his shoulders to the burden. When at length he actually entered on his task, he found the difficulties far greater than he had anticipated, so that he more than once thought of abandoning the undertaking in despair, to which the evident risk to his health almost compelled him. The death of Froben, too, struck down in the midst of his labour, filled him with alarm. On further consideration, however, this rather stimulated him to persevere, and it became a point of honour with him not to abandon his friend's children, on whom it devolved to complete this most laborious work. Accordingly he set himself resolutely to his task, and found that as it proceeded, the toil continually became less, owing, he believed, to the immediate help of St. Augustine himself.

The work was completed in ten volumes, and was dedicated to the Archbishop of Toledo, in a preface from which the above particulars are mostly taken.[58] Some years before—namely in 1522—Vives had edited the *De Civitate Dei*, with an admirable commentary, and this was adopted into the edition of Erasmus, where it formed the fifth volume. This edition has been frequently reprinted.

The "Augustine" appeared in the year 1529, after the removal of Erasmus to Friburg, whence the preface is dated. We must now glance at the causes which induced him to leave Basle.

[58] *Ep.* mlxxxiv.

CHAPTER XVIII.

PROGRESS OF THE REFORMATION AT BASLE — THE NEW DOGMA — CONRAD PELICAN — ŒCOLAMPADIUS — THE MASS ABOLISHED — ERASMUS REMOVES TO FRIBURG — INVITATION FROM FUGGER — LETTER TO PIRCKHEIMER — TROUBLES OF HOUSEKEEPING — ERASMUS'S HEALTH GIVES WAY — HIS EDITION OF ST. CHRYSOSTOM — THE DIET OF AUGSBURG — HIS APOPHTHEGMS — PREFACE TO ARISTOTLE — TO LIVY — EDITION OF ST. BASIL — HE BUYS A HOUSE — DEATH OF PIRCKHEIMER — AND OF WARHAM — VARIOUS WORKS — PAUL III. — THE "ECCLESIASTES" — ERASMUS RETURNS TO BASLE — HIS LAST ILLNESS AND DEATH — ESTIMATE OF HIS CHARACTER AND INFLUENCE.

THE reason why Erasmus left Basle will be readily surmised. Ever since the return of Œcolampadius, towards the end of 1522, the reformed doctrines had been making rapid progress in that city, and the more they gained ground the more equivocal, of course, his position must have become. Nor was it possible for him, with his habits of free utterance, and especially while the Protestants insisted on claiming him for their own side, to abstain altogether from expressing himself on the points in dispute between the two parties; and if sometimes he appeared to favour the new doctrines, his unguarded language being turned against him by the fanatics of either side, he was afterwards compelled, in self-defence, to make stronger protestations of his orthodoxy than he might otherwise have been inclined to do. Thus it was notably in regard to the most important question discussed during those years—the real presence of Christ in the sacramental elements—a point on which, it is well known, the Swiss reformers left Luther far behind. "A new dogma," wrote Erasmus, "has grown up here, that there is nothing but bread and wine in the Eucharist, and Œcolampadius has defended it with so many strong testimonies and arguments that it would be no wonder if the very elect were deceived."[1] And still more incautiously he wrote to his friend Pirckheimer, who had replied to Œcolampadius in a work in defence of the real presence, though rather in the Lutheran than the orthodox sense: "I should not be averse to the opinion of Œcolampadius, were it not that the consent of the Church is the other way. For I do not see what is the use of a body which is imperceptible to the senses, and which could confer no benefit, if it were perceptible, provided a spiritual grace be present in the elements."[2] He adds, indeed, that for all that he cannot possibly depart from the consent of the Church, but, if he talked in this way, as it is likely he did, there might be some excuse for the spiteful Farel whispering in the ear of a young Englishman—Thomas Grey's son, I presume—that Erasmus held right opinions, but had not the courage to profess them.[3] He was still more annoyed by a rumour which Conrad Pelican industriously spread to the effect that he held the same opinions with himself on the subject of the Eucharist. On hearing this he called Pelican to order pretty sharply in some letters which he wrote to him, and having invited him to an interview he at length compelled him to confess that his own opinion was that Christ's body is not substantially present in the Eucharist, and that he had never before expressed that opinion in his hearing,

[1] *Er. Op.* iii. 892, A.   [2] *Ib.* 941, A.   [3] *Ib.* 963, D.

nor heard any such sentiment from him. In a final letter which he wrote to Pelican Erasmus repudiates the reformed doctrine with unusual force. "I would rather," he says, "be torn limb from limb than profess the same as you profess, and I would rather endure every extremity than leave the world with such a sin upon my conscience."[1]

In order to obviate any evil effects which might arise from such reports Erasmus thought it advisable to write to the Council of the Swiss nation, which met at Baden in the year 1526, to assure them that he had not departed from the doctrine of the Church on the Eucharist, and it was no doubt a similar feeling which led him some years afterwards (1530) to publish an edition of Algerus, a Benedictine monk of the eleventh century, who wrote a work in confutation of the heresy of Berengar. In his preface to this work Erasmus, while deprecating curious inquiries as to the mode of transubstantiation, maintains that from the Apostles down the unanimous teaching of the Church had ever been that the true substance of the Lord's body and blood was present in the Eucharist. "I have never doubted," he concludes, "of the truth of the Lord's body, but somehow by the reading of this book my opinion has been confirmed and my reverence increased."[2]

All his protests, however, did not prevent Œcolampadius from quoting him in support of his own views.

---

[1] "Si tibi persuasum est in synaxi nihil esse præter panem et vinum, ego membratim discerpi malim quam idem profiteri quod tu profiteris, et omnia perpeti malim, quam tali flagitio contra meam ipsius conscientiam admisso, ex hac vita demigrare."—*Er. Op.* iii. 966, D.

[2] *Ep.* mxcv.

"I am greatly annoyed," he writes to Pirckheimer, "that Œcolampadius should mix up my name in his books without any reason, though he knows that I dislike to be named by him, dislike still more to be blamed by him, and dislike most of all to be praised by him."[*] And he was still more annoyed when the magistrates of Basle consulted him, privately however, as to the expediency of permitting Œcolampadius's book to be sold in the city. Berus, Boniface Amerbach, and another lawyer named Canzoneta, were joined with him in this deliberation, and their opinion, which, says Erasmus, was delivered without offence to Œcolampadius, must have been unfavourable, as he tells us elsewhere that the book was not on sale in Basle. The probability of being often appealed to in this way, when it would be impossible for him to avoid giving offence, or he might be betrayed into expressing sentiments that savoured of heresy, must have made him extremely uneasy. Accordingly, for some years past he had been thinking of a change of residence. At the same time, no doubt, he was very reluctant to leave a city where he lived beyond the reach of his monkish persecutors, surrounded by a circle of admiring friends, and, above all, where he had the command of the best printing-press on this side of the Alps. When, however, the mass was at length abolished by public authority, and the images removed from the churches, he felt that to remain longer would be to give his sanction to those innovations. His only hesitation now was where to fix his residence. He would indeed have received a welcome from any of the crowned heads in Europe, but he had never yet parted with his liberty, and he

[*] *Er. Op.* iii. 1028, A.

accordingly refused pressing invitations from Henry
VIII., who graciously reminded him that he had once
promised to choose England as a retreat for his old
age,¹ and from Ferdinand the King of Bohemia, who
offered him a salary of four hundred florins on the sole
condition that he would live in Vienna.⁸ He was
resolved, however, not to leave the Emperor's dominions,
and at length he fixed on the little town of Friburg, in
the Brisgau, where there was a university of some repute,
chiefly famed for its faculty of law, and where his friend
Zasius, his mind still unimpaired by his advanced years,
and several other learned men, were ready to welcome
him. Perhaps the chief recommendation of Friburg
was that there was there no religious dissension, but, on
the contrary, "the greatest unanimity between the
clergy, the magistrates, the people, and the university."
Immediately before his departure he also declined, on
the plea of his health and advanced years, liberal offers
from Anthony Fugger, the celebrated German merchant-
prince, who wished him to settle at Augsburg: he was
now, he wrote, too old a tree for transplantation, and,
though reluctantly compelled to leave Basle, he intended,
in the first place, removing only a short distance; he
had, besides, already sent his most valuable furniture to
Friburg, where a home was provided for him by the
corporation. His excuses were received in good part,
and Fugger sent him in reply a magnificent goblet, with
a request that he would make use of his services whenever he required them. The particulars of his departure,
and of the revolution at Basle which made it necessary,
are thus related in a letter to Pirckheimer:—

¹ *Ep.* dccccxxxvi.   ⁸ *Er. Op.* iii. 931, B. C.

ERASMUS *to his friend* BILIBALD.[9]

"*Friburg, May* 9, 1529.

"WHILE the rabble were in arms in the market-place, where they had their guns regularly arranged, everybody who had anything to lose at home, was in terror. For some time it looked as if there would be an armed encounter. The better part supported the cause of the Church, but they were numerically weaker, for the others had many strangers among them, besides a number of acknowledged ruffians whose only object was destruction. They began this tragedy close upon winter, when it was not easy either to take flight or to send for assistance. The Church party, finding that conventicles were held contrary to the order of the Council and the prescribed oath, took up arms, and soon the others followed their example, even bringing guns and other engines into the market. By the authority of the Council the Church party were made to lay down their arms, which the others also did reluctantly, but time enough; for on the order being issued for the destruction of the images, they assembled in the market, got their engines into order, built an immense pyre, and passed some nights there in the open air, amid the universal alarm of the citizens; however, they broke into no house, nor did they attack any person, though the chief magistrate, my next-door neighbour, a good speaker, and, as was proved on many occasions, an excellent public servant, was obliged to fly by night in a boat, and would have been killed had he not done so. Many others also fled through fear, who, however, were recalled by the Council if they wished to enjoy their

⁹ *Ep.* mxlviii.

rights as citizens, but all who favoured the old religion were removed from the Council, so as to put an end to all disunion there. So far the Council had kept the mob under control, and everything that was allowed to be removed from the churches was removed by smiths and workmen employed for the purpose; but they heaped such insults on the images of the saints, and the crucifix itself, that it is quite surprising there was no miracle, seeing how many there always used to be whenever the saints were even slightly offended. Not a statue was left either in the churches, or the vestibules, or the porches, or the monasteries. The frescoes were obliterated by means of a coating of lime; whatever would burn was thrown into the fire, and the rest pounded into fragments. Nothing was spared for either love or money. Before long the mass was totally abolished, so that it was forbidden either to celebrate it in one's own house or to attend it in the neighbouring villages. When I no longer feared the worst and there seemed reason to hope that no one's life or property would be attacked, this merciful course being recommended by Œcolampadius, notwithstanding new decrees continued to be issued every day by their synods, and so I began to think of moving, but without letting my purpose be known. I would have done so before Easter, but a violent stomach attack prevented me. Moreover I felt very anxious lest changing my residence should be bad for my health; I was rather afraid too that they would try to stop me on my departure, and accordingly I had procured from King Ferdinand two certificates, one inviting me to his court, and the other securing my safe passage through his own and the Emperor's entire dominions. First of all I sent secretly my money, my rings, and my silver plate, and whatever is most liable to be stolen. Some time afterwards I loaded two waggons with my books and papers, quite openly, and on this account Œcolampadius and the preachers are said to be incensed against me, for two reasons, which, as you will see by the enclosed letters, are perfectly frivolous. Considering, however, the present state of affairs, I wrote to Œcolampadius to pacify him, and at the same time begged him to come and see me. We talked together for a long time, but without falling out. He assured me of his sincere good-will, which I did not refuse provided he would allow me to differ from him on certain points. At last he began to urge me not to leave Basle. I answered him that I was going against my will from a city which I liked much for many reasons, but that I could not any longer endure the odium that my stay was causing, for I should be thought to approve of whatever is done here by public authority. When he continued to press me, I answered that it was useless, as all my furniture was at Friburg. He then urged me, if I must go, at least to return, to which I replied, 'I will stop at Friburg for some months, and thence will go whithersoever Providence shall call me.' So we shook hands and parted. This conversation, I suspect, he communicated to one of the magistrates, who had always taken a leading part in this business, a sensible and quiet man. He spoke to Beatus, and urged many reasons against my departure, but no one said a word to me. If I had said that I was going because I was offended, they would have promised me satisfaction; if because I could not approve of their institutions, they might have insisted on cross-questioning me, and for that reason I pleaded the displeasure of the princes and the envy of the theologians. Besides, some fierce and threatening expressions of the most influential men of this party had reached my ears, and some things had happened which seemed to forebode danger. Accordingly I did not think it prudent to remain in a city in which there was no one too poor to do me an injury. For it is not to be expected that the magistrates and people should favour any one who in his words and writings dissents from their dogmas.

" As I was about to get on board the boat, they raised some difficulty about the baggage of my servant-maid. In order to escape being stared at by the mob, I desired my boatman to loose from some retired place, but this the Council decidedly forbade, though previously it was free to set sail from any port belonging to the city. I submitted, and loosed from the bridge, accompanied by some friends. No one said a word to me. This change of residence has turned out better than I expected. The magistrates of this city offered me a hearty welcome of their own accord, before they saw King Ferdinand's letters of recommendation, and they have given me a royal palace to live in, one which was built for Maximilian but not finished. I intend remaining here for some months, unless war breaks out, which is not unlikely, for many are coming from Basle, and it is said that the whole college of canons will remove to this place, and that would soon draw down upon us the rage of our enemies."

In another letter to the same friend, written about two months later, he gives some further particulars respecting his departure:

". . . . Accordingly when I was determined to leave

Basle, I deliberated whether I should steal away in secret or go openly. The one was the safer course, the other the more honourable. I preferred honour to safety. I had already sent forward two waggon-loads of papers and baggage; for that could not be done secretly. The next day it was told me that all the preachers were very angry with me for two reasons: the first, because on my way to Froben's garden, on seeing them, I turned aside to the right hand, stopping my mouth with my gown, as if to express my abhorrence, when in reality I was covering up my mouth to keep out a nasty wind, which often gives me the toothache, and I turned to the right according to my usual custom, because the other street was narrow and full of bad smells; the second, because in my Colloquy entitled 'The Cyclops,' I had introduced a certain character with a very long nose, who carried a sheep on his head and a fox in his breast. Though this joke was intended for one of my clerks, who had a tolerably large nose and wore a sheepskin cap (for I had never heard of Œcolampadius wearing a cap of that kind), they thought it was a satire on Œcolampadius. Accordingly, in case they should get up any disturbance about it, especially as there was such an excitement of feeling, I wrote a short letter of apology to Œcolampadius, and invited him to a conference, if he desired to hear more. He came without delay, and I easily satisfied him, for he said he had taken no offence.[10] . . . ."

The rest of the narrative is much the same as before, but here is the characteristic letter which he had sent to Œcolampadius, and a copy of which was enclosed to Pirckheimer:—

[10] *Ep.* mlxvi.

Copy of ERASMUS'S *Letter to* JOHN ŒCOLAMPADIUS.[11]

"SEVERAL days ago I was anxious to invite you to a conference, but the weather was disagreeable, and I was suffering from a most troublesome stomach attack accompanied by fever. And I was afraid lest it might give rise to any talk among the people, as things were not then so quiet as they are now. To-day Jerome Froben told me that some people suspected me of unfriendly feelings towards you, on the ground that I had satirized you in my writings, and also turned aside out of my way to avoid meeting you. I assure you that both these charges are utterly groundless. I never wrote a single letter in which I intended to satirize you, or with the slightest thought of you. When my Colloquy of 'The Cyclops' was printing, some of Froben's workmen fancied that what is said of the sheep on the head, and the fox in the breast, and of the long nose, had reference to you, when it is clear that it was a joke against Nicolas Cannius, my servant, who was ambitious of being celebrated in my Colloquies. He wears such a cap, he has a long nose, he is of a dark complexion, and wears a black wig. That you wear such a cap I had never heard except on this occasion. I am not so simple as to indulge in trifling of that sort when speaking of men of repute. Polyphemus too, who used to carry about a beautifully bound copy of the Gospels, though his life was as impure as it could well be, was ambitious of being celebrated.

"So stands the case as regards my writings. Now as to the road, it is the one I am always accustomed to go by to Froben's garden, when the weather is fine,

[11] *Ep.* mlxvii.

because the other is narrower and full of bad smells. Therefore if no one had been by, I would nevertheless have gone that way. Nor was I aware at the time that you were coming; it was my servant that told me. And I would then have retraced my steps to meet you had there not been several others who were strangers to me, and on whose company I was unwilling to intrude; and I said so to my servant at the time. So much for the suspicion. But if there is any other matter, I shall be in Froben's garden to-day from about four till six, and if you will condescend to come thither, with one companion, or any other day you choose, I shall be glad to talk with you. In your tract in reply to Bilibald, you quote me as having said that your opinion on the Eucharist was far preferable. Possibly John Danus may have told you so, but he was mistaken. I said that yours was more simple and intelligible, as giving rise to fewer knotty questions. Otherwise, if I were convinced that your doctrines were preferable to those commonly received, so that my conscience could acquiesce in that persuasion, I would profess the same opinions that you do this very hour, and punish in my usual way certain mad monks and theologians of the stamp of Bedda. As it is, the only thing I can do is to wish and try that these troubles may have a happy issue. Farewell. The rest at our meeting, if you think good."

The result of this interview we have already seen. Œcolampadius, who was himself a scholar and a man of amiable character, never forgot the respect due to the great restorer of learning, and notwithstanding one or two hasty expressions, when he was specially nettled by the attempts to make him a Protestant, Erasmus seems always to have had a regard for the Basle reformer.

In another letter Erasmus tells an anecdote which shows that he was by no means a stranger to the troubles of bachelor housekeeping. Just as he was leaving for Friburg, a friend, recently married to Froben's daughter, came into his head, and he determined to make him a present of the only thing remaining in his house—namely, a cock and hen, with their brood of chickens. He accordingly gave orders for their delivery at the house of his friend, who was a Frenchman, and sent along with them a couplet punning on the word Gallus, which in Latin means at once "a Gaul" and "a cock." The verses were safely delivered, but not the fowls, on which he remarks, "I am sorry that my present was intercepted, and I cannot sufficiently admire the impudence of my old housekeeper, who often gives away my property to any one she pleases, so great is her familiarity, though we have never slept in the same bed!"[18]

Erasmus had been somewhat anxious about the effects of his change of residence on his health. He had always believed that the climate of Friburg, surrounded as it was by the Alps, and only open towards the west, was damp and vapoury, and he feared this would not suit his constitution. The torrents of rain, however, which fell during that spring, and which he commemorated in a stanza of no great merit, may have relieved the atmosphere, and contrary to his expectations, he felt much better and seemed for a time almost to recover his youth.

The year 1529 does not appear to have been very fruitful in work, though the publication of the splendid

[18] *Er. Op.* iii. 1224, D.

edition of St. Augustine, the preface to which was written at Friburg, would alone suffice to distinguish it. On the 1st of July he dedicated to the young Duke of Cleves two little works ascribed to Ambrose,[13] but on the approach of autumn his health again broke down, so that he was quite incapacitated for work. He suffered tortures from an abscess in his jaw, and for some months, he says, was unable to take either food or sleep.[14] The story first told by Simler in his Life of Bullinger, and repeated by Bayle, Jortin, and Butler, that Erasmus was cured of this abscess by the immoderate laughter provoked by the *Epistolæ Obscurorum Virorum*, which caused it to burst, does not appear to rest on any foundation; at least there is nothing to support it in the letters of Erasmus, and it is certain that this was not the first time he saw that amusing satire. On his recovery he attempted to continue his work on the art of preaching, but found he had such a distaste for his usual studies that he was obliged to throw it aside. His blood warmed, however, to another work which he completed in the course of the winter, and which was called forth by certain misrepresentations which had been made of his views to the Diet of Spire. The case was this. Gerard Noviomagus, a preacher of no great character,[15] had sent to the Diet some excerpts from his works to prove the unlawfulness of putting heretics to death, and this construction of his words Erasmus thought it necessary to repudiate. He had never, he said, denied the

---

[13] *Ep.* mlxii.

[14] "Autumnus me gravissimo dentium apostemate, non sine febri, parum humaniter salutavit."—*Er. Op.* iii. 1233, A. "Mensibus aliquot per juges cruciatus, nec somnum nec cibum capere licuit."—*Ib.* 1264, A.

[15] In a letter to Melancthon (*Ep.* mcxxvi.), Erasmus calls him "ebriolus quidam."

power of the sovereign to punish heresy capitally, but every one who fell into error was not forthwith a heretic, if there was no obstinacy or wilful perversity. In this piece, which he entitled a "Letter to certain who falsely call themselves evangelicals,"[16] he is very bitter against the reform party generally, but, as I shall have occasion to refer to it again, I will say no more of it here.

In the following spring (1530), the time of the year when his mind was usually most active, he was again laid prostrate by violent pains in the stomach, to which there succeeded a severe diarrhœa, and this again was followed by a dreadful abscess, which he describes as coiling round him like a serpent. Finding that the physicians aggravated rather than relieved his malady, he called in a surgeon of repute, who, after subjecting him to cruel and, as he thought, unnecessary torture, applied the lancet, after which he slowly recovered.[17] "I doubt," said he, "whether the pains of purgatory are so great as those I suffered." Fortunately his illness did not prevent the appearance this year of the complete works of St. Chrysostom, with a Latin translation, on which, with the assistance of Fisher, Bishop of Rochester, German Brixius and Simon Grynæus, he had been engaged for some time past. For this work, which equalled in splendour the Augustine, he wrote a life of Chrysostom; it was dedicated to the Bishop of Augsburg,[18] who had cordially invited him to that city, promised, at Erasmus's own request, to take the place of

---

[16] *Desiderii Erasmi Epistola contra quosdam qui se falso jactant evangelicos.*—Er. Op. x. 1573.

[17] *Ep.* mcxxiv. contains the most circumstantial account of this illness.

Compare, however, *Ep.* mcxvii. and mxciv., which last, to Sadolet, ought to be dated 1531, instead of 1530.

[18] *Ep.* mcl.

Warham, whose death could not be far off, as his patron, and who had gone to Friburg expressly to visit him.

His illness made it impossible for Erasmus to attend the Diet which met at Augsburg on the 8th of April, 1530, to which he was summoned as a councillor of the Emperor; but he could not fail to be an interested and indeed anxious spectator of the proceedings. If war should become imminent, it would be immediately necessary for him again to change his quarters, and indeed he was already thinking of leaving Friburg, where he found everything enormously dear, and where he was unable to procure his favourite Burgundy, or if he imported it, it was at a great expense and with the probability of its being watered by the way. He was advised, however, to wait to see the issue of the Diet. He does not appear to have expected much from its deliberations in the way of putting an end to the troubles which afflicted the Church—"God only," he wrote, "can do that, though ten councils were to meet." His influence, however, was exerted, as usual, in favour of peace and moderation, and Melancthon thanked him for having written to the Emperor, as he was informed he had done, to dissuade him from violent measures. To this Erasmus replied that Melancthon was misinformed. He had not written to the Emperor, but he had written to Cardinal Campeggio, to the Bishop of Augsburg, and other friends, to protest against settling questions of doctrine by the sword. "But why," he could not help asking, feeling no doubt that if his advice had been followed, there would never have been all this trouble, "why do you not request your own side to cease from exasperating the Princes by their abusive language?"[19]

[19] *Ep.* mcxvii. mcxxv. mcxxvi.

No doubt Erasmus was glad to have the plea of his bad health as an excuse for not attending the Diet. "I could not have gone there," he writes, "but at the risk of my life, and so I preferred to live. Besides, I knew well that if I went there, I should only bring new trouble on my own head, without being able to compose the troubles already existing. I also knew upon whose judgment the Emperor relied, and what sort of divines would be there, who think any one worse than a Lutheran the moment he dares to open his mouth in favour of true piety. And I cannot bear dissimulation, and I am somewhat free of speech. But if I had suited myself to the passions of certain people, I must have said many things against my conscience. So, I have some reason to thank my illness, disagreeable as it was, as it furnished me with an excuse for my absence." [20]

Early in 1531 he published the "Apophthegms of the Ancients," [21] a large work in six books, to which two more were subsequently added, and which must have kept him tolerably busy during the winter-days; but probably he had been collecting them for some time previously. It was dedicated to the Duke of Cleves. He had now nearly given up the duties of editor, being willing that the burden should fall upon younger shoulders, but he still sometimes wrote dedications for the works of others. Thus he wrote a preface to the "Aristotle of John Bebelius," [22] which he dedicated to John More, the not too brilliant son of his friend Sir

---

[20] *Ep.* melii.

[21] *Apophthegmata lepideque dicta principum, philosophorum ac diversi generis hominum, ex Graecis pariter ac Latinis auctoribus selecta, cum interpretatione commoda, dicti argutiam aperiente, per Desiderium Erasmum Roterodamum."—Er. Op.* iv. 93.

[22] *Ep.* melix.

Thomas; also one to Livy,[23] which, though frequently reprinted, was now increased by the addition of five new books recently discovered by Simon Grynæus, in a convent near Worms. It was about this time that he had the correspondence already referred to with Sadoleti, the Bishop of Carpentras, who, as we have seen, had recommended to him a little more caution in attacking usages which were not opposed to true religion, such as the invocation of the saints, and the worship of images, and a little more moderation in replying to the attacks of his adversaries. These indeed he advised him simply to treat with contempt. Erasmus, while admitting to some extent his need of such advice, yet justified himself on both points at some length, and courteously wished he had long ago had such an adviser.[24]

To this prelate he dedicated the works of St. Basil (1532).[25] He had resolved, he said, to resist the importunities of the printers and write no more prefaces; but he could not help making an exception in favour of St. Basil, for whom he seems to have had an extraordinary admiration, and whom he names "the Christian Demosthenes." This edition is remarkable as being the first instance of a Greek author not before printed—the New Testament writers of course must be excepted—being issued by a German press.

For nearly two years Erasmus had now lived in the unfinished palace of the Emperor Maximilian, when about the end of March, 1531, in consequence of some disagreement with a fellow-occupant, he received a three months' notice to quit, together with a demand for a considerable rent from the Christmas of 1529. This took him completely by surprise, as he had no notion

[23] *Ep.* mclx.   [24] See above, p. 292.   [25] *Ep.* mccxv.

that he was hiring the house. The result was, however, that he left at the appointed time, and bought a house for himself at what he considered an extravagant price. This was quite a new experience for Erasmus. "I am so wearied out," he writes, "with bargaining, contracting, stipulating, removing, and quarrelling with carpenters and thieves, that I would rather spend ten years in writing books than have this nuisance for a single month." And again, "If any one were to tell you that Erasmus, who is now nearly seventy, had married, would you not make the sign of the cross at least half-a-dozen times? I am sure you would; and yet I have done a thing which has brought on me no less annoyance and trouble and which is equally strange to my habits and pursuits. I have bought a house, a very nice-looking one, but it has cost me dear. Who need now despair of rivers returning to their sources, when Erasmus, after giving up everything all his life to the pursuits of literature, has become a bargainer, a buyer, a stipulator, a cautioner, and must exchange the society of the Muses for that of carpenters, smiths, masons and glaziers. These troubles, for which I never had the slightest taste, have all but finished me. I am still, however, a stranger in my own house, which, though roomy enough, has not a corner where I can lie down with safety. I have had one room made with a chimney and wooden rafters and with a tiled floor, but I cannot yet venture to trust myself in it, on account of the strong smell of lime. However, I must take possession in a short time, and I hope the change may turn out well: which has not hitherto been the case."[26]

[26] *Ep.* mcc.

During his stay at Friburg he lost two of his most valued friends. Pirckheimer died at the age of sixty, apparently in the first month of 1532, and Warham at a much more advanced age, on the 22nd of August, in the following year. The former seems to have been a man of rare excellence, upright, pious, constant, and liberal, a wise statesman and an excellent scholar. He left unfinished two works, an edition of "Ptolemy's Geography," which was afterwards published with a preface by Erasmus, and a translation into Latin of Gregory of Nazianzen. Almost his last thoughts were of his friends Erasmus and Zasius, to whom he was desirous of sending some message, which, however, death interrupted: his last words were, "After my decease may it be well with my country, may peace be restored to the Church."[n] On Warham, Erasmus wrote a beautiful eulogy in the preface to the third edition of his "Jerome," which appeared the year after his death. He describes him as a man of the most frugal tastes, who, amid the splendours of a sumptuous table, which he kept for his guests, lived himself on the plainest fare, and was so liberal that he left merely enough to pay his debts. A little before his death, being informed by his servants that he had no more than thirty gold pieces in his treasury, he replied, "It is well; it was always my wish to die thus: it is enough to carry me to heaven." Often he would say, "How I wish I might once more see Erasmus and clasp him in my arms, before I leave this world; I would never let him be parted from me." "The wish," says Erasmus, "was mutual, but neither of us obtained our desire. May Christ in his mercy grant

[n] *Ep.* mclxxxvii.

that we may soon embrace one another in that world where there shall be no more parting, and where no one will envy him to me or me to him."

Erasmus well knew the value of such a friend as Warham. Apart from the material advantages he derived from that friendship—and he says he would never accept nearly all that Warham was willing to give—he never felt for any one an affection more deep and sincere. Pecuniarily, Warham's death was no loss to him, for his successor in the see of Canterbury, Cranmer, undertook to continue his pension.[28] He was very differently affected by the death of two other celebrated men, the news of which reached him at this time. "It is a good thing," he said, "that two of their leaders have perished, Zwingle on the field of battle, and Œcolampadius shortly after of fever and abscess."[29] It must be regretted that Erasmus should have permitted himself to write thus of two great men who were not even his personal enemies, and who both had a sincere regard for him. But he was unable to think of them except as revolutionists and disturbers of the public peace.

It was a good omen, he thought, that the house which he first occupied adjoined a convent of friars, so that he could hear, and perhaps join in, their singing without leaving his room. Thus, literally as well as figuratively, he lived in perfect harmony with them, and there was one of their number who used sometimes to mention his name with honour in his sermons. He was not, however, secure against the malignity of his persecutors elsewhere. Some Franciscans, offended at the freedom with which he had treated their order in his

[28] *Er. Op.* iii. 1481, C.   [29] *Er. Op.* iii. 1422, B.

Colloquies, pretended or believed that he had been struck by lightning, thinking, no doubt, that he could not fail some day to meet with some such signal judgment. He took his revenge in a humorous narrative, in which he tells how St. Francis himself lately appeared to him in a dream, thanked him for having exposed the faults which he himself had always detested, and welcomed him as a friend of his order. "His dress," he continues, "bore no resemblance to that in which he is now painted; his gown was not of mixed colours, but of grey wool, as it is taken from the sheep, without being dyed; nor did he wear a pointed hood, but a cape fastened to his tunic behind, which he could pull over his head in case of a shower, like that which is worn at this day by some of the Irish. His rope had no carefully made knots, but was simply a common rope without knots; nor did his tunic reach the ground, but was a hand's breadth or more above his ankles. He had no sandals, and his feet were quite bare. Of the five wounds with which he is always painted, I saw no trace whatever. On going away he stretched out his right hand and said, 'Fight bravely: soon thou shalt be mine.'"[30] The story is told with an air of mock solemnity, which, incredible as it may seem, has induced some to believe that it records a fact.[31] One would have thought that only a very zealous Papist could believe in an actual epiphany of St. Francis, and that no Papist could possibly believe he would have appeared to Erasmus.

His change of lodging does not seem to have

[30] *Ep.* mccxxx.
[31] "Fleury" (says JORTIN, *Life of Erasmus*, ii. 34), "in his *Ecclesiastical History*, treats it as a true story. T. xvi. p. 574."

improved his health. From the end of February till September in 1533 he complains of having been in a state of great depression; his stomach would receive nothing, owing, he thought, to the want of wine that suited his constitution, for on changing his wine he recovered. His literary work, however, cannot have been long interrupted, for this year his pen was particularly active. He published quite a large work, in the form of a catechism on the Apostles' Creed, the Decalogue, and the Lord's Prayer,[82] which he dedicated to Thomas Rochford, Earl of Wiltshire and Ormond, father of the unfortunate Anne Boleyn, to whom he had previously sent, at his own request, an exposition of the twenty-second Psalm. He afterwards wrote for the same nobleman a short devotional work on preparation for death.[83] Notwithstanding his resolution already mentioned, he wrote prefaces for several of the Frobens' publications, his principal motive being his interest in his old friend's sons, for whose works he was willing to secure a sale by giving them the sanction of his authority. Besides, in the absence of original works, this was an opportunity of gratifying his patrons and forming new connections among the great. Thus he dedicated an edition of Demosthenes to John George Paungartner,[84] one of the four sons of John Paungartner, a wealthy citizen of Augsburg, to whom he was indebted for much kindness. For the same family he wrote several prayers.[85] He also wrote an exposition of the eighty-third Psalm

---

[82] *Dilucida et pia explanatio Symboli quod Apostolorum dicitur, Decalogi præceptorum, et Dominicæ precationis.*—Er. Op. v. 1133.

[83] *Desiderii Erasmi Roterodami Liber quomodo se quisque debeat præparare ad mortem.*—Ib. 1293.

[84] *Ep.* mccxxviii.

[85] *Er. Op.* v. 1197.

—" How amiable are thy tabernacles "—on the best means of producing harmony in the Church, dedicating it to Julius Pflug, now Bishop of Naumberg, who had begged from him some work tending to allay the present discord. Erasmus, with his usual learning, gives an account of some of the principal heresies which had infected the Church, and as some atonement, perhaps, for former admissions, is particularly hard upon the Arians. As a remedy for present evils, he advocates mutual forbearance and the correction of abuses.[86]

In 1534, on the death of Clement VII., the chair of St. Peter was at length filled by a Pope who was really in earnest about undertaking the reform of the Church. Paul III. signalized the first years of his pontificate by elevating to the Sacred College several men of moderate tendencies, and who had no claim to the honour save the legitimate one of distinguished learning or piety. Among these were Caraffa, Sadoleti, Reginald Pole, and afterwards Peter Bembo, all personal friends of Erasmus, and it is said that the elevation of Erasmus himself was seriously considered. This we have on his own authority, confirmed by that of Beatus, and it has also been inferred from a significant hint in a letter to him from Bembo.[87] That his name was mentioned we can have no difficulty in believing, but there were, no doubt, other very strong objections besides his bad health and the want of sufficient fortune—the difficulties which are said to have been raised. To elect into the Sacred College a man so obnoxious to a large portion of the Church, must have appeared on a moment's reflection altogether out of the question. At all events, the

[86] *De amabili Ecclesiæ concordia.*—*Er. Op.* v. 469.
[87] *Ep.* mcclxxxii.

offer was never actually made, and had it been, infirm
as Erasmus now was, and averse to public life as he
had always been, it is certain that he would not have
accepted it. "This would, indeed," he wrote, "be
putting a cat in petticoats." It was enough for him
that his influence—the influence of such writings, for
example, as his tract on the harmony of the Church—
was now felt in the Papal counsels, that the advice he
had given to Adrian was at last likely to be carried out
—too late, indeed, to save Germany to the Popedom,
but not too late to purge Rome herself of some of her
worst abuses.

And yet how characteristic of Erasmus that he
should begin to doubt the value of his own remedy for
the evils of his time the moment it seemed about to be
seriously applied! "This Pope," he writes, "seems to
be thinking seriously of a Council. But I don't see
how it is to meet, as long as there is so much dissension
between the different countries of Europe and their
rulers."[38]

On the accession of Paul III., Erasmus wrote to
him to exhort him to follow moderate counsels, and to
devote all his energies to the assertion of the true faith,
and the pacification of the Church. The letter, which
was conveyed to his Holiness by Louis Berus, would
seem to have been lost; but its contents may be gathered
from the Pope's reply, in which he thanks him for his
advice, and answers him that this was already his settled
purpose. "Nor are we ignorant," he adds, "how much
your extraordinary learning, conjoined with equal
eloquence, can aid us in rooting out those new errors
from the minds of many of our people." He begs

[38] *Ep.* mcclxxxvi.

therefore that "he will lend his assistance in this holy work, and in the defence of the Catholic faith, both before the Council and during the Council, which, with God's help, it is our intention to hold."[39] The letter, which bears the date May 31, 1535, concludes by assuring him that he will not find the Pope ungrateful or unmindful of him. It appears from the statement of Beatus, that the provostship of Deventer, a tolerably lucrative office, was pressed upon him, but declined, Erasmus thinking that he had enough to carry him to the grave.

Since the beginning of the year 1534 a new disease afflicted Erasmus, or the old trouble assumed a new form. Gout, or something like gout, shot through all his joints, putting him to intolerable pain, and for a time settled in his right hand, so that he could touch neither pen nor paper.[40] He was obliged to dictate his letters, of which, however, there are few for that year. Nevertheless he was able to go on with his great work on the art of preaching, which has been already referred to, as having been undertaken at the suggestion of his friend the Bishop of Rochester. It was printed by the Frobens, at Basle, and appeared in August in the following year. The *Ecclesiastes*,[41] in four books, is a very copious treatment of the preacher's duties and qualifications, but without as much order and method as would

---

[39] *Ep.* mcclxxx.

[40] "Dextram jamdudum totam occupat chiragra, sic ut ne chartam aut calamum possim tenere manu."—*Er. Op.* iii. 1489, E. "Me discruciat novum malum podagra, seu panagra verius; adeo prætentat omnes artus, aliunde alio migrans, ut vix unquam detur respirare. Negant esse podagram, sed sui generis esse malum, quo nunc hic laborent complures: vulgo *Souch* appellant."—*Ib.* 1491. F.

[41] *Ecclesiastes, sive Concionator evangelicus.*—*Er. Op.* v. 769.

be desirable in the discussion of such a subject. It is, like most of its author's productions, exceedingly diffuse, and, if I may judge from my own experience, most modern readers would find it somewhat tedious. But though written with more effort than was usual with Erasmus, I do not think it bears any marks of failing powers. Coming from his pen, it need scarcely be said, that it contains many excellent precepts, many wise and witty remarks, many sparkling anecdotes, and many lively sketches illustrating the manners of the time. It was dedicated to the Bishop of Augsburg.

Erasmus himself went to Basle, while his work was still in the press, having some finishing touches to put to it previous to its publication. He had, in fact, resolved to leave Friburg, and having received an invitation from Mary, the Queen Dowager of Hungary, and now, since her aunt's death, Governess of the Netherlands, together with money for his journey, it was his intention, after making a short stay at Basle, should his health permit, to proceed down the Rhine to Brabant. He accordingly sold the house at Friburg, and brought his furniture, which, says Beatus, consisted chiefly of books, to Basle, where he was hospitably received by Jerome Froben. Probably he foresaw that he would never proceed further. It may be, indeed, that he was unwilling to die among comparative strangers, and that he went to Basle on purpose that he might breathe his last amid that circle of friends in which his warmest attachments were to be found. Everything seemed now to point to the approaching end. Shortly after his arrival in Basle, the melancholy news reached him of the bloody death of his friend Fisher. The King, it was reported, hearing that Paul III. had proposed making him one of his new

cardinals, had the more speedily hurried him to the
scaffold. "That," said Erasmus, "was the red hat
which *he* gave him." News of More's death came at the
same time, but as yet needing confirmation. The pains
in the joints from which he had suffered at Friburg now
returned with renewed violence, and confined him to his
room, and often to his bed. When they somewhat
abated, he was able to creep about with the help of a
stick, but only once through that winter did he leave
his apartment. Yet in the intervals of his sufferings he
never ceased to write. During the last months of his
life he composed an essay on the purity of the Church,
in the form of a commentary on the fourteenth Psalm,[41]
which he dedicated to his old friend, the customs-col-
lector of Poppard, revised the text of Origen, and
prepared a new and enlarged edition of his letters.
This last work he was anxious to complete as a protection against the spurious compositions which were
sometimes fastened upon him. In turning over his
papers with this view, he was struck to observe how
many of his correspondents had passed away, and as
each familiar name presented itself, he exclaimed, "And
he too is gone!" At last he added, "Neither have I
any desire to live longer, if it please the Lord."[42] His
last letter, written, it seems, with his own hand, for it is
subscribed "*Eras. Rot. ægra manu*," is dated June 28,
1536. He speaks in it of having intended, after his
business in Basle was finished, to go to Besançon, which
he had sometimes thought might suit him better than
Friburg. "For," he adds, "though I am with the
kindest friends here, such as I had not at Friburg, still

[41] *De Puritate Ecclesiæ Christianæ.—Er. Op.* v. 291.
[42] BEAT. RHEN.—*Ep. Cor. Cas.*

on account of our difference about doctrines, I would rather end my life elsewhere. I wish Brabant was nearer!" " And now the time was indeed at hand when the great scholar, quite broken down by disease, worn out with his long life's work, might honourably lay down his burden and pass to his rest. For nearly a month he was laid up of a dysentery, and on the 12th of July, continually exclaiming, "O Jesus, have mercy; Lord deliver me; Lord, make an end; Lord, have mercy upon me!" and in the German language, "Lieber God," a little before midnight, he breathed his last. For months previously he had been accustomed to prophesy that he would die this year, and he foretold his death three days, and again two days, before it took place. His reason remained unimpaired to the last, nor were his sufferings able to check the play of his always kindly and genial humour. When a few days before his decease his three friends, Boniface Amerbach, Jerome Froben, and Nicholas Episcopius, entered his apartment, he reminded them of Job's three comforters, and playfully asked them where were their torn garments, and the ashes that should be sprinkled on their heads. Beatus, we may presume, was with him to the end.[45]

And thus died Erasmus of Rotterdam, the greatest luminary of his age, the greatest scholar of any age, mourned by all lovers of wit and learning, honoured and esteemed by every sovereign in Europe, by the head of his Church, and by almost all who took a leading part in the memorable events of that period; hated and feared only by the ignorant monks who were wholly incapable of appreciating his merits. He died, after all, in a Protestant town,—died as the monks said before, and as

" *Ep.* mccxcix.   [45] BEAT. RHEN.—*Vita ex Ep. ed.*

they no doubt said again, *sine lux, sine crux*,—without those consolations which the Roman Church provides for her faithful sons. It was better so. There would have been a strange incongruity in the presence of priestly mummeries round the death-bed of Erasmus. Grateful Basle did not refuse him a resting-place in her principal church. His remains lie buried in the cathedral, on the left side, not far from the choir, whither they were borne by students of the university, many of the magistrates and all the professors following them to the grave. The place is marked by a stone tablet, erected by his heirs, above which is an enlarged copy of the figure on his favourite seal, the head of the god Terminus.

The will of Erasmus is an interesting document, and shows, what might be otherwise inferred, that he spent his last years in comparative wealth. It is said that he died possessed of 7,000 ducats. The Nicholas Episcopius referred to above, and also remembered in the will, was Froben's son-in-law, married to his daughter Justina, and it is pleasant to think that the womanly hands of his old friend's daughter may have tended the old man in his last moments. The will is as follows:—
" 'In the name of the Holy Trinity, I, Desiderius Erasmus, of Rotterdam, in virtue of a diploma of his Imperial Majesty, a papal brief, and the permission of the magnificent magistracy of the illustrious city of Basle, by this writing under my hand, renew my last will, which I wish to be performed, declaring all contrary dispositions made by me to be void. In the first place, being certain that I have no lawful heir, I appoint that most excellent man, Boniface Amerbach, heir of all my property, and Jerome Froben and Nicholas Episcopius my executors.

A considerable time ago, I sold my library to John à Lasco, Baron of Poland, but by the contract made between us, the books are not to be delivered to him except on payment to my heir of two hundred florins. If he refuse to accede to these conditions, or dies before me, it shall be free to my heir to dispose of the books as he may think proper. To Louis Berus I bequeath my gold watch; to Beatus Rhenanus my gold cup and my gold fork; to Peter Vetereus one hundred and fifty gold crowns; and as many to Philip Montanus. To my servant Lambert, should he be in my service at my decease, I bequeath two hundred gold florins, unless I shall have paid him that sum in my lifetime. I bequeath to John Brisch my silver bottle; to Paul Volzius one hundred gold florins; to Sigismund Telenius one hundred and fifty ducats; to John Erasmius Froben two rings, the one without a stone and the turquoise. I bequeath to John Froben all my clothes and all my furniture, in wool, linen, or wood, also my cup engraved with the arms of the Cardinal of Maintz; and to his wife the ring with the figure of a woman looking behind her. I bequeath to Nicholas Episcopius the cup with the lid, which has some verses engraved on its foot; and to his wife Justina two rings, the diamond one and the smaller turquoise. I bequeath to Everard Goclenius my silver cup with the figure of Fortune at the top. If any of my legatees die before me, I direct that what I have bequeathed to him shall return to my heir, who, in addition to what I have given him by will shall take my remaining cups, rings, or other articles of the same kind, besides my coins, medals, and Portugal crosses with the image of the King of Portugal and Severinus Bonerus, and other similar articles; and also all my double and quadruple ducats. As to the money deposited by me with Everard Goclenius, my heir is to leave it with him to make that disposition of it in Brabant which I have recommended to him. If anything of mine remains in the hands of Erasmus Schetius, my heir will ask it of him; and, according to the best of his judgment, and in concert with my executors, he shall dispose of it, and of all the residue of my property, for the benefit of the aged and infirm poor, in marrying young girls, and educating young men of promise, and generally for the benefit of any other person whom he shall think deserving of assistance. I have written this, my last will, that there may be no mistake about it, with my own hand, and I have sealed it with the god Terminus, my true seal. At Basle, in the house of Jerome Froben, on the twelfth day of February, in the year of our Lord 1536."

Having thus brought the life of Erasmus to a close, it might perhaps be well that I should now simply leave it to make its own impression on the mind of the reader. I am unwilling, however, to abandon what must be considered the most responsible, as it is also the most ambitious, part of the biographer's task, and I therefore venture to subjoin a few remarks by way of estimating his character, and helping to the formation of a right judgment on his relations to the age in which he lived.

What Erasmus was as regards his outward man has been already described in this work,[46] and must be sufficiently known to every one who has studied his expressive features as they present themselves on Holbein's canvas. It was very unwillingly, it is said, that he allowed himself

[46] See above, vol. i. p. 31.

to be prevailed on by his friends to have his portrait taken,[47] but, his reluctance once overcome, he sat for it repeatedly. He was first painted in the year 1517 by the celebrated Flemish artist, Quintin Matsys, in the same picture with his friend Peter Giles, in which Erasmus is represented beginning his Paraphrase of the Epistle to the Romans, while Giles holds in his hand a letter from More.[48] Matsys also made a bronze cast of him. He was afterwards taken by Albert Dürer, but according to his own statement, in one of his letters, the portrait bore no resemblance to the original, an assertion, however, which he elsewhere qualifies by observing that "it is no wonder if the likeness is not a good one, for I am not the same as I was five years ago."[49] One of the earliest of Holbein's portraits is a profile in which the hands are especially conspicuous, the left richly adorned with rings on the second and fourth fingers, the right holding a pen with which he is writing the Paraphrase of St. Mark. It belongs, therefore, to the year 1523. The best known and most pleasing likeness is that which is reproduced at the beginning of this work, but during his stay at Basle he was frequently taken by the same artist, previous to the year 1526, when Holbein went to England, furnished with a letter of introduction from Erasmus to Sir Thomas More. The fine bronze statue of Erasmus at Rotterdam was erected in the year 1622, to replace the previous one of stone erected in 1557, and that again was a substitute

[47] *Comp. Vit.*
[48] *Er. Op.* iii. 1635, B.
[49] *ib.* 1073, F. "Si minus respondet effigies, mirum non est: non enim sum is, qui fui ante annos quinque."—*Er. Op.* iii. 944, F. Conf. *Ib.* 1073, F. As both passages belong to the year 1528, we thus obtain 1523 as the date of Dürer's portrait.

for the original wooden statue decreed by the authorities of Rotterdam in 1549, on the occasion of the visit of Philip II. to that city.[50]

If we now endeavour to picture Erasmus to ourselves as he was in life, a man among men, or as he reflects himself in his writings, the faithful mirror of his soul, we receive at once the impression of a nature flexible, sensitive, transparently open; a heart warm, generous, and full of the milk of human kindness; a mind highly cultivated, possessed of great and ready resources, keenly observant and unceasingly active. Of quick sympathies, he could not bear the infliction of pain, and detested alike the cruelties of war and the barbarities of the petty tyrants of the schoolroom. This last circumstance, together with the many kindly references to the boyish age with which his writings are interspersed, may show that, like his friend Colet, he had a special fondness for children. That he was ever charitable to the poor, we have the testimony of his friend Beatus, who assures us that he seldom went to mass without, on his way, bestowing an alms, while he himself has stated that he often gave more of his own accord than Eppendorf attempted to extort from him under the pretence of charity. To young men he was particularly kind, and would frequently supply them, out of his own purse, with the means of prosecuting their studies.[51]

He was, as he himself maintained, neither covetous of gold nor ambitious of worldly honours. We may readily believe him. Beyond the means necessary for carrying on his studies, for making his various journeys in safety, and for living in such comfort as his delicate

[50] BAYLE: art. "Rotterdam."
[51] BEAT. RHEN. *Ep. Car. Cæs.: Er. Op.* iii. 1089, A.

constitution required, what need had he for great wealth? What title or office could have added anything to the man who was already the acknowledged head of the literary world? No pope, no cardinal, or bishop, was ever held in greater honour, or received warmer or more willingly offered adulation than Erasmus.

Great-souled, perhaps even his most enthusiastic admirers would scarcely venture to call him. Neither physically nor mentally was he cast in the heroic mould. Of nervous temperament and sickly constitution, of refined, if not even somewhat finical tastes, keenly sensitive to every change of climate, food, or persons, and for many years of his life a prey to disease and suffering, he was little qualified to play a great part on the field of action; in his own apartment, on the other hand, surrounded by his books, his pen in his hand, and with the consciousness that the whole learned world was anxiously waiting for every word he should utter, he reigned supreme and triumphant. He could not, like Luther, have stood alone against the united power of Church and State. The armed men, the pomp and display, the imperial crown, would have overawed him. He was, besides, too broad, too liberal, he saw too much good in things the most evil, too much evil in the best things, to be sternly consistent or absolutely unyielding. His barbed sarcasms flew forth against sin, ignorance, and error, not against men or institutions. Of these last he always hoped the best, and laboured not for their destruction, but for their reform.

Not altogether a great man in his public action, in the sense in which Luther was great, in the sense of standing simply and absolutely upon conscience, and upon conscience alone, against all the power of the world, must we admit that there was in his private character a touch even of something not far from meanness—a meanness originating in his birth, nurtured in the monastery, and witnessed in his desperate shifts to raise money by begging in the days of his poverty, in his consenting to humiliate himself before Eppendorf, and, finally, in his anxiety to anticipate his best friend, Warham's death, by securing another patron in his place?[82] Perhaps the worst evidence of all is that of none of these things does he seem to have been the least ashamed. And yet, let us not be too severe in judging Erasmus in this respect. He lived, we must not forget, in an age when mendicancy was a virtue. The atmosphere of the convent in which he was educated was not very well fitted to inspire gentlemanly feeling, or the nicest sense of honour. And we may be sure he was as much above the coarse monks of his day in delicacy and refinement of mind as he was their superior in learning and genius.

And to think that with all this he must have, too, his little touch of aristocratic pride! He quite disdained the rich but unlettered merchant whom he supposed Cardinal Canossa to be that time he met him, *incognito*, at the house of his friend Ammonius. Or was this simply the humour of the moment? For we certainly find him on other occasions corresponding with merchants on familiar terms and treating them as his equals.

Erasmus has been freely accused of sycophancy in his relations to the great, but the charge has no special

---

[82] "Spero equidem illum mihi superstitem fore, sed timeo: si quid secus acciderit, animus est tuam celsitudinem in illius locum surrogare." —Erasmus to the Bishop of Augsburg.--*Er. Op.* iii. 1292, E.

foundation, and his own trouble was that he was far too free of speech to make a dexterous courtier. In the dedications which he prefixed to his works, it was not to be expected that he would abstain altogether from lauding those whose patronage he sought; but generally he is far too full of the subject of his work to spend much time in flattery, and when he does praise, his commendations are judicious and moderate, never fulsome or extravagant. His letters in this respect are models of good taste. Certainly no one knew better than he how to please a friend or conciliate an opponent; and if he wishes to expose a fault or correct an error, he does it with a delicacy and a skill which go far to avoid offence.

No man, according to himself, was ever more free from jealousy; but that is a temptation by which they are little affected who sit on the topmost pinnacles of fame. Erasmus was certainly keenly sensitive to every attack on his reputation either as a scholar or as an orthodox divine. "So thin-skinned that a fly would draw blood," as the Prince of Carpi expressed it, he rushed into controversy with an eagerness which perhaps may be accounted for by his mere delight in using his pen as much as by any fear of the harm that could be done him by his opponent. He was never backward to do justice to the merits of others, not even to those of the one man who could really compete with him for the palm of scholarship, and in this respect his conduct contrasts favourably with that of Budæus who, as we have seen, carefully abstained from mentioning his rival's name in his works. How far, like some other great wits, he was indifferent to all wit but his own, may perhaps be doubtful. He always spoke contemptuously of the *Julius Exclusus* and the *Epistolæ Obscurorum*

Virorum, but this was probably not from any unwillingness to acknowledge their merits as literary performances, but simply in order to disclaim their authorship, which some wished to thrust upon him, and because he felt that he had already sufficient odium to bear.

Bitter enough he could indeed be in controversy, when he was once fairly provoked, and no regard for the feelings of others, or even fear of their resentment, induced him to spare an opponent. It would be impossible to imagine anything more exasperating than his manner of dealing with Hutten, or his sarcasms on his poverty, his debt, his disease; which must have been all the more keenly felt, as there was no appearance of anger, but even the profession of continued friendship.

When we proceed to examine the mental qualities of Erasmus, we find it impossible to place him in the first rank, or perhaps even near the first rank, of intellectual greatness. Original genius, or creative power of any kind, cannot be ascribed to him, nor was the time ripe for the appearance of any such qualities, when the apparatus of literary workmanship had still to be got into order. Learning which embraced nearly all the books that ever were written in either Latin or Greek, including the classical and patristic writers, the schoolmen and the moderns, a memory retentive and exact, an admirable taste, classical but without pedantry, indefatigable industry, extraordinary command of language, and a power of facile expression which, however, often made his style exceedingly verbose—these were his most marked characteristics, these were the qualities which placed him at the head of the literary world of his time, and which give him the chief place in the history of the restoration of literature. His productiveness was simply wonderful. He would sometimes, he tells us, write forty letters in a day, besides the other compositions in which he might be engaged. To the astonishment of Aldus, he could compose in the midst of the greatest noise;[53] and on one occasion he had a contest with Froben to try whether he could write or Froben print the faster.[54] When we consider the mere bulk of his works, albeit that is certainly the last thing which we ought to consider; but when we think further of the vast range of literature which they cover, of the spirit and vigour and life which make them still most delightful reading, of the exact and varied knowledge, the rich humour, the grace and eloquence with which they abound, if we refuse to call Erasmus a great man, we must at least place him at the very head of those who are not great.

If we would seek in Erasmus any faculty, not the result of culture, but simply original, we shall find it no doubt in his faculty of humour. In this, indeed, he had Lucian and Jerome for his models; but in the exercise of such a weapon no mere imitation will avail, or rather the weapon itself must have been forged in nature's workshop, before it can be brought into use. Erasmus poured out on the vices and superstitions of his day a stream of light pleasantry peculiar to himself, by which he succeeded in making them infinitely ridiculous, without, however, attempting to excite against them the fiercer passions of our nature. He was only occasionally bitter, never cruel or vindictive, nor did he at any time forget that it was his duty to reform his fellow-creatures, not to plunge them in despair. Such, indeed, is the true

[53] *Er. Op.* ix. 1137, B. [54] *Ib.* iii. 417, E.

object of satire—to make men better by tearing away the mask which hides their real features, and showing them as they are, both to themselves and to others, by laying a vigorous hand on the weak spot and remorselessly rubbing off the paint which gives to vice the semblance of virtue. But too often does the continual probing of weak places induce the habit of regarding the whole body as diseased. With Erasmus it was not so. If he did not wield the terrors of a Juvenal, he was still farther from exhibiting the fierce disgust with all things human which we observe in Swift. Always he preserved his faith in human nature, nor would he have felt any satisfaction in ridiculing folly and superstition apart from the practical object of correcting them. Of irony he was a perfect master, and it was a weapon of which he made the most unsparing use. Under cover of elegant compliments, or modest self-depreciation, he would make the most terrible home-thrusts, and he must have been especially provoking whenever the humour would take him to speak disparagingly of himself as a man of no importance, neither a theologian nor a philosopher, and with hardly any pretensions to learning, in contrast with the vast erudition and immense talents of such opponents as the Syndic Bedda or the Prince of Carpi.

Erasmus was preserved from the dangers of the satirist by his faith in humanity and his sincere and heart-felt piety. Never, even in his most galling exposures of superstition, does he forget what is due to real religion. His writings abound in devotional sentiments, obviously introduced not for mere display, but as the honest expression of his feelings, and some of his treatises directly concerned with religious subjects are still charming from their tone of earnest practical piety.

In pursuing our attempt to estimate the intellectual character of Erasmus, it may be well to place it at once in the light afforded by the relations which he occupied towards the Papist party on the one hand and the reformers on the other. In this respect his conduct has been frequently misunderstood or misrepresented. In his own lifetime the partisans of either side would fain have made him a Lutheran against his will, the reformers because they thought he ought to be with them, and the Papists because they knew he was not with *them;* and thus he endured all the evil effects of occupying a neutral position at a time when half-measures were no longer permissible. Nor, since his death, has the world's judgment been much less severe. Erasmus has been very commonly regarded as a reformer who feared to declare himself, as one who, for worldly considerations, or else from mere infirmity of purpose, chose to remain in a Church whose principles and practice he disapproved, rather than cast in his lot with the younger and bolder spirits who openly renounced the thraldom of Rome; in short, as a kind of theological *bat,* neither a beast nor a bird, and yet capable of representing himself, according as it might serve his turn, both as one and the other; therefore deservedly pleasing to neither party and persecuted by both.

Now, it is certainly not to be denied, that Erasmus had very substantial reasons of a purely worldly nature against leaving the communion of Rome. By taking such a step he would have forfeited the consideration which he enjoyed with the dignitaries of that Church, he would no longer have corresponded on intimate terms

with archbishops and cardinals, with popes and kings;
he would have been deprived of his pensions and
compelled, it may be, to seek a livelihood by taking a
professor's chair in some university where the reformation had triumphed. Nor need it be denied that such
considerations had their full share of influence on his
mind. In no age has the comfortable Churchman been
much disposed to revolutionary principles, and Erasmus,
it must be confessed, was not the man from whom a
great sacrifice for conscience' sake was to be expected.
Still we are surely not entitled to assume, without the
clearest evidence, that he was influenced by no higher
than worldly motives, or, if we believe this in his case,
how many among the liberal thinkers of all Churches
must fall under the same condemnation. We have his
own assurance, moreover,—and why should we not believe
him?—that his conscience alone prevented him joining
the Lutherans, into whose arms he sometimes felt
almost driven by the persecutions of the monks.⁶⁶ After
all, he had only a few short years to enjoy his
emoluments before he must be called to his final
account, and is it for a moment to be supposed that he
would not instantly have abandoned them, if he had
once seen it in the light of a clear and unquestionable
duty? The vulgar scandal that Luther and the other
reformers renounced their monastic vows with no higher
object than that they might freely indulge their passions,
appears to me scarcely more unjust than to suppose that
Erasmus acted from purely sordid motives in adhering
to the Catholic Church.

⁶⁶ "Sola conscientia me revocat a Lutheranis, alioqui declararem illis Furiis, quales sunt. De emolumentis leviter laboro, jam hinc migrare meditans."—*Er. Op.* iii. 1089, E.

But Erasmus, it will be said, agreed far more nearly with the reformers than with the Papal Church, and was bound, as an honest man, to give his support to that side on which his sympathies lay. This statement, however, requires very serious qualification. It is quite true that there were many questions deeply involved in the reformation—such as the virtue of celibacy, the nature and number of the sacraments, the excellence of the monastic life, auricular confession and others—in regard to which he not merely agreed with Luther, but had long anticipated him. No one ever inveighed more bitterly than he against the usurpations of the priesthood, and the pride and luxury of the successors of the Galilean fishermen. No one ever exposed with more ample knowledge or more pungent wit the superstitious worship of imaginary relics. No one ever wrote more earnestly against the false trust in the Virgin or the saints, which had almost superseded the worship of Christ. And even on the capital question of all—the Primacy of St. Peter and the authority, temporal and spiritual, of the Roman Pontiff—there is no doubt that he expressed sentiments which were far from orthodox according to the standard of the time. He seems, indeed, to have regarded the Pope as merely the first among bishops—the head of that great organisation which constituted the Church, placed there for the sake of order and completeness, but not necessarily endowed with any supernatural character or divine right. All this is quite true; but besides the important fact that many points in connection with such questions which have been since decided were then open, there was a great difference between the way in which these questions were dealt with by Erasmus, and the way in which they were dealt with by the reformers. They dogmatised about them. He never did. He merely expressed doubt and denounced abuses; but he never set up his own opinion against the authority of the Church. He might doubt, for example, whether confession was instituted by Christ, but if not, he never called in question the power of the Church to establish or to abolish it. He might ridicule the extremes to which the practice of invoking the saints was sometimes carried, but he never denied that the saints ought to be invoked. He might sneer at the wonderful fondness of the monks for the fires of purgatory, so useful in keeping their kitchen hot, but he no more denied the existence of purgatory than he denied the existence of hell. In short, whatever opinion he expressed, it was always with entire submission to the judgment of the Catholic Church, and the Catholic Church in his eyes was the Christian people, speaking through the voice of a general council.[66]

In other respects it would be the greatest mistake to suppose that Erasmus ever adopted the principles of the Reformation. So far as those principles embraced the right of private judgment, he would certainly have repudiated them in the strongest terms. But it is now generally admitted that the Reformers never intended to assert the right of private judgment except in the most

---

[66] No doubt Erasmus conscientiously believed that he had never impugned any doctrine of the Roman Church. "At interim nullus exstitit vel Lutheranus, vel Antilutheranus, qui liquido vel unum improbatum dogma potuerit in libris meis ostendere, quum tot greges coorti sint hoc summo studio molientium," &c.—*Er. Op.* iii. 1095, B. His expressions of attachment to the Church are very strong:—"Me certe neque vita neque mors distrahet ab obedientia ecclesiæ, et a sinceritate fidei Christianæ."—*Ib.* iii. 777, A.

qualified sense. They repudiated the authority of the Church, but for that they substituted Scripture and their own interpretations of Scripture. Erasmus, like many since, felt the difficulty of making Scripture a rule of faith, without some tribunal of appeal against false interpretations, and foresaw, moreover, that the result of doing so must be to endanger many doctrines —such as the personality of the Holy Spirit—which the Reformers had no thought of calling in question. On the other hand, so far as the Reformation was based distinctively on dogma, as to a large extent it was, it had even less of his sympathy. The reader does not require to be reminded that the one point which immediately rose into prominence as the distinguishing doctrine of the Reformation, and which has ever since remained as a corner-stone of what is called evangelical Protestantism, was the sufficiency of Christ's sacrifice as an atonement for sin. Faith in that great atonement was the one thing which the monk of Erfurth proclaimed must be substituted for the vain rites and penances prescribed by the priesthood, without which, he said, human righteousness was rottenness, and by means of which the deepest scarlet of sin could be made white as the driven snow. Now what was it that Erasmus wished to put in the place of the monkish practices which he so unsparingly ridiculed? It was by no means this impalpable faith in a metaphysical transaction, this vicarious righteousness, this trust in another's merits. He accepted, of course, the dogma of justification as it was taught by the Fathers and Councils of the Church, but he probably accepted it merely because they taught it. What he believed in, what he insisted upon as the one thing needful, was precisely that righteousness which Luther utterly scorned.[37] With him, faith in Christ meant to follow the example of Christ, and to obey his commandments. "To be a Christian," he says—to take a single example out of numbers that might be quoted—" is not to be baptized or anointed; not to attend mass; but to lay hold on Christ in one's inmost heart, and show forth his spirit in one's life."[58] One of the finest passages in the "Praise of Folly" is that in which the writer pictures the monks appearing before the judgment-seat at the last day, and pleading the various forms of asceticism, or other religious practices, by which they have sought to make themselves worthy of heaven. One will produce a

[37] I think this language will not seem too strong to those who are acquainted with the subject. The question whether Luther was an Antinomian has been warmly debated, and the late Archdeacon Hare has attempted a vindication of the reformer against the attacks of Hallam, Sir W. Hamilton, and others. These writers may have expressed themselves too strongly upon the point, or they may have shown—as Dr. Hare maintains—that they possessed but a very slight acquaintance with the writings of Luther. But the charge, it may be remarked, does not depend upon any extensive knowledge of those writings. For the question surely is, not whether Luther uniformly and consistently denied the value of the moral law--for that probably no one would maintain—but whether he ever uses language which, taken in its plain meaning, and with every allowance for the exigencies of controversy, cannot fairly be made to bear any other construction. If this be the question, one example is obviously as good as a hundred. And if the following words, from the *De Babylonica Captivitate Ecclesiæ*, are not Antinomian, it may be doubted whether any words can be found in all literature that are so. "Jam vides," says Luther, "quam dives est homo Christianus, sive baptizatus, qui etiam volens non potest perdere salutem suam quantiscunque peccatis, nisi nolit credere. Nulla enim peccata eum possint damnare, nisi sola incredulitas."

[58] "Christianus est, non qui lotus est, non qui unctus, non qui sacris adest, sed qui Christum intimis complectitur affectibus, ac piis factis exprimit."—*Inst. Principis Christiani.—Er. Op.* iv. 576, C.

vessel filled with all the fish on which he has starved himself. Another will reckon up the fasts which he has practised. A third will fling down before the tribunal as many rites and ceremonies as would sink half a dozen merchant-ships. A fourth will boast that for sixty years he has never fingered a piece of coin except through two pair of gloves. Another will hold up his hood, so coarse and dirty, that the poorest wretch on earth would not condescend to wear it. And so on. But Christ, interrupting these empty boasts which else would never end, shall say, "What new kind of Jews are these, and whence come they? I left you one law which I acknowledge to be mine indeed, but which seems to be quite forgotten now. Plainly, and without parable, I promised the inheritance of my Father's kingdom, not to hoods, prayers, or fasts, but to the offices of charity." It is remarkable that an *aliter* reading in this last sentence gives "faith and charity;" but if that was the correction of Erasmus himself, it would still remain certain that his first thoughts were of practical righteousness, nor would it by any means follow that he used the word "faith" in the same sense as Luther. In fact, Erasmus himself confesses his inability to understand Luther's doctrine. In one of his "Apologies," he declares that he "doesn't know what Luther means by saying that good works follow necessarily from faith." It is clear, therefore, that he was altogether out of sympathy with the cardinal doctrine of the Reformation.

Erasmus was in truth, in his own age, the great apostle of common sense and of rational religion. He did not care for dogma; and accordingly the dogmas of Rome, which had the consent of the Christian world, were in his eyes preferable to the dogmas of Protes-

tantism, which destroyed the unity of the Church and
threatened to open the way for every sort of extravagance. What he did care for was practical Christianity,
and that he advocated with an earnestness and eloquence, and an unwearied devotion, which have perhaps
never been surpassed. Peace, good-will, justice, righteousness, charity,—in pleading the cause of these virtues he
knew neither fear nor favour. If he showed no mercy
to the poor monk who had barely enough Latin to
know when he was ridiculed, he was equally unsparing
of bishops, popes, and kings. Whether his notions, so
far as they touched upon public matters, were always
correct, is of course another question. In common with
many wise men of his time, and following the doctrine
of Aristotle, he held it a sin to take interest for money.
Kings, as a rule, he looked upon as no better than
robbers, and taxation in his mind was synonymous with
spoliation. But there was quite enough of tyranny and
oppression in high places in those days to justify much
of the strong language which he used; and if his earnest
pleadings for peace, justice and moderation had been
listened to, the world would have been spared many a
fiery trial. But by no power was it possible to avert
the tremendous crisis through which Europe had to pass
before the cause of liberty and light could triumph. If
Erasmus desired that that cause should triumph without
the disunion of the Church, he wished what was impossible, what, upon the whole, would not have been
for the highest good of mankind. But the wish was
perfectly natural to one educated in the cloister,
held in honour by the chief authorities of the Roman
Church, and who had never dreamed of the disunion of Christendom until he saw it actually accom-

plished before his eyes when he was verging towards old age.

Whoever will impartially weigh these considerations will, I think, admit that, whatever inconsistency Erasmus may justly be chargeable with for remaining a member of the Roman Church, it was simply impossible for him to join the party of Luther; and the best answer that can be made to any charge of dishonesty or cowardice that may be brought against him on this ground is simply this, that he never concealed his sympathy with the Reformation as long as it only went his own length, but the moment it went farther he declined to follow it. From the beginning to the end of his career he remained true to the great purpose of his life, which was to fight the battle of sound learning and plain common-sense against the powers of ignorance and superstition, and amid all the convulsions of that period he never once lost his mental balance. It is no small thing to be able to say of any one that his mind was never hurried into excess and never suffered reaction. But that is the simple truth as regards Erasmus. When his friend Sir Thomas More had abandoned the generous principles laid down in his "Utopia," and was writing in no gentle language against Tyndale and others of the reformed school, Erasmus quietly continued his work, scarcely moved by the changes around him. What he had been at the first he continued to be to the last. He had always declared that he desired to teach nothing that was at variance with the doctrines of the Church, and that, if any such proposition could be pointed out in his works, he was ready to retract it; he never ceased to attack and ridicule the corruptions of the Church, and to labour for the reform of its manners and discipline.

In some of his later writings, it may be, his tone is slightly altered, his remarks are a little more carefully qualified than in his earlier compositions. But this is the case far less than might be expected, if we supposed that his main object was to keep on good terms with his own Church and avert from himself the suspicion of heresy. If the "Familiar Colloquies," for example, the most important work of general interest which he published in the latter half of his life, and the best known and most characteristic of all his works, be compared with the "Praise of Folly," which appeared long before the monk of Wittenberg was ever heard of, it will be found that there is no difference at all in the spirit of the two works, and that the one is to the full as severe upon the corruptions of the Church and the superstitions of the people as the other. Nor, certainly, is there any ground for accusing Erasmus of cowardice in his personal relations with Luther. When the latter wrote to him, claiming his sympathy, he replied in such courteous terms as to offend even the less extreme supporters of the Papacy; only he took occasion to counsel moderation—advice of which Luther stood much in need—and intimated that he was no partisan of either side. But when the great Reformer publicly burned Leo's ill-timed bull, and proposed to throw the Pope and his whole pack of Cardinals into the Tuscan Sea, Erasmus very naturally asked what devil had taken possession of him. Can we wonder that to a man so eminently moderate, and so guided in all his sayings and doings by the principles of common-sense, conduct such as Luther's seemed little short of madness?

No one, indeed, with any enthusiasm in his nature

can help admiring the invincible energy and heroic courage of Luther, without which the Reformation could not have been accomplished. But, in order to do justice to Erasmus, we must not contrast him with Luther, but rather consider what his own work was, and how far he would have improved its prospects of success by declaring for Luther. When the breach with Rome took place he was upwards of fifty. He had been labouring all his life to reform the Church, but he had never had the least thought of quitting her communion. And next to the reformation of the Church, the other great object which he had at heart was the advance of learning. The question arises, then, whether he would have been in a more favourable position for attaining either of these objects as an avowed ally of Luther than as a Romanist. It would be difficult to show that this would have been the case. As a member of the Roman Church he had found as much freedom of speech as he desired. His contributions to the study of the classics had been received with an applause in which the yelpings of a few captious monks were completely drowned. His attacks on the corruptions of the Church were nowhere more bitter or galling than in the Annotations on the New Testament; yet that work had the express sanction of the head of Christendom. Had Erasmus, therefore, joined the party of Luther, he would undoubtedly have contributed to the success of a movement which, in its remote consequences, was, indeed, destined to save mankind from spiritual slavery; but he would neither have extended his own influence, nor would he have acquired any advantage which he did not already possess in fighting his battle with ignorance and superstition. In fact, it is clear that he regarded

Luther—and with some reason—as a man who had stepped in, not to carry on his own work, but to mar it by going to extremes which he had never foreseen, and which it was impossible for him to sanction.

So far indeed was Erasmus from thinking the Reformation favourable to the objects which he had in view as the work of his own life, that he regarded it as directly adverse to them. It seemed to him to tend neither to the improvement of life nor the advancement of learning, nor to greater freedom in the discussion of doubtful points. This he has made abundantly clear in his little tractate against the pseudo-evangelicals, which has been already referred to,[40] and which is especially interesting as explaining his reasons for distrusting the reformers. "I have never entered one of their churches," he here declares, "but I have sometimes seen them returning from meeting, looking as if they were possessed by an evil spirit, with their faces inflamed with anger and ferocity; nor was there one of them who showed me, or the friends by whom I was accompanied, the most common politeness, except one old man." And again, "it may be my misfortune, but I have never yet known one of them who has not been changed for the worse." Erasmus often complains of the injury done to the cause of learning by the reform movement. "There have arisen," he here says, "some of them who teach, both privately and in public, that human studies are no more than devil's nets, and with such success, that it is very rare to find any of their society giving their time seriously to literature, either sacred or profane; but profit and pleasure are eagerly pursued." And lastly, in regard to liberty of speech, he observes that the effect

---

[40] See above, p. 323.

of the Reformation has been directly unfavourable to it.
"Formerly," he says, "it was permissible to agitate
various questions on such subjects as the Pope's power,
indulgences, visitations, purgatory; on which it is now
unsafe to open one's mouth even to speak the truth."
No doubt the composition in which these sentences occur
was written at a time when he was a good deal embittered against the reformers. Still there is much truth
in what he here urges. Neither in the sixteenth
century, nor any other, has evangelicism been very
favourable either to human culture or to freedom of
discussion.

The true key to the position of Erasmus, we are
now probably prepared to admit, is to be found in the
character of his intellect. His mind was essentially of
the sceptical and inquiring, by no means of the affirmative or dogmatic order. Of this he was himself fully
conscious, and he has stated it in pretty plain terms.
"I have such a horror of dogmatism," he says in his
treatise on Free-Will, "that I could easily declare myself a member of the sceptic school, whenever I am not
met by the inviolable authority of Holy Scripture and
of the Church, to which I willingly submit my reason
in all things, whether I understand what it prescribes
or do not understand."[60] It was probably this consciousness, the consciousness that if he once made
his private judgment the standard of his faith, he must
inevitably be led much farther from the safe paths of
orthodoxy than even the most extreme reformers had
yet gone, that caused Erasmus to feel the necessity for
some external standard from which there should be no
appeal. That this would have been the case, and that

[60] *Er. Op.* ix. 1215, D.

his natural tendencies were towards the most rational views on every subject, must be evident to every one who has the slightest acquaintance with his writings. Even the mysterious doctrine of the Trinity, protected though it was by the Creeds of the Church and the decrees of so many Councils, formed no exception to this rule. It was all very well for him to talk of the "execrable impiety of the Arians," [61] as he does in one of his later Apologies, but as he more than once betrays a strong leaning towards the Arians, and as he interprets all the texts usually relied on in proof of the doctrine of the Trinity in an Arian sense, it is not unfair to infer that he was not an Arian merely because he had resolved never to deviate—to use his own expression—by so much as a hair's breadth from the doctrine of the Church, but would have been one if he had permitted himself to follow his own judgment.[62] Indeed, he himself has used an expression which, though ambiguously worded, it is difficult not to interpret in this sense. "So great," he says, "is my respect for the authority of the Church, that I could agree with the Arians and Pelagians, if the Church had approved of their teachings." [63] What can this mean but that, apart from the authority of the Church, the views of those heretics commended themselves to his mind rather than the dogmas of the Catholic faith? With the Pelagians it would indeed seem that he agreed, as he implies, if he does not expressly teach, that original sin consists in

---

[61] *Er. Op.* ix. 8:8, C.
[62] "So irresistible, indeed, is the tendency of Erasmus towards Arianism, that on one occasion, in repelling the imputation of it, he actually begins arguing in its favour, maintaining that Christ is never called in Scripture *verus Deus*," &c. —*Er. Op.* ix. 1175, A, B, C.
[63] *Er. Op.* iii. 1029, A.

following Adam."[64] How disinclined he was to the stern Augustinian and Lutheran doctrine of predestination is evident from his treatise on Free-Will. He was accused, indeed, of having written on this subject contrary to his real sentiments, and some modern writers have been unjust enough to repeat the charge;[65] but it is only necessary to reflect that the doctrine of the Roman Church which he undertook to defend was much more in accordance with the common sense of mankind than the doctrine of Luther which he impugned, in order to be sure that Erasmus was perfectly sincere.

That his relation to the doctrine of the real presence in the Eucharist was precisely the same as to the doctrine of the Trinity, is clear from expressions which I have already quoted.[66] He would rather be torn limb from limb than doubt the doctrine of the Church, but for all that he cannot conceal his personal leaning towards the rational teachings of the Swiss reformers. The following sentence, which may be added to those previously quoted, is not the language of one who had any strong personal faith in the miracle of transubstantiation. Referring to the tracts of Carlstadt he observes, "The

---

[64] See especially Par. on Rom. v. 12, where he says, "Ita factum est, ut malum a principe generis ortum, in universam posteritatem dimanaret, dum nemo non *imitatur* primi parentis exemplum;" and compare Art. ix. of the Articles of the English Church.

[65] The charge is founded on a somewhat ambiguous passage in a letter to Vives: "Verum ut ingenue dicam, perdidimus liberum arbitrium. Illic mihi aliud dictabat animus, aliud scribebat calamus."— *Er. Op.* iii. 985, D. There is nothing whatever in these sentences, nor in their context, to lead any one to suppose that reference is made to the treatise *De Libero Arbitrio*. Mr. Hallam has given the true explanation in a note to his *Lit. Hist.* vol. i. p. 362.

[66] See above, p. 310.

laity are very angry at losing their God, as if God was nowhere but under that sign."[67] In another place, however, and perhaps in a more serious mood, it may be proper to notice that he argues for the truth of the Catholic doctrine on the ground that he cannot believe that "Christ, who is truth and love, would ever have permitted his beloved spouse to continue so long in such abominable error as to worship a piece of bread in his own place."[68]

The sceptical character of his mind appears farther in his tendency to allegorize Scripture rather than accept it in its literal sense, in his unwillingness to credit stories of miracles, in his disposition to refer extraordinary events to natural, rather than supernatural, causes. A remarkable instance of this last occurs in a letter, in which he gives a long description of the blowing up of a tower, the explosion of which startled him one day as he was taking his afternoon's *siesta* in Froben's garden. On this he remarks, "There are some who say that this catastrophe portends some future event; but I, who am no prophet, think it means nothing but the carelessness of those who took no precautions against an accident which has not been hitherto so very rare."[69] We have seen how he could express his sarcastic wonder that the reformers were permitted to do their destructive work in the churches of Basle, without any interference on the part of the saints whose altars they overturned. In another passage he speaks still more pointedly, as follows:—"When we read how enraged St. Francis was with the man who laughed at his five wounds, when they tell of the horrible punishments inflicted by other saints for dis-

[67] *Er. Op.* iii. 834, D.   [68] *Ib.* iii. 1180, C.   [69] *Ep.* dcccxl.

respectful language addressed to them, I could not help wondering that among so many there was none to take vengeance on the authors of this great destruction; for I am not surprised at the gentleness of Christ and the blessed Virgin."[70] That Erasmus carried his rationalizing spirit so far as to doubt even some of the miracles of Scripture is not improbable, though on such a subject he would naturally be very cautious. He speaks boldly enough, however, of the myths in the book of Genesis, and in referring to the New Testament, he places the spiritual miracles wrought in man's soul above the mere external miracles presented to the senses. "We all wonder at the power which called Lazarus back to life, after he had been four days dead, even though we know that he must die again. How much more wonder is it that at the voice of one man so many tares should be changed into the Lord's good wheat, that every day the secret energy of the Spirit, working through the ministers of the Church, should restore corpses sixty years old to everlasting life!" At any rate there can be no doubt that Erasmus was very far from the common evangelical view of Scripture, which holds every word to be inspired and every book to be genuine. On the latter point, he remarks, that so far as his human understanding goes, he does not believe the Epistle to the Hebrews to be Paul's or Luke's, nor second Peter to be Peter's, nor the Apocalypse to be by John the Apostle, the author of the Gospel.

And yet it is curious that with all his liberal and rational tendencies there was in Erasmus also a certain vein of superstition. It is curious, because in studying his writings we so often forget that he lived on the very

[70] *Er. Op.* iii. 1223, D.   [71] *Eccl.* lib. i.: *Er. Op.* v. 828, D.

borders of mediævalism, but when we recall that fact we are ready to confess that the real marvel is that he was not more superstitious. The vow to St. Geneviève, the vow to St. Paul, the pilgrimage to the shrine of Walsingham, all assume a certain grotesqueness in his handling of them; but it is clear that beneath the humorous colouring with which he invests them there is an under-current of seriousness, which those who know on what familiar terms the devout Catholic can be with his patron saints will not find it hard to understand. The same remark applies to two stories which have been quoted in proof of his credulity, but in the truth of which, it must be confessed, he does not seem to have any very implicit faith. One of these was how, in the town of Schiltach, about eight German miles from Friburg, a demon carried a woman aloft into the air and placed her on a chimney-top, when he gave her a flask, which by his command she upset, and within an hour's time the whole town was burned to ashes. The story is told with all apparent gravity, but it is prefaced with this significant remark, "Whether all the reports about it are true, I will not venture to affirm, but it is too true that the town was burned and the woman executed after confessing." The other story is as follows. In his house in Friburg he was tormented with a plague of fleas, so small that it was impossible to catch them, which bit his neck and filled his clothes and even his very shoes as he stood writing, and which he used to tell his friends in jest were not fleas but evil spirits. "This," he continues, "was really no joke, but a divination; for some days ago a woman was burned, who, though she had a husband, had carried on intercourse for eighteen years with an evil spirit, and who, among other crimes, confessed that she had sent some large bags of fleas to Friburg by her paramour." In days when women could be burned for their supposed connection with such transactions, it would not have been wonderful if even the strong sense of Erasmus had succumbed to the popular faith. Still, one cannot help suspecting that he was laughing in his sleeve as he recorded these things. Probably, the truth is that, as his mood changed, he fluctuated between belief and doubt.

It would be easy to multiply passages in illustration of the character and opinions of Erasmus, but probably enough has been said to indicate the right point of view from which to judge him. It is, however, impossible to conclude without turning for a moment to our own times, and glancing at the parallelism they present to the period of which we have been speaking in these volumes. The struggle against the tyranny of dogmatism belongs, in truth, to no single age in the world's history, but is renewed from century to century, wherever there is the assumption of Infallibility on the one hand and any degree of intellectual activity on the other. There is no essential difference between orthodoxy in its Roman and orthodoxy in its Protestant form. The Roman Church claims an infallibility which resides in itself, or in its supreme head, the representative of Christ on earth. Evangelical Protestantism ascribes Infallibility to the Scriptures, which, inasmuch as the Scriptures require an interpreter, virtually comes to the same thing. Each holds up an authoritative standard of truth, from which it is the most fatal error to dissent. There is, accordingly, no essential difference between the struggle which is now maintained by the liberal thinkers among the clergy of the various Protestant denominations against the bigotry of the majority, and the contest which Erasmus conducted with such consummate skill against the fanaticism of the sixteenth century. Circumstances are changed, but men are not greatly changed with them. No reflection, indeed, occurs so frequently to the student of that period as the reflection that he is studying under other names the history of his own times.—

> Mutato nomine de te,
> Fabula narratur.—

Bigotry and superstition are, it is true, less formidable now than they were then; but that may be, perhaps, because they have lost the power rather than the will to do harm. They have not the less, on that account, fiercely resisted every step in the onward march of knowledge, closed men's eyes against the advancing light, and endeavoured to drown with hideous clamour every accent of truth which might seem to clash with ancient prejudice. If, then, Erasmus were alive now, he would have to direct his satire against very nearly the same objects as actually engaged his pen. He would still have to rebuke those who rely for salvation upon costly rites or wearisome ceremonies—upon anything rather than personal righteousness. He would still have to aim the shafts of his ridicule against pretentious ignorance or unscrupulous malice. He would still have to complain of those who stop their ears against reasoning which they cannot refute, denounce books which they have never read, and resort to calumny and abuse whenever better arguments fail them. The position of Erasmus was obviously very similar to that of the

Broad Churchmen of our own day. Like them, he had outgrown the Church in whose fold he was born, whose sacraments he had received, and whose orders he had taken, no doubt in the most perfect good faith; and like them, notwithstanding the pressure put upon him on all sides, he refused to separate himself from her communion. Although it would be cruel not to make great allowance for the difficulties of such a situation, it is impossible to maintain its consistency. Erasmus, however, had one plea of which the Protestant might well hesitate to avail himself: he never admitted, at least in theory, the principle of free inquiry, but, as we have seen, always professed to hold his individual opinion in subordination to the judgment of the Church. He was not, therefore, called upon to attempt the difficult task of reconciling his own views with the acceptance of propositions which plainly excluded them.

Erasmus could not have left the Church of Rome without identifying himself with the Reformers; and if he felt that he was not at one with them, he is scarcely to be blamed if he preferred holding his ground. Even from the evangelical point of view it is absurd to denounce him, as Farel did, as a coward who held right opinions but feared to confess them; while it is unjust to regard him, as others have been inclined to do, as a mere mocker, who sought to turn everything into ridicule. He had an unwavering faith in goodness and in God, but on all speculative points he was willing that the Church should decide for him, simply because without her authority he would never have known how to make up his mind. On all such questions he tended to be, essentially, if not theoretically, a sceptic

and a free thinker. He had doubts on nearly every
subject — not indeed on those principles which are
admitted to lie at the foundation of all religion, the
existence of God and the moral law—but on everything
short of these. He had doubts about the Trinity, the
Eucharist, the Confessional, the sacramental character
of marriage, the damnation of unbaptized infants, and
various other points of divinity. He condemned the
long pilgrimages which were often undertaken, to the
neglect of duties nearer home, for the expiation of some
sin, or in hope of some blessing; found fault with the
excessive homage which was paid to the Virgin Mary
and the saints, to the exclusion of Christ; and, in short,
put love to God and love to man far above all the
ceremonies of the Church. But then, assuredly, the
breadth of Erasmus was his weakness, just as the narrowness of Luther was his strength. No man ever made
himself a martyr for a doubt, and whatever doubts
Erasmus might entertain, he knew well how to convey
them without committing himself to any positive
statement. It was surely no heresy to say that
Christ was distinctly called God only once or twice
in the New Testament, nor that St. Hilary nowhere
teaches the separate personality of the Holy Spirit,
especially if he was willing to retract even these
statements, so soon as the Church should pronounce
them erroneous. If he declared himself ready to
become an Arian the moment the Church should decide
in favour of Arianism, his submissiveness might be
thought excessive; or if he asserted that the arguments
of those who maintain that there is nothing but bread
and wine in the eucharist were so strong that they might
deceive the very elect, the concession might be deemed

unwise; but in neither case could he be charged with making any affirmation contrary to the Catholic Faith, for in fact, so far as points of faith were concerned, he affirmed nothing whatever. It was thus that Erasmus started doubts and difficulties at every turn, and by so doing prepared the way for the entire abandonment of the scholastic theology, and a return to a simpler and more scriptural faith. Of the Roman Church he continued a member, simply because she was to him the representative of Christian peace, and he hoped that the corruptions which had crept into her bosom in the course of centuries might not prove ineradicable. Intellectually, he belonged neither to the Papal Church nor to evangelical Protestantism, but was equally in advance of both. Far before his own age, he embodied in himself what we now call the modern spirit—the spirit of doubt, of inquiry and investigation, which, it is certain, is the only path to whatever truth may be attainable by man.

Device on Erasmus's Seal.[1]

---

[1] The seal-ring given to Erasmus by Alexander, Archbishop of St. Andrew's, had no inscription on it, but having been informed by an Italian antiquary, that the head represented the God Terminus, he had another seal made with a somewhat similar head, and the inscription, as above. The account of Erasmus himself in his Apology does not make this very clear, but see the plate in Jortin's third volume, from which our engraving is taken.

INDEX.

ADAGES, the, of Erasmus, i. 95, 113, 271. History of, 272-280. Description of, 280-306
Adolphus, son of Lady de Vere, i. 45, 54, 55
Adrian VI.; Principal of the University of Louvain, i. 123. Elected Pope, ii. 101. Correspondence with, 102-109. His death, 189
Agricola, Rodolph, i. 9. Commends Erasmus, 10. His writings, 105
Albert, Cardinal Elector; his admiration for Erasmus, ii. 32. Letter to, 33
Alberus, Erasmus, ii. 149
Aldington, Rectory of, i. 241
Aldridge, Robert, i. 233
Aldus Manutius; his reception of Erasmus, i. 171. Prints the "Adages," 279
Aleander, Jerome; his intimacy with Erasmus, i. 171, 279. A maniac, ii. 76. Letter to, 209
Alexander, Archbishop of St. Andrews, i. 173
Alexander, Pope, i. 130
Algerus, ii. 311
Ambrose, St., edition of, ii. 283
Amerbach, John, Froben's predecessor, i. 256. His edition of St. Augustin, ii. 306

Amerbach, John, the brothers, i. 268
Ammonius, Andreas, i. 208. Sends Erasmus wine, 209. Latin secretary to Henry VIII., 227. Letters from, 225, 228. Letters to, 230, 248, 368, 378. His death, 385
Andreas, Bernard, i. 224. Epigram on, 225
Andrelinus, Faustus; his character, i. 33. Intimacy of Erasmus with, 53. Letters to, 86. Anecdote of, 354. Supposed author of the *Julius Exclusus*, ii. 28
Anti-barbarians, The, i. 25, 407
Antipolemus, the, of Erasmus, i. 180
Apophthegms, the, ii. 325
Aquinas, St. Thomas; studied by Erasmus, i. 83. His view of Scripture, 121, *note*. Heresy to dissent from him, ii. 44
Aristotle, i. 2. Translations of, 67. Preface to, ii. 525
Arnobius on the Psalms, ii. 102
Atensis, John, Vice-chancellor of Louvain, i. 379; ii. 91. His character, 134
Athanasius, St., translations from, ii. 283
Augsburg, Diet of; Erasmus summoned to, ii. 324
Augustine, St., order of, i. 14
———, edition of, ii. 306-308

BAD

BADIUS the printer, i. 376; ii. 291
Balbus, Jerome, i. 33; ii. 28
Barbirius, Peter, letter to, ii. 79
Basil, St.; his commentary on Isaiah, i. 206, 213, 215. Edition of, ii. 326
Battus, James, a friend of Erasmus, i. 32, 44. Letters to, 45, 51, 53, 94, 100, 102, 108. Death of, 111
Becket, St. Thomas à, shrine of, i. 234
Bedda, Natalis, Syndic of the Sorbonne, ii. 220. Notes the errors of Erasmus, 228. Letter from, 229. Letter to, 230. Defence of Erasmus against his charges, 238, 239. Reply to his criticisms, 240-244. Makes the *amende honorable*, 251
Bembo, Peter, i. 177; ii. 292, 332
Beraldus, Nicholas, letter to, ii. 70
Bere, Louis, a Paris divine, i. 365. Letter to, ii. 74
Bergis, Anthony à, Abbot of St. Bertin, i. 32. Letter to, 235
— Henry à, Bishop of Cambray, takes Erasmus into his service, i. 30. Sends him to Paris, 32. His stinginess, 37. His death, 112
Bernard, St., the devil entrapped by, i. 192
Berquin, Louis de, gentleman of Artois, ii. 221. Corresponds with Erasmus, 222. Persecuted by the Sorbonne, 224. Burned for heresy, 226
Bersala, Anna, Marchioness de Vere, i. 44. Erasmus visits her, 50. Her virtues, 51. Patroness of Erasmus, 94. Letter to her, 104. Entreated for money 110, 111. Her marriage, 112
Boethius, preferred to Cicero, i. 67
Boier, Baptista, chief physician to Henry VII., i. 163

CHA

Bolduc, Erasmus at, i. 13
Bologna, Erasmus's adventure at, i. 167
Bombasius, Paul, i. 169, 170. Letter to, ii. 82
Brunfels, Otto von, ii. 148
Budæus, William; his life and works, i. 372. Correspondence with Erasmus, 373-377. Offence of, ii. 291
Bullock, Henry, Fellow of Queen's, i. 210
Busch, Hermann, i. 395; ii. 148
Busleiden, Jerome, i. 380

CAMBRIDGE, Erasmus a B.D. of, i. 141. University of, 207. Erasmus professor at, *ib.*
Campeggio, Cardinal, letter to, ii. 61
Canossa, Cardinal, interview of Erasmus with, i. 245
Capito, Wolfgang, public preacher at Basle, i. 365; ii. 32
Caraffa, John Peter, i. 267; ii. 332
Caranza, Sanctius, Spanish divine, i. 341
Carondiletus, Archbishop of Palermo, ii. 186, 195
Carpi, Albert, Prince of; his satisfaction with Erasmus's reply to Luther, ii. 208. Calumniates Erasmus, 251. Correspondence with, 252, 253. His attack, 254. Reply of Erasmus, 255-258. His death, 259
Carteromachus, Scipio, of Pistoia, i. 177
Catherine, grandmother of Erasmus, i. 5
— St., of Sienna, i. 17
— Queen, ii. 281
Ceratinus, James, i. 381
Chalcondyles, Demetrius, i. 68
Charity; its true nature, i. 118

INDEX.

CHA

Charles, Prince; Erasmus councillor to, i. 235, 259. Succeeds to nineteen kingdoms, 366. Crowned Emperor, ii. 60

Charnock, Richard, head of St. Mary's College, i. 66. Urges Erasmus to undertake the *Adages*, 273

Christian, pupil of Erasmus, i. 41. Letter to, 57

Christopher, St., i. 190

— Bishop of Basle, letters to, ii. 189, 191

Chrysoloras; lectures on his grammar, i. 207

Chrysostom, St., translations from, ii. 283. Edition of, 323

Cicero, enthusiasm of Erasmus for, ii. 154. Preface to the Tusculan Questions of, 294

Ciceronians, the, ii. 286

"Ciceronian," the, of Erasmus, ii. 287–291

Clement VII., ii. 189. His character, 190. Letter to, 194. His death, 332

Colet, John; his birth and education, i. 70. Lectures on St. Paul, 71. Greeting to Erasmus, 73. Disputation on Christ's agony, 76–81. Opinion of Aquinas, 82. Invitation to Erasmus, 84. His asceticism, 89. Letters to, 135, 160, 211, 214, 218. His school, 212. His death, 385

Confessional, work on the, ii. 277

Conon of Nuremberg, i. 268

Contempt of the World, essay on, i. 24

Cop, William, Dr., i. 56, 95, 354

Copia, the, of Erasmus, i. 212. Its dedication to Colet, 219

Cornelius Lopsen; his friendship with Erasmus, i. 27. Correspondence with him, 28

— Werden; brought up with Erasmus, i. 17. Persuades him to enter a convent, 18

ERA

Cranmer, continues Erasmus's pension, ii. 329

Craston; his Greek lexicon, i. 8

Curtius, Quintus, edition of, i. 406

Cyprian, St., edition of, ii. 93

DEVENTER, the school of, i. 8. Erasmus at, 9, 10

Disputatiuncula de tædio et pavore, the, i. 77–81

Donatus, the grammarian, i. 274

Dorpius, Martin, his controversy with Erasmus, i. 203–205. His death, ii. 272

Dover, adventure of Erasmus at, i. 91

Dürer, portrait of Erasmus by, ii. 268, 339

ECCLESIASTES, the, ii. 334

Eck, Dr., ii. 46

Egmund the Carmelite, ii. 52. His dispute with Erasmus, 53–58. His death, 272

Elias, grandfather of Erasmus, i. 5

Enchiridion, the, i. 114–123. Object of Erasmus in writing it, 137. Froben's edition, 407

Encomium Moriæ, the; origin of the work, i. 184. Analysis of, 186–200. Its reception, 201. Attacked by Dorpius, 203

Epimenides, his sleep, i. 60. Revived in Scotus, 63

Episcopius, Nicholas, Froben's son-in-law, ii. 337

Eppendorf, Henry of; his character, ii. 115. Foments quarrel between Erasmus and Hutten, 116, 117. Satire on, 172. Threatens Erasmus, 295. Makes terms with him, 298. Complains to the Duke of Saxony, 302

Erasmus, St., i. 191.

EUR

Euripides, the Hecuba and Iphigenia in Aulis of, i. 112, 173
Everard, Nicholas, letter to, ii. 75

FABER Stapulensis; his controversy with Erasmus, i. 322-325
Faith, what it is, i. 115
"Familiar Colloquies," the, ii. 151-179. Condemned by Sorbonne, 246
Farel, William; his character, ii. 198. His dispute with Erasmus, 199
Fasting, treatise on, ii. 96
Fisher, Robert, letter to, i. 83
— John, Bishop of Rochester; his character, i. 149, 150. Letters to, 364; ii. 210. His death, 335
— Christopher, apostolic protonotary, i. 307
Flodden, battle of, i. 226
Fonseca, Archbishop of Toledo, ii. 261
Fox, Richard; Bishop of Winchester, i. 144
Francis I. invites Erasmus to Paris, i. 360. Appealed to by Erasmus, ii. 245
— Wolsey's physician, letter to, i. 386
— St.; his gentleness, ii. 177. Epiphany of, 330
Frederic, Elector of Saxony, ii. 60
Froben, John, the printer of Basle, i. 4, 244. Reception of Erasmus by, 257. Reprints the "Adages," 280. Offers to print the New Testament, 308. His character, ii. 273, 274. His last illness, 275, and death, 276
— Jerome; Erasmus at his house, ii. 335. At death-bed of Erasmus, 337
Fugger, Anthony, ii. 313.

HEN

GAGUIN, Robert, professor of rhetoric at Paris, i. 33. Acquaintance of Erasmus with, 44
Garland, John à, stanzas of, i. 9
Gaza, Theodore; his grammar, i. 207. Translated by Erasmus, 406
Gellius, Aulus, i. 273
Geneviève, St., library of, i. 35. Erasmus's vow to, 56
George, Duke of Saxony, urges Erasmus to write against Luther, ii. 203. Sends him a silver cup, 260
Gerard, the real name of Erasmus, i. 4
— father of Erasmus, i. 4. Ordained a priest, 6. His death, 11
Ghent, adventure at, i. 254
Goclenius, i. 381
Greek, studies of Erasmus in, i. 9, 91, 97, 99, 112, 139
Gregory of Tiferno, i. 33
Grey, Thomas; a pupil of Erasmus, i. 42. Letter to, 60. At Basle, 270
Grimani, Cardinal, visit of Erasmus to, i. 177. Letter to, 265
Grocyn, William, i. 68, 84, 138, 147
Groot, Gerard, i. 8
Grunnius, Lambertus, apostolic secretary, i. 253
Grynæus, Simon, ii. 323, 326

HEBREWS, Epistle to the, not in St. Paul's style, i. 317
Hegius, Alexander, i. 9
Henry VII.; poem in praise of, i. 87. His aversion to Linacre, 224. Saying of, 288
— VIII.; Erasmus introduced to him as Duke of York, i. 87. Accession to the throne, 182. His answer to Luther, ii. 80, 92. Invitation from, 313

INDEX.

HER

Hermann, William; his intimacy with Erasmus, i. 21. His odes, 23, 102. Letter to, 40
Hermonymus, George; teacher of Greek, i. 33, 274
Heyen, Bertha de; funeral oration on, i. 24
Hilary, St.; introduction to, ii. 180-186
Hochstraten, the Inquisitor, i. 261. Letter to, ii. 29
Holbein, portraits of Erasmus by, i. 31; ii. 339. His illustrations of the *Moria*, i. 202
Horace, i. 9, 67
Hunting, satire on, i. 189
Hutten, Ulrich von; his first acquaintance with Erasmus, i. 383. His treachery, ii. 46. Career, 110, 111. Arrival at Basle, 113. Quarrels with Erasmus, 116. His "Expostulation," 124-130. His death, 146
Hyperaspistes, the, ii. 218

IGNATIUS Loyola; his opinion of the *Enchiridion*, i. 123
Indulgences, the, ii. 14-16
Ingoldstadt, Erasmus invited to, i. 363, 365
Irenæus, edition of, ii. 282

JEROME, St.; Erasmus copies the letters of, i. 28. Begins, 220; and completes his labours on, 244. Compared with Erasmus, 346, 347. Edition of, 348-360
Jonas, Jodocus, letter to, ii. 71
Julius II.; his triumphal entry into Bologna, i. 166, 167. Incident at his court, 180. Forms the Holy League, 226. His death, *ib.*
Julius Exclusus, the, ii. 24, 27
Juvenal, i. 24

LUT

LASCAR, Constantine; his Greek grammar, i. 8, 99
—, John, i. 279, 372, 380
Lasco, Baron à, ii. 269
Latimer, William, an excellent Grecian, i. 68
Latomus, James, his defence of scholasticism, i. 326
Laurinus, Marcus, Letters to, i. 389; ii. 94, 118
Lee, Edward; his character, i. 327. Controversy of Erasmus with, 328-335
Leo X.; letters of Erasmus to, i. 265; ii. 47. New Testament dedicated to, i. 310. His bull against Luther, ii. 49. His death, 100
Letter-writing, treatise on, i. 54
Libanius, translation from, i. 112
Lilly, William, Head Master of Colet's School, i. 212
Linacre, Thomas; his learning, i. 68. His taste, 84. Letter to, 161. His translation of Proclus, 224. His death, ii. 272. A translator of Galen, 282
Listrius, Gerard; his commentary on the *Moria*, i. 201. Welcomes Erasmus to Basle, 256
Livy, preface to, ii. 326
Longolius, ii. 272
Louis XII. of France, in league with Julius II., i. 166. Attempts to recover Milan, 226
Lucian; admired by Erasmus, i. 112. His Mycillus, 142. Estimate of, 143. His *Toxaris*, 144. His "Timon," 145. Other dialogues of, 145, 146. Erasmus compared with, 185
Luke, St.; his style, i. 317
Lupset, Thomas, a pupil of Colet, i. 220, 385
Luther, Martin, at Erfurth, ii. 3. His doctrine of justification, 10. His propositions against the Indulgences, 14. Letters from,

MAC

19, 203. Letters to, 20, 205.
Defence of, by Erasmus, 35-42.
His extravagances, 72. His doctrine of free-will, 201. Treatise of Erasmus against, 205-207.
His reply, 215-217

MACROBIUS, i. 44, 273
Margaret, mother of Erasmus, i. 4. Her fidelity, 7. Her death, 10
— More's daughter, i. 158; ii. 279
Matsys, Quintin, portrait of Erasmus, by, ii. 338
Melancthon, letters to, ii. 114, 212
Method of study, the, i. 213
— of true theology, the, i. 325; ii. 186
Michael, St., Ode to, i. 22
Montaigu, College of, i. 34, 35
More, Sir Thomas; Erasmus captivated by, i. 68. Intimacy of Erasmus with, 150. Portrait of, 151-157 Erasmus at the house of, 184. His Utopia, 362. His death, ii. 336
Mosellanus, i. 381; ii. 46
Mountjoy, William Lord; a pupil of Erasmus, i. 42. Letters to, 48; ii. 87. Anecdote of, i. 55. Invites Erasmus to England, 64, 83. The "Adages" dedicated to, 276
Musurus, Marcus, i. 175, 279

NEW Eagle, Count of, i. 397, 398
Nicholas, provost of Burgundy, letter to, i. 93
Noviomagus, Gerard, ii. 322

ŒCOLAMPADIUS; his regard for Erasmus, i. 259.
Marriage of, ii. 271. Returns to Basle, 309. Letter to, 319.
His death, 329

PSA

Origen, the text of, revised by Erasmus, ii. 336
Oxford, university of, i. 66-69.
Erasmus at, 72-85

PACE, Richard; his acquaintance with Erasmus, i. 175. Letters to, ii. 77, 80
Paludanus, John, orator of the University of Louvain, i. 133
Paraphrase of New Testament, the, i. 410-412
Paris, the University of, i. 33, 34, 38
Paul III. made Pope, ii. 332.
Erasmus exhorts him to moderation, 333
Paungartner, John, citizen of Augsburg, ii. 331
Peace, The Complaint of, i. 402
Pelican, Conrad, ii. 310
Peter, brother of Erasmus, i. 7.
His character, 15. His existence questioned, 16, *note*
Pflug, Julius, ii. 302
Philip of Burgundy, i. 134
Pirckheimer, Bilibald, of Nuremberg, i. 259. Anecdote of, ii. 59. Letter to, 314. His death, 328
Plautus, edited by Erasmus, i. 173
Plutarch; his Moral Essays translated, i. 112
Poggius, i. 27, 159
Politian, i. 68, 159, 273
Poncher, Bishop of Paris, i. 370
Popes, the, satire on, i. 198
Prieras, Sylvester, ii. 43. Letter to, 191
Prince, the Christian, i. 260
Priscian, i. 67
Pronunciation, dialogue on, ii. 284, 285
Proverb, definition of, i. 280
Psalms, exposition of the, ii. 280

RAP

RAPHAEL, Cardinal of St. George; his intimacy with Erasmus, i. 177. Letters to, 263
Ravenna, battle of, i. 226
Rescius, Rutgerus, i. 381
Reuchlin, John, persecution of, by the Dominicans, i. 261. Defended by Erasmus, 264, 268. His acquittal, 383. Meeting with Erasmus, ii. 26
Rhenanus, Beatus, i. 256. His learning, 268. Letter to, 394
Rochford, Thomas, Earl of Wiltshire and Ormond, ii. 331
Romboldus, teacher of Erasmus, i. 13
Rome, Erasmus at, 170, 176-180
Rotterdam, birth-place of Erasmus, i. 3
Ruthall, Thomas, Bishop of Durham, i. 145. Makes Erasmus a present, 249
Rutier, Nicholas, Bishop of Arras, i. 134

SADOLETI; his correspondence with Erasmus, ii. 292, 326. Made a cardinal, 332
Sampson, Richard, Bishop of Chichester, i. 361
Sapidus, John, i. 256, 407
Scaliger, Julius Cæsar; his oration, ii. 293
Schoolmen, the, satire on, i. 194, 195. Their contentions, 402
Schurer, Matthias, printer of Strasburg, i. 258
Scotists, the, i. 34. Ridiculed by Erasmus, 63, 215. Described by Colet, 82
Scotus, Duns, i. 34, 63
Scriptures, the; a variety of senses in them, i. 80. Not to be understood literally, 120
Seneca, edition of, i. 257; ii. 303-306
Servatius, Father, letter to, i. 250

TYN

Sintheimius, John, or Zinthius, i. 10
Sion, College of, i. 14
— Cardinal of, ii. 99
Sixtine, John, of Friesland, i. 76
Socrates, anecdote of, i. 216
Spalatine, ii. 60
"Sponge," the, of Erasmus, ii. 130 -146
Standish, Dr., Bishop of St. Asaph, i. 342. Anecdotes of, 343, 344
Standonck, John, Principal of Montaigu, i. 35
Steyn, monastery of, i. 17. Erasmus an inmate of, 18-30. Refuses to return to, 250-253
Stunica, James Lopez, i. 335. Defends the Vulgate, 336. His attacks on Erasmus, 337-341.
Suetonius, edition of, i. 406
Suidas, i. 279
Sutor; his attack on Erasmus, ii. 229. Reply to his ravings, 235
Sylvagius, the Chancellor, i. 368, 384

TERENCE familiar to Erasmus, i. 9. Edited by him, 173
Terminus, Erasmus's seal, i. 176
Testament, the New; Erasmus finishes the collation of, i. 220. First edition of, i. 310. Second, 312. The criticism of, 317. Notes on, 318-321. Controversies about, 322-342
Theophylact, i. 315, 316
Thomists, the, i. 34, 67
Tongue, work on the use and abuse of, ii. 279
Tonstall, Cuthbert, Bishop of London, i. 361; ii. 92
Turin, Erasmus made D.D. of, i. 165
Tutor, James, i. 44. Letters to, 96, 98, Dedication of Cicero's "Offices" to, ii. 93
Tyndale, William, i. 123

U

URSEWICK, Christopher, i. 142. Letter to, 364

V

VALLA, Laurentius, a forerunner of Erasmus, i. 26. Epigram on, 27. Defence of, 28. Work by, 307. Critic of New Testament text, 345
Vespasian; his favourite proverb, i. 287
Virgil, Polydore, discussion with, i. 277. Letter to, ii. 267
Vitellius, Cornelius, i. 33
Vitrarius, John, the monk of St. Omer, i. 123-133
Vives, Ludovicus, i. 379, 380
Volzius, Paulus, letter to, i. 407
Vulgate, the, quoted as if inspired, i. 81. Not good enough for Erasmus, 314

W

WALSINGHAM, pilgrimage to, i. 232
War, satire on, i. 187. Erasmus condemns, 237
Warham, William; Erasmus at his palace, i. 146. His character,

Z

148. Letter from, 210. Letter to, ii. 271. His death, 328
Watson, John, i. 210, 367
Wentford, Roger, letter to, i. 163
Werner, Nicholas, i. 30, 43
Whitford, Richard, Fox's chaplain, i. 144. Dedication to, 151
Wickliffites, the, ii. 107
"Widow, the Christian," ii. 281
Wimphilingus, James, i. 256. Delivered by Julius II., 265
Winckel, Peter, Erasmus's guardian, i. 12, 14, 26
Wolsey, Thomas, at Oxford, i. 69. Courted by Erasmus, 239. Letter to, ii. 25

X

XIMENES, Cardinal, i. 308. Rebukes Stunica, 337

Y

YOUNG, Dr. John, Dean of York, i. 231

Z

ZASIUS, Udalric, professor at Friburg, i. 258; ii. 313
Zwingle; his visit to Erasmus, i. 258. His death, ii. 329

www.ingramcontent.com/pod-product-compliance
Lightning Source LLC
Chambersburg PA
CBHW030342230426
43664CB00007BA/499